PARLIAMENTARY DEMOCRACY IN BHUTAN

A Journey from Tradition to Modernity

Sarish Sebastian

Adroit Publishers
New Delhi

Published by

ADROIT PUBLISHERS

4675/21, Ganpati Bhawan, Ansari Road,
Daryaganj, New Delhi-110 002

INDIA

Phone : 011-23266030

Distributors

AKHIL BOOK DISTRIBUTORS

email: akhilbooks@yahoo.com
akhilbks@gmail.com

ISBN : 978-81-87393-15-3

Printed in India on behalf of M/s Adroit Publishers by Design Unit, Delhi-110092

Contents

Foreword

In the modern globalised world, the term 'democracy' is a often discussed topic. For many centuries, political scientists have analysed the democratic aspects and its genesis in every corner of the world. In recent years, sustaining democracy has became a major concern of every third world nations and world organisations.

Being a landlocked nation between India and China, the two giants of Asian continent, Bhutan has successfully transformed its political system from a century old hereditary monarchy to a parliamentary constitutional monarchy. In the book "parliamentary demo", the author has successfully illustrated the peaceful transformation of the political system in Bhutan. It provides a great input into the influence of modernisation process on various political institutions and how the rulers have successfully managed to preserve their traditions and culture even after embracing the principles of modernisation in the transformative world.

The author has tried to present the transformation in a systematic way by presenting the historical background of the origin of the political institutions in Bhutan and how each monarch has initiated the process of modernising these institutions based on the unique principle of 'Gross National Happiness'. The author also discusses about the future challenges that the nation might face or is facing at present due to the introduction of modernisation process in the traditional society and how Bhutan as a nation could handle onerous challenges successfully.

It is my immense pleasure to write a foreword for such an extra ordinary effort made by the author in this book. I am sure this book will be abiding interest to students, research scholars as well as general public in the field of international relations and South Asian studies.

12 January 2015

Professor Dr.Mohammed Badrul Alam
Head, Department of Political Science
Jamia Millia Islamia, New Delhi

Preface

It is interesting to note that a small country in the Himalayas transform its political system into a parliamentary constitutional monarchy from a traditional hereditary monarchy in a peaceful manner when in the neighbouring states faced a violent movement for democratic governments. In the history of democratic movements, it is surprising to witness a monarch give up his powers voluntarily to establish a democratic government.

The process of Modernisation plays an important role in the transformation of political system of the developing nations. Adopting the principles of globalisation and Modernisation of the society requires a change in the political structure to cope with the new issues and challenges of the country and lead the nation in the right direction on the road to development. The present work is to understand the influence of modernisation process in the country in the political transformation to be a parliamentary democracy.

Before understanding the political changes that took place in the country, it is important to know the history and cultural aspects of Bhutan. The first chapter is an attempt to make the readers understand the historical perspective of the nation and how the state is culturally unique in the political discourse. Hence, the first chapter is titled *'Situating Bhutan in the Political Discourse: Introduction and Overview'*. This chapter provides an outline of the history, social structure, geography and economy of the country. Being a Buddhist nation, how Bhutan's socio-political sphere was shaped by religious values and was kept isolated for centuries. It is very important to study and know the nation's history, geography, economy and social structure to get a better knowledge about how far the process of modernisation affected the nation's growth in the globalised economy.

The second chapter, *'Explaining the Historical Basis of Bhutan's Administrative Systems'* discusses the growth of political institutions in the country, the beginning of political organizations, political offices and the development as it took place in Bhutan. The chapter discuss the democratic changes that each rulers of the country brought forward for modernising its political system

The third chapter titled, *'Analysing the Trends towards Modernisation in Bhutanese Politics'* makes an effort to understand and examine the Modernisation process in the political structure in Bhutan. Emphasis will be given to the importance of the effect of Modernisation on various aspects such as political structure, public administration, human rights, good governance and sustainable development.

Chapter four, *'Bhutan and the World: with Special Reference to India'* discuss the growth of foreign relations of Bhutan with special references to India. In the world of Globalisation and Modernisation, no country can remain isolated from the rest of the world for long, as every nation requires a helping hand from others. The growth of globalisation in the whole world created a condition in which every nation is dependent upon its neighbours or other nations.

The book will be incomplete without discussing the future challenges that the nation may face in the new modernised era. Thus, chapter five titled *'The Future Challenges Ahead of Bhutan'* will discuss about the major challenges the nation faces in its administrative setup, social life and economic system as well as in the traditional cultural sphere. In this chapter, I will also deal with the problems of refugees and the challenges they cause to the governing system in Bhutan.

The last chapter titled, *'Conclusion'*, evaluates the transformation of political system in Bhutan. As said by Niccolo Machiavelli, *"Whosoever desires constant success must change his conduct with the times"*, the Kingdom of Bhutan also striving to attain its success through following the unique principle of Gross National Happiness (GNH). Though being a land-locked nation, sandwiched between two Asian giants, Bhutan successfully adopted and changed to a modern nation without losing its tradition and culture following this principle.

CHAPTER 1

Situating Bhutan in The Political Discourse

Introduction and Overview

Introduction

The Himalayas meaning the "abode of the snow" is home for different culture and traditions profoundly shaped the culture of South Asia. A snowy, lofty and glistering peaks with verdant forests and flowing rivers clearly states the Himalayas is different from the rest of the world. At the eastern end of the Himalayas one gets the feeling of being in an exotic and unmolested or undisturbed by human settlements which showcases a blend of natural beauty and tradition. A tiny nation at the eastern end of the Himalayas takes our attention with limited human settlements and far from the crowded urban-industrial settlement which gives predominant considerations to its nature and tradition, which is called as the dragon kingdom. Looking at the tiny nation here, everyone literally admits that it is the Last- Shangri-La on earth with perfect blend of nature and its seducing beauty.

Having lived in the self-imposed isolation for centuries and cut off from the larger world, the Kingdom of Bhutan is creating a new history in all walks of life and moving faster towards a social, political and economic development in the 20th century. The introduction of modernisation and democratic processes in the country accelerated this growth and changed the traditional notion of the nation. Knowing the history and social standards of Bhutan is necessary for understanding the process of change that happened in the country. One should have an idea about how the social structure and values in the country are been functionalised and must know the economic aspects of the nation to evaluate the movement towards modernisation. This chapter provides an outline of the history, social structure, geography and economy of the country.

Being a Buddhist nation, Bhutan was shaped by religious values and it was kept isolated for centuries. It is very important to study and know the nation's history, geography, economy and social structure to get a better knowledge about how far the process of modernisation affected the nation's growth in the globalised economy.

The Early History of Bhutan

The Kingdom of Bhutan is a landlocked nation in the South Asian region, located at the Eastern end of the Himalayan Mountains, sandwiched between two emerging world powers, the Republic of India and the People's Republic of China (Tibet). Bhutan shares its border in the east and west with India, the world's seventh largest nation and to the north by the fourth largest- China. The early history of Bhutan is deeply concealed in the mystery of the past. Excavations and studies revealed that Bhutan was inhabited as early as 2000 BC. The archaeologists have unearthed Stone tools, weapons and large stone structures from Bhutan which belongs to that period. Historians believes that the state of *Lhomon* (meaning 'Southern Darkness') or *Monyul* (meaning 'Dark Land') believed to be inhabited by aboriginals of Bhutan known as *Monpa*, may have existed in this region between 500 BC and 600 AD. The ancient Bhutanese and Tibetan Chronicles have also mentioned the names of *Lhomon Tsendenjong* (meaning 'Sandalwood Country') and *Lhomon Khashi* (meaning 'Country of Four Gateways' or Southern Mon).[1]

The history of Bhutan remains as a mystery due to number of reasons. The people of this region once believed to be predominantly a pastoral-nomadic community, who practice *transhumance*. Such a nomadic and transhumant community is basically very rich in oral transmission of records and tradition due to the absence of a written language. In such a society and community, the facts and fictions of history may get mixed up with other traditions or sometimes many of the historical facts in those periods may be ignored by the people giving way to damaging an authentic background of the history. With the establishment of a theocratic society in the country, the significance of the family genealogy lost its relevance along with the clan organisations. Nomadism and migration of people facilitated this process further by losing their family genealogy and tradition. The very basic characteristics of *Lamaist* society, which is a mixture of Buddhism, animism, mysticism, tantric cult, and a battery of practices known as the '*Bon*', further accelerated this effect by linking the rulers and culture supernatural, merging them into the realm of mystique, sacred and other-worldliness. Moreover, the studies show that the records in the ancient time were kept in the *dzongs* (fortress), which emerged as the centre for religious, military, administrative, and social activities. These huge structured buildings were made of wooden edifices and it was mainly used to keep the historic records, wool, cereals, butter, other consumer goods and hide from enemies. Being made up of wood and built mostly on hilly areas without an architectural plan, it is prone to destruction by fire, earthquakes and attacks from other region or invaders along with the archival materials. In such conditions, it is natural to lose an authentic chronology of the country's ancient history. Thus, the early history of Bhutan can be gauged from its rich religious and mythical texts and legendary stories.[2]

Fire, earthquake, flood, and internecine warfare unfortunately destroyed whatever records may once have existed. The accidental burning in 1832 of the *Dzong* (monastery-fortress) in Punakha, one of the capitals of Bhutan at that time, and the widespread destruction caused at the same site by an earthquake in 1897, were especially responsible for the destruction of Bhutanese historical documents relating to the ancient period. The non-availability of historical documents on Bhutan resulted in its obscurity to the rest of the world. With given available artefacts preserved and kept in some of the ancient monasteries and archaeology departments, one finds that *Bonism*, shamanistic ritual, were followed in Bhutan prior to the advent of Buddhism in the country. These traditions are still practiced in some parts of the nation.[3]

The geographical situation of Bhutan and its policy of isolation by the early Monarchs kept the world at bay. Its ancient history, which is a mixture of the oral tradition and classical literature, tells of a largely self-sufficient population that had a limited contact with the outside world until the turn of the century. The earliest notable relics visible of the history of Bhutan, today, are the two monasteries, the

Kyichu Lhakhang in Paro and *Jambay Lhakhang* in Bumthang which were built in the 7th Century A.D.

Medieval Period of the Kingdom of Bhutan

The ancient and medieval histories of Bhutan have been described as the period of warlords, feuds, giant fortresses and castles, with intrigue, treachery and extraordinary pageantry. According to the historians, the earliest notable event happened in Bhutan was the passage of *Guru Rinpoche,* who is also known as the Buddhist saint Padmasambhava, in 747 A.D. One salient features of Guru Padmasambhava's religious policy was his incorporation of the Bon deities into the Buddhism pantheon, having, as the legend relates, bound them through oaths not only to serve the Buddhist faith, but also, in the process and necessity, to becomes its protector. During the medieval history of Bhutan, many of the Buddhist Monks (*Lamas*) in Tibet fled to Bhutan as a result of persecution by the rival *Gelugpa* lineage in the 9th century A.D. They settled down in Western Bhutan and established Buddhist Monasteries in the region. Since then, Buddhism has largely shaped the history of Bhutan and the way of life of its people. Many saints and religious figures, over the years, helped shape Bhutan's history and develop its religion.

The influence of Buddhism in the political scenario of Bhutan was more visible by the 10th century. By the 14th century A.D., the competition between the sects and sub-sects in the region mainly led by the Mongol and Tibetan overlords in the area witnessed the political and religious mix-up and fight for absolute power. In the 12th century, the *Drukpa Kagyupa School* (the Bhutanese form of Tibetan Buddhism) was established by Lama *Phajo Drukgom Shigpo* (1184-1251), who came to Bhutan from Ralung and defeated Lama *Lhanangpa* establishing a *Dzong* on the banks of Wang Chu River. Between the 13th & 16th centuries, the *Drukpa Kagyupa* tradition flourished in Bhutan becoming a dominant force.[4] Lama *Phajo Drukgom Shigpo's* four sons further spread the *Drukpa Kagyu* traditions in the country. Nevertheless, the *Drukpa* School continued until the 17th century, when it was totally crushed by *Shabdrung Ngwang Namgyal*.[5]

The arrival of Guru Shabdrung Rimpoche in the region heralded the most dynamic era in the history of Bhutan. In the 16th century, Bhutan remained fragmented with many feudal lords and religious figures competing for influence over one another. Lama Ngawang Namgyal (1594-1651) came to Bhutan from Ralung in Tibet, and travelled in Western Bhutan teaching his religious and political views. Soon, he established himself as the religious leader of Bhutan with the title Shabdrung Rimpoche. He developed the system of *Dzongs* which were the key to unifying Bhutan as a single nation. The *Dzongs* combined the three domains such as religious, political, and social functions. The Dual System of Government-the temporal and theocratic- worked with *Je Khenpo* (chief abbot) as the religious head and the political leader known as the *Druk Desi*. He was not only a great spiritual personality and a statesman but also left his indelible legacy as a great architect and a builder. The Shabdrung's Dual System of Government was ruled by 54 *Druk Desis* and 60 *Je Khenpos*, which steered Bhutan from 1651 until the birth of the Wangchuck Dynasty and establishment of a Hereditary Monarchy in 1907.[6]

Religious and secular powers were not clearly separated until the 17th century, when Shabdrung Ngwang Namgyal established a new Dual System Government. Even today, it is evident that the supreme head of the religious institutions known as the *Je Khenpo*, holds a prominent place in the social, cultural and political life of the Bhutanese people. The Shabdrung defeated many Tibetan invasions in this period to keep his region safe and united. In 1634, in the Battle of Five Lamas Ngawang Namgyal prevailed over the Tibetan and Bhutanese forces allied against him and was the first to unite Bhutan into a single country. In 1635 Punaka *Dzong* was completed becoming the home of the *Sangha* (Body of Monks) of Bhutan headed by the *Je Khenpo*. By 1639, Shabdrung Ngawang Namgyal was recognized as the Supreme Authority of Bhutan. In 1644, the Shabdrung defeated another Tibetan army and built *Drukgyel Dzong* on the upper part of the Paro valley to commemorate the victory. Further incursions in 1648 and 1649 were repulsed and the Shabdrung's influence spread throughout Bhutan.

Shabdrung Ngawang Namgyal went into retreat in Punaka *Dzong* in 1651. According to the reports he most likely died early in his retreat. His death was concealed through an elabourate ruse to be revealed in1705. The 'Desi' or secular ruler of this period felt the Shabdrung's influence would continue to keep Bhutan unified and keep the Tibetans at bay. During the period from 1656-1730 the Tibetans invaded several times. The third Desi Mingyur Tempa ruled for twelve years from 1668 and expanded Bhutan's western border to Kalimpong (India). The announcement of the Shabdrung's death began nearly two hundred year period of struggle and civil war in the country.[7]

State Building in Modern Bhutan

The nation which was also known as *Druk Yul* – The Land of the Thunder Dragon, has a unique history of religious and political stream which is steeped in mythology. The emergence of Bhutan as a state in the South Asian region is a story of continuous strife and structural reshufflement in religious, cultural and political spheres.[8] Known to its people as the Dragon Kingdom (*Drugu-yul*), the nation has always kept its tradition by keeping the country as other-worldly tradition of *Lamaist* Buddhism (the last *Shangri La*). With its *Lamaist* religion, Mythical Traditions and a unique pattern of culture, Bhutan impresses her visitors and people giving them a reluctantly Modernising, future-oriented and environment-friendly country. It provides a very different view of an imaginary world (*Shangri La*) scenario compared to the other nations in the South Asian Region. This is the Dragon Kingdom- Druk-yul- which the people like to call *IHo-mon-Khabzi* (the Southern Mon country of four Approaches) in the medieval Tibetan tradition.[9]

Until the 17th century, Bhutan was not a separate entity, as it was jointly ruled by a Buddhist spiritual ruler and a temporal ruler and the evolution was shrouded in mystery and ambiguity. Bhutan's political evolution to be a unified nation began from the establishment of political ascendancy of **Shabdrung Ngawang Namgyal** (1594-1651) who is considered as the great historical figure of Bhutan. He defeated all his rivals and became the King of Bhutan gaining full control of spiritual and temporal power. He began with a dual system of administration in the country known as *Chossi*. To look after the entire administration, the King appointed two Tibetan Monks. (1) *Je Khempo* (Dharma Raja) whose duties were to enforce the strict observation of priestly vows amongst the monks and presides at religious ceremonies. (2) *Druk Desi* (Deb Raja) who has to oversee the general administration of the state, mainly the functions related to foreign affairs, economy and financial matters and the needs of the Lamas.

As a process of change, he divided the country in to many administrative units known as *Dzongs* in which each unit was headed by a local governor known as *Penlop*, who had to obey the central authority. He established the council of states consisting of the *Je Khempo, Deb Raja, Penlops* and other high ranking religious and secular officers. Its function was to guide the affairs of state by offering concrete suggestion and laying down board guidance for policies to be implemented. In practice, all the major decisions were taken by the King, thus making the decentralised administrative structure a normal one.

From the death of Namgyal in 1651 till 1904, the political history of Bhutan is known as the history of rivalry, war and struggle. The system of governance was changed in 1907, when the temporal joint ruler became the King of Bhutan. The emergence of **Ugyen Wangchuk** (1907-1926) who was also called as *Tongsa Penlop* (Governor or *Penlop*) proved to be a good sign for a change in Bhutan's political history. He defeated his political enemies and rivals in the region and united the country following several civil wars and rebellions in 1882–1885. Being a powerful leader in the Central Bhutan, he was been "elected" as the Hereditary King (*Druk Gyalpo*) of Bhutan by a council of lamas, abbots, councillors, and laymen. With the emergence of Ugyen Wangchuk, the country entered in to a hereditary monarchical system of governance. He was an able administrator and a wise diplomat and took several reforms in the country and introduced the system of western education in Bhutan. By 1865, British forces invaded from India, annexing some border regions of Bhutan. In 1910, King Ugyen and the British signed the Treaty of Punakha which provided that British India would not interfere in the internal affairs of Bhutan unless the country accepted an external intervention.

In August 1926, with the death of Ugyen Wangchuk, his son **Jigme Wangchuk** (1905-1952) became the second King of Bhutan. He was a guiding force and a progressive ruler. During his reign, he too continued to maintain the policy of isolation from the outside world following his predecessor's policy. The only foreign relations the nation under the Majesty was with the British India. In 1949, shortly after gaining independence from the British Colonial rule, India recognized Bhutan's independence and returned the territories annexed by the British force in 1865. In the same year, the power to determine its foreign relations has been transferred to Bhutan.[10]

His Majesty Jigme Wangchuk was succeeded by his son, **Jigme Dorji Wangchuk** (1928- 1972) as the third King of Bhutan in October 1952. He was considered as the architect of modern Bhutan and responsible for bringing the nation in to international realm. During his reign, he changed the policy of isolation and began to open the nation's borders to the outside world. The idea of a *Tshogdu* (National Assembly) was conceived by Him in 1952. With His wisdom and foresight, the King realized that for the rapid progress of the country, all sections of the people must participate in the deliberation on national issues and must advice on the formulation of many policies which would have an impact on the country and the people of Bhutan.

The history of Bhutan from 17th century to 20th century provides a clear picture of Bhutan's political activities and its struggle to survive as an independent state in the world and especially in the South Asian Region. Up to 1952, the institution of monarchy in Bhutan centralised its power and integrated all the other areas of administration. It was only under the guidance of Jigme Dorji Wangchuk, that the discretion of this institution had deviated from its traditional way. Thus since 1952, Bhutan moved towards a new direction of more liberal and modern administrative system seeking recognition as a sovereign independent country with its own distinct identity and unique culture.

King **Jigme Singye Wangchuck** (1955-2006, abdicated) emerged as the fourth hereditary Monarch of Bhutan in 1972 at the age of 17 due to the sudden death of his father Jigme Dorji Wangchuk and was formally crowed as the King of Bhutan on June 1974. He also continued his father's policies of slow modernisation while trying to preserve the unique culture of Bhutan. He made changes in the socio- economic conditions of the nation. Under his reign, the nation went through tremendous progress in the field of communications, hydro-electric power development, education, health, financial sector, environmental protection, and industrial and infrastructural development.

Bhutan became member of a large number of international organisations under the leadership of His Majesty Jigme Singye Wangchuck. In September 1971, Bhutan became a full member of the United Nations Organisation and maintained a diplomatic mission in New York and Geneva. In the year 1972, Bhutan became a member of the ESCAP and NAM in 1973, IFAD, IMF, IBRD, IDA and FAO in 1981. Membership to the World Health Organisation, UNESCO and ADB has been taken in the year1982, UNIDO in 1983, ITU in 1988, ICAO in 1989 and ECOSOC in 1992. During his reign, Bhutan established diplomatic relations with Switzerland, Denmark, Sweden, EEC, Norway and Netherlands Kuwait, Japan, Finland, South Korea, Austria, Thailand, Bahrain, Hong Kong, Singapore, Macaw, Maldives, Sri Lanka, Pakistan, Bangladesh, India and Nepal.[11]

The National Assembly of Bhutan took a major step to Modernise the administrative system when it officially sanctioned the formation of the Council of Ministers in May 1968 under his reign. In 2005, steps began towards the introduction of a democratic constitution in 2008. On December, 2005, His Majesty King Jigme Singye Wangchuk announced that from 2008, he would abdicate the throne in favour of the Crown Prince of Bhutan Jigme Khesar Namgyal Wangchuk. In the last year of his reign the King prepared a draft constitution for the nation. He made a historical change in his last period by proclaiming an election in 2008 to elect a parliamentary democratic government to rule the nation.

In December 2007 and in March 2008, the elections took place in Bhutan to the National Council and National Assembly respectively, which made the hereditary King as a constitutional monarch. The changes in the political system of Bhutan from absolute to constitutional monarchy were aimed at giving the people a decisive voice in the countries affairs. Contrary to any of the monarchical system, Bhutan shifted its political structure to a parliamentary democracy in 2008 which was supported and initiated by the country's ruler- His Majesty the King in pursuit of attaining Gross National Happiness (GNH). With the establishment of the new political system, the administration in the nation fostered people's capacity to participate in decision making through various decentralisation programs towards promoting GNH.[12]

In November 2008, **Jigme Khesar Namgyal Wangchuck** was officially crowned as the fifth continuous and first Constitutional Monarch of the nation. After the establishment of a democratic parliamentary government the responsibility of ruling the nation has been transferred to the Prime Minister from the century old Hereditary Monarchical rule. However, the King still holds a vital role in the country's policy making.

Geographical Condition of Bhutan

Situated in the Southern slop of Eastern Himalayas, Bhutan gives an impression of snowy mountains, verdant forests, snaking rivers and a very low population density to the other world. The country presents a striking evidence of how the geographical setting of a nation influences social, political and economic life of its people. Topographically, Bhutan is been viewed as a nation surrounded by mountains and ridges of varying heights and widely differing altitudes disclosing various climatic conditions.

Natural Geography

Nestled towards the eastern extreme of the Himalayas mountain range Bhutan lies between 26°45′N-28°10′N latitude and 88°45′N-92°10′E longitudes of the northern hemisphere sandwiched between China and India. Being a compact nation of an approximate area of 46500 square kilometres, Bhutan is landlocked by its neighbours and its maximum east-west extension is 300 km and the north – south extension is 150-170 km.[13] Owing to its land locked nature, not only trade and commerce but various other development activities have been severely constrained. The Himalayas dominated the north part of Bhutan at a height of approximately 7570 meters. Weather is extreme in the mountains: the high peaks have perpetual snow, and the lesser mountains and hewn gorges have high winds all year round, making them barren brown wind tunnels in summer and frozen wastelands in winter.

The Kingdom of Bhutan is located on the southern slopes of the eastern Himalayas surrounded by the Tibet to the north and the Indian states of Sikkim, West Bengal, Assam and Arunachal Pradesh on the west and south (see figure). The geographical terrain of Bhutan consists mostly of steep and high mountains crisscrossed by a network of swift rivers which form deep valleys in the region. The elevation of the region starts from about 200 meters int he southern foothills to more than 7000 meters in the north.

Such a great geographical diversity combined with equally diverse climate conditions contributes to the nation's remarkable range of biodiversity and ecosystems. The northern region of Bhutan consists of a number of Himalayan shrub and meadows reaching up to the mountain peaks at the highest elevations. The highest point in Bhutan is Gangkhar Puensum with a hight of 7570 meters which is considered to be one of the highest unclimbed mountains in the world. Most of the country's peaks int he northern region are situated over 7000 meters above sea level. The lowest point is in the valley of Drangme Chhu at 98 meters near Indian boarder.

FIGURE 1.1
Geographical Map of Bhutan

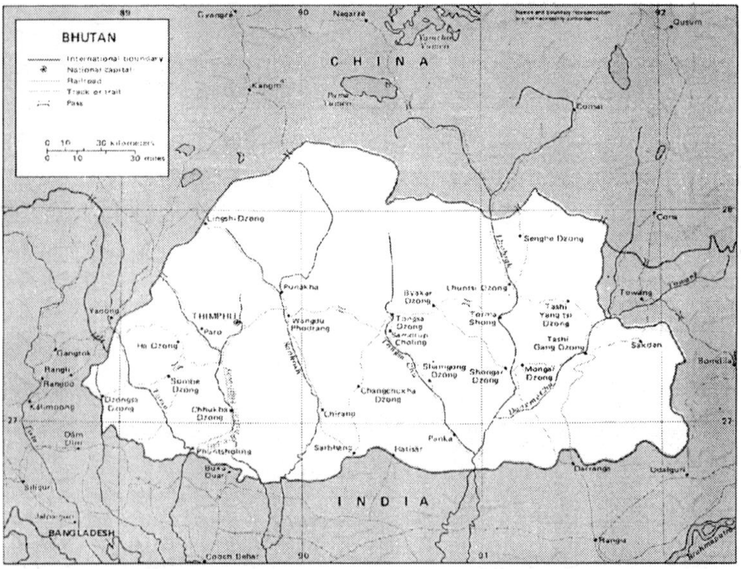

Bhutan's Ecology and Environment

Physically, Bhutan has been divided in to three lateral ones from north to south, such as, the great Himalaya, the

FIGURE 1.2
Physical Map of Bhutan

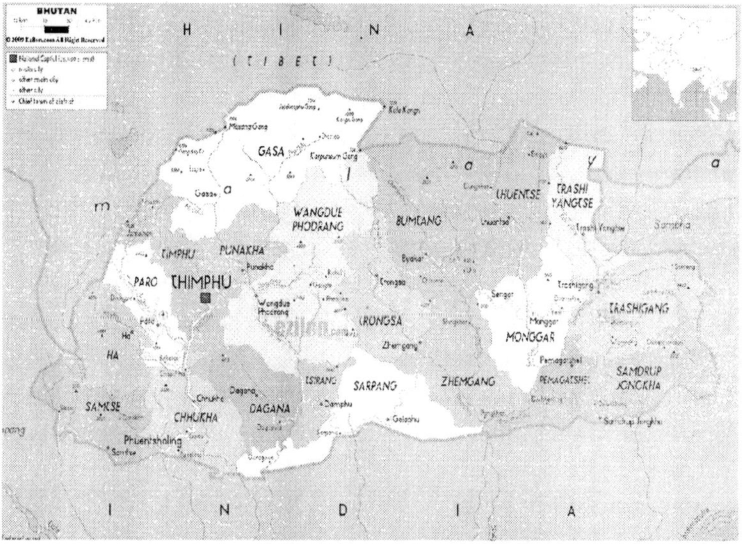

inner Himalaya or the middle range, and the sub-Himalaya or outer-most range. Each of these zones has a different ecology of its own: sub-tropical, temperate and alpine.[14] Around 72.5 percent of Bhutan's total land is under forest cover providing home to about 7000 species of plants, 165 species of mammals and 700 species of birds. Approximately 35.23 percent of the nation's land lies under protected areas and biological corridors which created to connect different protected parks. This keeps Bhutan as one of the nations with a highest percent of land area under protected area and forest cover in Asia. Bhutan has been rated as one of the top ten countries with the highest density in the world.[15] Centuries of isolation, a small population, and topographical extremes have led to Bhutan maintaining one of the most intact ecosystems in the world.

Unlike other South Asian nations, Bhutan is successful in preserving and conserving its rich bio diversity and been declared as 'hotspots' globally. The history of Bhutan shows that the people have tried to preserve its natural environment. Under the influence of strong Buddhist beliefs, they always lived in harmony with nature and this relationship has been inbound within the lives of Bhutanese in moral, cultural and ecological aspects. The people in Bhutan believes in giving back to nature what has been taken from it and respect all forms of life as Buddhism teaches about the interdependence among all life forms.[16]

Bhutan is been gifted with a verity of forest types like, Fir Forests, Mixed Conifer Forest, Blue Pine Forest, Chirpine Forest, Broadleaf mixed with Conifer, Upland Hardwood Forest, Lowland Hardwood Forest, and Tropical Lowland Forests. Bhutan is also home for 46 species of Rhododendrons and over 300 types of medicinal plants. Bhutan is also a heaven for a wide range of animals like Snow leopard, blue sheep, red panda, tiger, takin, marmot and musk deer in high altitude and Tiger, leopard, goral, gray langur, Himalayan black beer, red panda, sambar, wild pig, and barking deer in the temperate zone. The tropical forests in the south is a home for clouded leopard, elephants, one horned Rhinoceros, water buffalo, golden langur, gaur, swamp deer, hog deer and horn bills.

The country is also considered as a place favourable for birds. More than 670 species of birds have been found in the area so far. Most of the inhabitant birds are altitudinal refugees which move up and down the mountains depending upon the weather and seasons. Around 50 species are known to be winter migrants and 40 species as summer visitors. Bhutan is also privy to 16 species of internationally vulnerable birds like Pallas's Fish Eagle, White bellied Heron, Satyr Tragopan, Grey bellied Tragopan, Ward's Trogaon, Blyth's King Fisher, Chestnut breasted Partridge, Blyth's Trogon, Wood Snipe, Dark

Rumped Swift, Rufous Necked Hornbill, etc.

The nation is also an important wintering ground for the rare Black Necked Crane which is also known as *Thrung Thrung Karmo*. It is considered as a Heavenly Bird (*lhab-bja*), which harmoniously coexisted with the people due to strong Buddhist beliefs. This can be clearly visible in the Phobjikha valleys, where even today no electricity (except solar and mini-hydro) or telephone lines been established out of fear that stringing up power lines could injure the cranes. The nation has begun some environmental organizations for the preservation and protection of the rich environment.[17] The southern strip of Bhutan mostly consists of Himalayan subtropical broadleaf forests that come under the tropical plains of the Terai-Duar savanna and grasslands. These lands are largely used for agricultural purpose producing mostly rice.

In the southern region of Bhutan, the Shiwalik Hills are covered with dense Himalayan subtropical broadleaf forests, alluvial lowland river valleys and a number of mountains with varying heights at 1500 meters above sea level. The foothills in the country are descended into the subtropical Duars Plain which has its strip extended to Bhutan to 10 to 15 km. The Bhutan Duars are divided in to two parts such as the northern Duars and the southern Duars. The Northern Duars has rugged, sloping terrain and dry, porus soil with dense vegetation and abundant wildlife. The southern Duars has moderately fertile soil, heavy savannah grass, dense and mixed forests and many freshwater springs.

Road and Air Transport

Bhutan is one of the most mountainous and sparsely populated countries in the world providing social and other infrastructure very costly. Bhutan has a very limited road and air transportation. Until 1961, the transportation in Bhutan was mainly by foot or on muleback or horse because of the lack of roads and transportation facilities. The modern road transportation facilities began during the First Development, Plan (1961-1966) under the Third King of Bhutan His Majesty Jigme Dorji Wangchuck. The first ever paved road was completed in 1962 from Thimphu (Trashigang) to Phuntsholing. By the mid of 1970's, about 1500 kilometres of roads had been built in Bhutan connecting some of the important places in the country. However, the mountainous terrain in the nation makes the transportation very difficult from one valley to the next despite these road networks. The country has an international airport at Paro with a paved single runway and a domestic airport at Trashigang with an unpaved single runway. Drukair is the national carrier connecting Bhutan (Paro) with Thailand, Nepal, Bangladesh and India.

Climate

Bhutan, perhaps one of the most beautiful gifts of nature to the world, which is been called as the *Last Shangri-la* by many writers, has an outstanding picturesque environment on the earth. Like any of the South Asian countries, Bhutan's climate is also varied depending on the monsoons. The climate in Bhutan varied depending on the geographical features of the nation as it is humid and subtropical in the southern plains and foothills, in the inner Himalayan valleys of the southern plains and central regions it's temperate and the climate in the north if cold as it's covered by snow. The temperature also varies according to the elevation of the plains. Most of the central parts of the nation experience a cool and temperate climate throughout the year. The northern range of the country experiences an extreme cold climate in winters. In the south, the climate is of a hot, humid and the temperature sometimes reaches up to 40°C in summer.

River System

The country has four major river systems; the *Drangme Chhu*, the *Puna Tsang Chhu*, also called the Sankosh, the *Wang Chhu* and the *Amo Chhu* flows southwards through the Duars to join the Brahmaputra River in India. Among this the Drangme Chhu is the largest, which flows south-westerly and has three major branches like the Drangme Chhu, Mangde Chhu, and Bumthang Chhu. The Puna Tsang Chhu river which is of 320 kilometers long begins in north-western Bhutan fed by the snows from the Great Himalayan Range. The Wang Chhu River flows through west-central Bhutan draining the Ha, Paro and Thimphu valleys. Among this three the smallest river system, the Torsa Chhu, known as the Amo Chhu flow through the western Bhutan before it reaches India.[18] The fast-flowing rivers in the Black Mountain range nearly about 1500 to 4925 meters above sea level, have carved out deep gorges in the lower mountain areas.

Society and Culture of Bhutan

Culture: Situating in the folds of the Himalayas, Bhutan has been always been protective of its tradition and culture from the outside cultural influence. The policy of isolation that the rulers kept till recently helped the nation to keep its culture unique and the economy independent. This way Bhutan has successfully preserved and promoted its culture which dates back to thousands of years. The lack of contact with the outside world forced Bhutan to establish its own distinct forms of civilisation, socio-economic life and religious and political institutions. The Buddhist religious influence is clearly visible in Bhutan's culture and social life. Every aspects of Bhutanese people's life such as the language, architecture, drama, dance and music, ceremonies, festivals, etc. have a direct impact and roots from the Buddhist teachings.[19]

The present modern Bhutanese culture is derived from its ancient culture and religion which has an immense role in the early growth of the country. The Bhutanese languages, *Dzongkha* and *Sharchop*, have a close relation with the Tibetan language known as *Chhokey*. The genealogy the Bhutanese people are similar to that of the Tibetans.

The Tradition of Sectarian Myth

Bhutan has been given an image of *Shangri-la*, an image of being other –worldly society, situated in the snowy Himalayan ranges and forested ravines, is the only *Lamaist* country in the world wrapped in myths, legends and hoary past.[20] The Mahayana School of Buddhism of Bhutan assimilated most of the pre-Tibetan Buddhist religious practices, myths, legends and theology in to it. The traditional dances and the instruments used are closely related to Buddhist religion which can be traced back to the 17th century.[21] The western part of Bhutan is considered as the cultural region of the nation as it is the base for important cultural-political centres like Paro, Punakha, Thimphu and Wangdi Phodrang.[22]

Religion and Festivals

The religious practices of Bhutan are basically centred on the concepts of *Tantric Buddhism*. Religion has an important role in everyone's life in the country. Mahayana Buddhism is the state religion of Bhutan. Each valley or districts has a huge *Dzong*, or a high-walled fortress, which is basically used as the religious and administrative centres.

Majority of the population are Buddhist which comes to two-third to three-quarters of the population, mostly from the *Drukpa Kagyupa* or *Ningmapa* Buddhism, and nearly one quarter of the population is Hindus who are ethnic Nepalese. Other religions like Christianity, Islam and non-religious groups constitute less than one percent of the total population. The nation celebrates many festivals especially in the village communities. Local *isechu* festivals are practiced to honour Guru Rinpoche. Most of the festivals are held in the courtyards of the *dzongas*. The *Chaam* dances are the special features of these festivals. The other characteristic of the festival is the archery contests for which the rules are different from that of the international competitions.[23].

National Dress Code

The nation's government has maintained a law stating that the ethnic Bhutanese must wear the traditional dress, which is known as the national dress code (*Driglam Namzha*) in public. Shabdrung Ngawang Namgyal established this dress code in 17th century attempting to create a unique identity to the people of Bhutan. According to *Driglam Namzha* men in the nation wear a heavy knee length robe known as *Gho*, tied with a woven cloth belt called *'Kera'*. The national dress code of women in Bhutan is called *'Kira'* generally made of woven fabric which is a floor-length rectangular piece of cloth and wears it over a blouse called *'Wonju'*.[24] Both men and women wear scarves or shawls, white for commoners and carefully specified colours, designs, and manners of folding for higher ranking individuals. Only the *Druk Gyalpo* and the *Je Khenpo* were allowed to wear the honorific saffron scarf. Other officials were distinguished by the colour of the scarves they wore: orange for ministers and deputy ministers, blue for National

Assembly and Royal Advisory Council members, and red or maroon for high religious and civil officials, district officers, and judges (anyone holding the title of *Dasho*). The ethnic Nepalese citizens in the southern part of the country near Indian border showed resistance to the national dress code of Bhutan.[25]

The Bhutanese People and Society

Society: Bhutan, the land of migrants, comprises of a population of multi-ethnic, multi-religious and multi-lingual society consisting of four major groups. They are the *Ngalop*, the *Sharchop*, several aboriginal peoples, and Nepalese origin. Each ethnic group of Bhutan has lived clustered together in separate regions and places. The major three ethnic groups such as the *Ngalop*, the *Sharchop* and the Nepalese origin people migrated to Bhutan at different periods of the history. Besides these groups, there are other smaller ethnic groups having their own distinct characteristics in terms of language, culture, religious practices, etc such as Tibetans, *Doyas, Khengs, Adivashis, Brokpas Monpa, Gongduk Lhop/Doya, Kurteops*.

The *Ngalops* are those people who migrated to Bhutan as early as 9th century from Tibet. They are often referred as *Bhote* (people of Bhotia or Tibet) in some literatures. They introduced a Tibetan culture and Buddhist religion in Bhutan and began political and cultural element in modern Bhutan. The *Ngalops* (*Drukpas*) are concentrated in the north-western region of the nation. They are called as *Drukpas* as they follow the *Drukpa Kargyupa School* of Buddhism. Being an agrarian society, they cultivate rice, wheat, barley, maize etc.

The *Sharchops* which means easterner, are Indo-Mongoloid people who are migrated from Assam or possibly Burma during the past millennium, comprise most of the population of eastern Bhutan is the second largest ethnic group in Bhutan. They practice slash-and-burn and *tsheri* agriculture. They practice *Nyingmapa* sect of Mahayana Buddhism and belong to Tibeto-Burman ancestry. They speak *Sharchopkha, Tsangla, Kurteop, Kheng and Brokpa* dialects.

Aboriginals and Indigenous Tribal people consist of small aboriginal or indigenous tribal peoples living in scattered villages throughout Bhutan. Historically they believed to be culturally and linguistically part of the populations of West Bengal or Assam. They embrace the Hindu system of endogamous groups ranked by hierarchy and practice wet-rice and dry-rice agriculture. They include the *Drokpa, Lepcha,* and *Doya* tribes as well as the descendants of slaves who were brought to Bhutan from similar tribal areas in India.

The Nepalese Origin the remaining 28 percent of the population were of Nepalese origin. The first small groups of Nepalese, the most recent major groups to arrive in Bhutan, emigrated primarily from eastern Nepal under Indian auspices in the late 19th and early 20th centuries. Mostly Hindus, the Nepalese settled in the southern foothills and are sometimes referred to as southern Bhutanese. Traditionally, they have been involved mostly in sedentary agriculture, although some have cleared forest cover and conducted *tsheri* agriculture.

Bhutan also had a sizable modern Tibetan refugee population. The Tibetan expatriates became only partially integrated into Bhutanese society, however, and many were unwilling to accept citizenship. Although Bhutan traditionally welcomed refugees and still accepted a few new ones fleeing the 1989 imposition of martial law in Tibet—government policy in the late 1980s was to refuse more Tibetan refugees.[26]

Social Structure

The traditional society of Bhutan has been defined as both patriarchal and matriarchal in its form. In the absence of a strong social stratification in the society the nation also has been described as a feudalistic society. As in every culture, Bhutan's society also divided in to a three-tire system, the monastic community, the rulers or civil servants, who ran the government and the farmers living in villages.[27] This classification of community later added the class of prisoners of war and their descendants in the medieval period of war and conflict. The ancient and medieval social structure was characterized by joint family units and occupational and social status based class division. With the introduction of modernisation and globalisation in the present modern Bhutan the joint family structure has been changed in to nuclear family units. The caste system was absent in Bhutan except in the southern part where Nepalese Hindus reside.[28]

Language: Dzongkha the national language of Bhutan is an offshoot of Tibetan language. The Nepalese impact in the language is also visible in the nation. The country has mainly nineteen dialects spoken by the people besides *Dzongkha*. English is been establish as the official language of Bhutan. There are mainly four types of languages used in different parts of Bhutan. They are (1) Dzongkha which is spoken in the western and northern parts of Bhutan (2) Bumthankha used in central Bhutan (3) Sarchapkha in eastern parts and (4) Nepali and Hindi in the southern parts of the country.

Women: Contrary to the neighbouring countries Bhutanese women occupies more rights than men especially in the land ownership rights. Throughout the tradition the property of each extended or joint Bhutanese family is been controlled by an "anchor mother" assisted by the other women in the family. She passes her position to her sister, daughter or niece known as matrilinearity by the anthropologists. Men and women in Bhutan work together in the field and own shops and businesses individually. The culture of Bhutan allows both men and women to be the monks, but the number of women monks are relatively less in the country. The traditional joint family system is changing to a nuclear family where the husband as breadwinner and wife as home-maker where in the joint family system men take a full part in the household management.[29]

Marriage: Marriages in the country are based on mutual affection than the traditional pattern based on family and ethnic ties. Being arranged by the partners, the minimum age is sixteen for women and twenty-one for men. The institution of child marriage had in a large extent wiped out from Bhutan as the nation Modernised in the late 20th century. Interethnic marriages are now being encouraged by the late 1980's. The practice of polyandry and polygamy was restricted in the mid twentieth century, but the law in the country allows one to have as many as three wives, provided he had permission from first wife. Divorce is not uncommon, and new laws provided better benefits to women seeking alimony. The marriages are registered officially only after the couple live together for more than six months.

Family: Family life in Bhutan, both traditionally and in the contemporary modern period, insists in providing self-sufficiency by making own clothing, bedding, etc. land ownership and possession varied depending on the wealth and size of the individual families. The key element of family life in Bhutan was the availability of labour as joint family system in villages existed. The married couple move to one home depending on the strength of the labour in that family. Newly wedded couples normally move to that side where labour is less and if both sides have enough they are free to set up their own individual families.[30]

Economy and Development of Bhutan

Bhutan's economy is one of the world's smallest and least developed economies. The nation's economy is based on agriculture and forestry, which contribute more than 60 percent to the Gross Domestic Product (GDP). The agricultural economy largely consists of subsistence farming and animal husbandry. The economy of Bhutan is closely related with India's trade and monetary links and depends on India's financial assistance. Being a landlocked nation, the rugged terrain across the Kingdom had made the development activities slow and difficult. Since the development activities in 1960's, Bhutan began to develop dramatically in its socio-economic sphere within a short span of time. The economic development programs were closely monitored by the rules so that the countries environment and cultural heritage are not been damaged. Bringing the country out of its geographic and economic isolation was the prior development strategy of Bhutan. Every economic program in Bhutan takes into account the government's desire to protect the country's environment and unique cultural traditions.

The Monetary System

Since the 18th century, Bhutan had its own coinage system. The monetary system of Bhutan was based on the decimal-system *Ngultrum* which was established as the nation's currency and used to keep financial accounts. Prior to 1957, a nondecimal system using both Indian and Bhutanese rupees was in usage and this was the standard currency till 1974. However, until 1960's, most of the financial transactions were carried out using barter arrangements in the nation. Bhutan's Ministry of finance, which provided foreign exchange for most currencies and capital transactions till 1985, delegated most of this function to the Royal Monetary Authority.

Agriculture

The Bhutanese economy is largely an agrarian society and most of its livelihood comes from farming. However, the arable land in the nation is only a small fraction of the total geographical area of the country. The adverse climate, poor soil, and steep slopes in much of Bhutan have made it necessary to leave a large land area covered with forest growth, meadows, and grasslands. The central Bhutan which is relatively low, well-watered and fertile soil has the largest percentage of the cultivated land. Being the back born of the economy, agriculture contributes about 33percent to the GDP and near about 70 percent of the population depends on it for livelihood.[31]

The agriculture sector provided 22.3 percent of GDP in the year 2006. The growth rate of 2010th GDP consisted of a high production of crops and a well planned economic activity in the forestry sector and livestock production. While self-sufficient in maize, barley, millet, and buckwheat, Bhutan is only 50 percent self-sufficient in rice and 30 percent in wheat. In total the country is around 60 percent self-sufficient in cereals. Other key crops which are actually exported are potatoes, spices (mainly cardamom and nutmeg), and fruit which in 1997 consisted mainly of oranges (54,000 metric tons) and apples (13,600 metric tons). In total, agricultural goods provided 13.7 percent of Bhutan's total exports in 1997.

Bhutan was traditionally self-sufficient in food production. Most of Bhutan's citizens and a significant amount of its GDP were devoted to the agricultural sector in the late 1980s. About 87 percent of the population was involved in agriculture, and a projected 30.5 percent of GDP was expected to be produced through farming, animal husbandry, and fishing in 1991. Most agriculture was carried out with traditional methods and at the subsistence level. Faced with constraints of a shortage of cultivable and pasture land, lack of technical knowledge, logistical difficulties, and a shortage of skilled labour and managerial expertise, agricultural development was difficult. Government interest in agriculture was ensured during the First Development Plan (1961-66), with the establishment of agriculture and animal husbandry departments to oversee model farms, research, and crop and herd improvement, a trend which continued through subsequent development plans.[32]

Agriculture is hampered due to irrigation problem, rough terrain, poor soil quality and limited number of arable lands. But several other factors have contributed in the development of agriculture. These factors include improved quality of various cereal seeds, oil seeds, and vegetable seeds, use of fertilizers, mechanisation process and trained agricultural experts. In several areas, the shifting cultivation is being replaced by the orchard cultivation. Progressive changes in farming and forestry practices have been introduced in Bhutan since the late 20th century to increase the productivity of the agricultural sector. A large number of orchards have been established, and thousands of fruit plants have been distributed to farmers to popularize fruit growing. Emphasis also has been given to the development of small-scale irrigation schemes. In the early 21st century the sector remains a leading contributor to Gross Domestic Product (GDP) and a top employer of Bhutan's labour force. Most Bhutanese farms are small in size, and terraces are used extensively to raise crops on hillslopes. Corn (maize), potatoes, rice, citrus fruits, apples, and various spices, including nutmeg, mace, and cardamom, are among the chief crops. Cattle, pigs, and horses are the principal livestock raised on Bhutan's scattered pastures. About two-thirds of Bhutan is covered with forests. Consequently, timber production emerged as an important component of the economy, and there are many sawmills situated throughout the country. Growth of the forestry industry has been restrained, however, by legislation aimed at preserving the country's extensive forest cover.

Industry

The industrial sector of Bhutan is technologically backward and in a nascent stage due to its isolation policy by its rulers in the beginning. Most of the production sectors in the nation are of a cottage industry type. Manufacturing, which began in Bhutan about 1970, has grown considerably, with four industries -producing cement, chemicals, wood products, and processed foods-arising as pillars of the sector by the early 21st century. Nearly all Bhutan's manufacturing centres are located in the south, close to the Indian border. Phuntsholing, with nearly half of Bhutan's manufacturing activity, is the largest industrial centre.[33] Craft manufacture is the predominant industrial occupation, and homespun textiles—woven and embroidered cottons, wools, and silks—are the most important products. Other Bhutanese handicrafts include Daphne paper; swords; wooden bowls; leather objects; copper, iron, brass, bronze, and silver work; wood carvings; and split-cane basketry. The industrial sector provided 37.9 percent of GDP of Bhutan in the year 2006. The subject 'industries' covers the whole range of industrial activity carried out by businesses in all fields including mining, manufacturing, wholesale and retail trade, and other service industries. In Bhutan, the industrial sector has until recently, played a relatively small role in the economy of the Kingdom.

The economy in the 21st century has become increasingly dominated by the hydroelectric sector, and the building of new power projects has led to double-digit growth in the transport and construction sectors, including a number of local cement operations. The country's first cement plant was completed in the border town of Penden in 1982 by India, to which the bulk of its output is exported. Bhutan's first mega power plant, the 336-MW Chukha Hydroelectricity Project (CHEP), came on line in early 1987, having been first agreed to as a turn-key operation with India in 1961, on what has become a standard arrangement of 60% grant and 40% concessional loan. In 1988, in conjunction with the country's sixth economic plan (1987–1992), the Bhutan Development Finance Corporation was established to promote small- and medium-scale businesses. A second cement plant was established in Nanglam by the late 1980s, and another, in 1995, in the same town, by an Indian investor, along with several manufacturing plants producing carbide, particleboard and other products destined for the Indian market, but Bhutan industrialisation was hobbled by stridently anti-foreign, anti-modernity policies.

There are a large number of small, privately owned sawmills throughout Bhutan since most of its domestic energy actually comes from firewood, not electricity. Industrial estates have been set up at Phuntsholing and Geylegphug, and the Ninth Five Year Plan (2002 to 2006) calls for five more to be located around the country. Besides cement, there is a narrow range of other manufactures exported—Ferro-alloys, calcium carbide, processed foods and particleboard—which tend to rely on energy-and capital-intensive methods and expatriate labour. Bhutan Ferro Alloys Ltd., which makes ferrosilicon and exports to India and Japan, began operations at a new plant at Pasakha in April 1995. It is likely that with the emphases in the Ninth Five Year Plan on commercial and private sector development as means of achieving economic self-sufficiency and generating employment, this share will continue to grow.[34]

Only 1 percent or less of the work force was involved in industry and construction in the late 1980s, and industrial production and construction represented only 14.2 percent of GDP projected for 1991. Handicrafts, cement, food processing, wood milling, and distilling were the major industries. Most of the larger industries, established since Bhutan's economic Modernisation began in the 1960s, were themselves modern and used a considerable amount of labour-saving technology. The largest industries employed no more than sixty or seventy workers. Many of the newly developing industries began making public stock offerings in the late 1980s.[35] The mining industry in Bhutan is as yet relatively undeveloped. The Kingdom has significant deposits of a number of mineral resources, including limestone, coal, graphite, gypsum, slate and dolomite. Most mining activity is limited to relatively small operations, mainly involved in the mining of limestone, coal, slate and graphite.

Service Sector

Like the industrial sector the service sector in Bhutan is also backward and in a beginning stage. After the introduction of modernisation and getting out from the policy of isolation, the nation saw a progressive change in the service sector. The nation began to move into an era of

Modernisation and development in the late 20th century. The service sector in Bhutan includes the banking sector, education, the tourism and hospitality sector, the printing and publishing sector and information and communication technology, etc. The nation had witnessed a successful change and development in all this fields in the last few decades. The nation began to accept foreign tourists to Bhutan and started providing them hospitality since 1970's. The media in the nation got a new life in the modernising era, especially after the general election in 2008. The internet and web services in Bhutan made the people to think globally and helped them to connect with the outside world. The service sector in Bhutan had provided around 39.8 percent to the nation's GDP and economy and expecting a bigger contribution by 2010 with plans to construct a domestic airport at Youngphula and the opening of Merak and Sakteng to the tourists, many resorts and hotels are sprouting in Trashigang.

Tourism has been an important industry and the country's largest foreign-exchange earner since its inception in 1974. Most tourists visit cultural sites-particularly *dzong* and temples-and observe seasonal festivals featuring masked dances and archery contests or go on trekking expeditions on foot or mounted on horses or yaks. The government then decided to limit the number of tourists to around 2,000 a year and restricted access seasonally and to certain historical, cultural, and scenic sites. These restrictions resulted in decreases to 2,199 tourists and to revenues of US$1.9 million in 1988. Opened to increasing tourism, Bhutan planned to turn over its government-run hotels to private management to improve its lodging accommodations.

In the early 1990s, however, the tourism industry was privatized, and since that time the volume of tourists, tourist facilities, and tourist income increased monumentally. In the early 21st century there remained a government-imposed daily tourist tariff to ensure significant tourist input into the economy. With greater government expenditure on education and social services, as well as increased allowance to civil servants, government and financial services also expanded since the late 20th century. The services sector—including primarily public administration and defence, finance, trade and restaurants, and public utilities—generates more than one-third of Bhutan's GDP.[36]

Trade and Commerce

Trade: Traditionally, majority of the nation's foreign trade was with Tibet before 1960's. But after this period, following the closing of the Bhutan-China border and the development of closer ties with India, Bhutan began to have more trade relations with India replacing Tibet. The nation, since 1960 achieved a continuous growth in its export and import with India. There were no import duties on Indian imports, but customs fees had to be paid on imports from other nations. Bhutan is an integral part in the South Asian trade and commerce in the 21st century. Being the smallest economy in the world as well as in SAARC community, the nation is trying to make itself in to a developing economy and establish bilateral and multi lateral trade relations with the other nations. Bhutan predominantly had trading relations with India for a long period since 1960's. The nation's trade, export and imports have flourished during the last few decades under its 8th and 9th Five Year Plans. Since 2002, Bhutan has diversified its imports to African countries and Latin American nations. Bhutan imports crude marbles from Egypt, vegetable products from Brazil, copper wires from Cyprus and medical equipment from Finland for the last few years. In the year 2007, the nation began to import cars and cell phones from Kuwait and Sudan.[37]

Both imports and exports increased steadily during the 1980s, from a total of Nu805.9 million in 1983 to more than Nu2.9 billion in 1990. The balance of trade also improved as the decade progressed. Although there was little trade with the United States, in recognition of its economic status Bhutan was granted an exemption in 1985 from the competitive trade requirements provided by the United States' Generalized System of Preferences. In the year 2007, Bhutan's main export partners were India with 58.6 percent, Hong Kong with 30.1 percent and bilateral trade with Bangladesh touched 7.3 percent. The main import was mainly with India with 74.5 percent and Japan stood second with 7.4 percent followed by Sweden with a small percent of 3.2 in the year 2007.

Exports, which reached almost Nu1.2 billion in 1990, consisted primarily of cement, talc, fruit (mostly oranges) and fruit products, alcoholic beverages, resin, cardamom, lumber products, potatoes, and handicrafts. Although most trade was with India, such specialties as timber, cardamom, and liquor were exported to Bangladesh, Singapore, and countries in the Middle East and Western Europe. The opening of thirteen border crossings with customs facilities for Bhutan's exports and imports also eased trade with Nepal and Bangladesh. Imports amounted to nearly Nu1.8 billion in 1990. They consisted of raw materials; textiles; cereals; fuel; investment goods, including motor vehicles; and other consumer goods, primarily from India.

The year 2007 saw a significant surge in the import and export of Bhutan wit compared to 2006. Bhutan's trade with India in the year witnessed and increase in terms of imports and exports by 16.13% and 33.49%, respectively. The country's imports from third world countries increased by 11.55%, while the exports grew by 19.9% in the year 2007. The export items of Bhutan included electricity, software, cables and vegetable oils in the year 2008 which came to a total of $513 million. This year was a milestone in the export trade of the nation by joining its hands with the country's biggest partners like India and Bangladesh, and to an extent, Italy. The export value stood at Nu 27.86 billion the year 2007 for Bhutan.

The total value of import in electricity stood at Nu 21.74 billion in the year 2007 with top imports of Cars, crude oil and machinery. Marking a significant increase in imports in the year 2008 at $533 million with that of a $320 million in 2006. Bhutan's main import partners were India (63%), Japan (12.3%) and China (5.1%). According to industry trade experts the bilateral trade with India and Bhutan is expected to grow by 15% in 2009-2010. The main areas of trade were identified as power, roads, health, tourism, environment management, horticulture, automobiles and agro processing.[38]

Commerce: Commercial services were projected to generate 7.4 percent of GDP in 1991. Much of Bhutan's commerce revolved around tourist oriented hotels and restaurants, and wholesale and retail trade made up the balance. The Bhutan Chamber of Commerce and Industry served as a formal conduit between government and private-sector businesses. The chamber was established with government sanction and leadership in 1980, but it made a slow start. In 1984 the first meeting was held between chamber members and heads of government departments, and the Trade Information Centre was established as a unit of the Department of Trade and Commerce to provide trade and commercial information to both the public and private sectors. Despite these initiatives, the Bhutan Chamber of Commerce and Industry had to be reorganized in 1987;

the intent was that the chamber would play a "vital role" in coordinating activities in the government and private sectors and promoting socioeconomic development. The Druk Gyalpo himself criticized the chamber in 1988 for its "extremely poor and disappointing performance" and urged it to take on a greater role in national development and to help build a strong and dynamic economy. Despite these initiatives, the Bhutan Chamber of Commerce and Industry had only forty members in 1989.[39]

Conclusion

Bhutan, the land of the thunder dragon, is indeed a treasure house of precious and colourful traditions, culture. The nation successfully preserved this rich inheritance even in the environment of modern technological progress and development. To conclude this chapter, the people in Bhutan have gone and are still going through many social changes and reforms to form their new identity as an independent nation, but on the basis of old religious and cultural traditions. The country has made tremendous changes, some out of deliberate reforms to change the present condition and others happened with the increasing contact with the outside world. The rulers have tried to make the changes friendly with the century old traditions and culture of Bhutan.

NOTES

1. Explore Himalayas, *Ancient History of Bhutan.* Available at: http://www.himalaya2000.com/bhutan/history/early-history.html
2. Sinha, A. C. (2001) *Himalayan Kingdom Bhutan:Ttraditions, Transition and Transformation*, Indus Publishing Company, New Delhi. pp. 37-38.

3. Key to Bhutan, History of Bhutan. Available at: http://www.keystobhutan.com/bhutan/bhutan_history_pre.php
4. Bhutan Siam.com, History of Bhutan. Available at: http://bhutansiam.com/history.html
5. Key to Bhutan, n.3.
6. Ibid.
7. Bhutan Siam.com, n.4.
8. Choudhury, Tapash and K. Roy, (1993) *State Building in Modern Bhutan (1616-1990): A Structural Functional Analysis*, in Manis Kumar Raha, Iar Ali Khan (ed) Polity, Political Process and Social Control in South Asia: The Tribal and Rural Perspectives, Gyan Books, New Delhi. p. 61
9. Sinha, A. C. (2001), n.2, pp. 9- 17.
10. Marshall Cavendish Corporation, (2007) *World and its People: Eastern and Southern Asia (part II)*, Marshall Cavendish, New York. p. 498.
11. Bhutan Majestic Travel, Bhutan Celebrates 100 Years of Monarchy. Available at: http://www.bhutanmajestictravel.com/bhutan-100-years-of-monarchy
12. Tshering, Kuenga *Gross National Happiness: Its Assumptions And Applications in Bhutan.* Available at: http://www.friendsof-humanity. ch/uploads/pdf/article_gnhinbuhtan_feb09.pdf
13. Bhradwaj, Vinod Kumar, (1996) *Geography as a Factor in Bhutan's Development*, in Ramakant and R.C.Mishra, Bhutan: Society and Polity, Indus Publishing, New Delhi. p. 22
14. Sinha, A. C. (2001), n.2, p. 19.
15. Unique Bhutan Adventures, Bhutan. Available at: http://advbhutan.com/about-bhutan.htm
16. Ibid.
17. Bhutan 2008, Flora and Funa. Available at: http://www.bhutan2008.bt/en/node/276
18. Savada, Andrea Matles (ed) (1991) *Bhutan: A Country Study*, GPO for the Library of Congress, Washington. Available at: http://countrystudies.us/bhutan/21.htm
19. Unique Bhutan Adventures, n..15.
20. Sinha, A. C. (2001), n.2, p. 37.
21. Marshall Cavendish Corporation, (2007), n.10, p. 505-506.
22. Sinha, A. C. (2001), n.2, p. 23.
23. Marshall Cavendish Corporation, (2007), n.10, p. 506.
24. Ibid, p. 507.

25. Savada, Andrea Matles (ed) (1991), n. 18.
26. Ibid.
27. Sinha, A. C (2001), n.2, p. 32.
28. Savada, Andrea Matles (ed), 1991, n.18.
29. Upreti, Sonia, (1996) *Status of Women in Bhutan*, in Ramakant and R.C.Mishra, Bhutan: Society and Polity, Indus Publishing Company, New Delhi. p. 52-53.
30. Savada, Andrea Matles (ed), 1991, n.18.
31. Unique Bhutan Adventures, n. 15.
32. Savada, Andrea Matles (ed), 1991, n.18.
33. ibid.
34. Enclyclopedia of Nations, Bhutan- Industry. Available at: http://www.nationsencyclopedia.com/Asia-and-Oceania/Bhutan-INDUSTRY.html
35. Savada, Andrea Matles (ed), 1991, n.18.
36. Encyclopedia Britanica, n.33.
37. Economy Watch.com, Bhutan Trade, Exports and Imports. Availabel at: http://www.economywatch.com/world_economy/bhutan/export-import.html
38. ibid.
39. Savada, Andrea Matles (ed), 1991, n.18.

CHAPTER 2

Explaining The Historical Basis of Bhutan's Administrative Systems

Introduction

A change in social, economic, political, religious and cultural elements in the life of human beings is a natural process and eternal phenomenon. Being a social animal and always living in cooperation with his fellow beings, change is a necessary factor for realizing common good in any society. Core and important factors of this complex interaction plays a vital role in changing the entire socio-economic and political factors in the life of the nations. The change is visible in all the above said aspects of the people of that country.

Bhutan, the Dragon Kingdom, which initiated the Modernisation process in 1960's had a far reaching impact on all these factors of life of the Bhutanese people. The nation began to transfer the ancient and medieval past of strict religious socio-economic and political structure in to the modern world, but by giving prior importance to the old religious and cultural traditions. It was in 1960's, that the nation ended its self-imposed isolation and started to move on the path of Modernisation and development which resulted in introducing many changes especially the democratic changes in the political set-up.

Contrary to other monarchies in the world history where monarchs have restricted any political change or democratic processes, Bhutan is an exceptional case with its Kings themselves have been the leading force of change in the nation. This chapter will discuss the growth of political institutions in the country, the beginning of political organizations, political offices and the development as it took place in Bhutan. The changes that each ruler brought forward for change will be discussed as any of the global political concepts such as socialism or communalism and liberal or democratic revolutions were irrelevant in its politics. The political behaviour in the Kingdom had always been different from the western political theories.

Political History of Bhutan: Overview of Bhutan's Political Structure

Political history of Bhutan is unique in the entire world, where the King himself gave-up his right of monarchical rule for the peoples' elected representatives to rule the people. June 10, 1998, probably will remain a milestone in the history of international politics and especially in South Asian political history. Contrary to any monarchs in the entire political history, His Majesty Jigme Singye Wangchuck, the Fourth King (Druk Gyalpo) of Bhutan, issued a Royal Charter (Kasho) through which he transferred his executive powers to an elected cabinet and introduced the principle of his own political responsibility to the parliament. Still politically Bhutan is really dependent on its King. The National Assembly (Tshogdu) hardly overturns the decisions of the King.

The political development and Modernisation of the governing system of Bhutan from the 17th century to the 21st century paints a vivid picture of the nation's struggle to survive as an independent state in international politics. The centralization of power under the monarch which was a feature till 1952 began to change to a more liberal and decentralised one with the full participation of the people. The Kings of Bhutan wanted to form a government including both the democratic and monarchical system of administration for ensuring the stability and solidarity of the nation. With the elections in 2007 and 2008, the position of the King has been changed to a constitutional monarch and His powers have been delegated to the democratic parliament which is elected by the people.

Bhutan's political history began in A.D. 747 when a Buddhist saint Padmasambhava (Guru Rimpoche) came to the nation. By the 10th century, the country's political development was highly influenced by the religious believes. Various sects of Buddhism emerged in Bhutan which basically developed as an administrative system and dominated in this era. The basic structure and beginning of political system in Bhutan began in the 17th century when a Tibetan Lama of Drukpa sect, Shabdrung Ngwang Namgyal, established a political ascendancy in the country. He established a dual system of administration known as Chhosi in 1651 after defeating all his rivals in the country. Rivalry and struggle between the Penlops began in the country after the death of Namgyal making the political history of Bhutan under threat. The emergence of Tongsa Penlop, Governor Ugyen Wangchuk, in the year 1907 provided a new era in the political history of Bhutan. He was unanimously chosen by the people of Punaka, the Old

Capital of Bhutan, as the hereditary Monarch of the country. He was succeeded by his son Jigme Wangchuk in the year 1926 after the death of his father Ugyen Wangchuk and ruled the country till his death in 1952. He also maintained his father's policy of isolation, but maintained a relationship with the British India. In October 27, 1952 His Majesty the King Jigme Dorji Wangchuk succeeded his father and began a revolutionary change in the political system of Bhutan. He is known as the architecture of modern Bhutan and bringing the nation in to the international level by opening its borders for Modernisation and development. The King introduced the idea of a Tshogdu (National Assembly) in 1952 to provide the people an opportunity to participate in the deliberation of national issues and formulation of policies in the country.

Political Developments under Shabdrung Ngwang Namgyal

Bhutan was divided in to various warring fiefdoms before 16th century. Shabdrung Ngawang Namgyal who came to the political stream of the nation unified the country under his reign for the first time in 1630s and created a unique cultural identity for Bhutan. He was born at Ralung in Tibet on 1594 from the family of Drukpa Lineage. He was enthroned as the Eighteenth Drukpa and hereditary prince of the traditional Drukpa seat being recognized as the re-incarnation of the forth Lama Kunkhyen Pema Karpo. However facing an arrest from the Tsang Desi and the Gelugpa sect in Tibet, in 1616 he fled to Bhutan and established a new base in western Bhutan by founding Cheri Monastery at the Thimphu Valley. In 1630, Shabdrung built Simtokha Dzong[1] in Thimphu Valley and began to control the nation.

In 1634, in the Battle of Five Lamas, he defeated all his rivals in the country and conquered unifying all of Bhutan under one ruler and established a single political and religious authority. With the subsequent organised resistance of both the internal and external, especially from Tibet, rival made him to strengthen his political and religious powers in the country. He constructed many Dzongs in Bhutan such as Simtokha in 1630, Punakha Dzong in 1631, Wangdue Phodrang Dzong in 1639, Tashicho Dzong in 1641 and Darkar Trashiyangtse Dzong in 1651to spread his powers and Drukpa sect. He constructed Punakha Dzong which was named Punthang Dechen Phodrang Dzong or 'the Palace of Great Bliss', and served as the capital of Bhutan.

Dual System of Administration

Inorder to keep his power unquestioned and keep his reign he began to rule the nation under a system of dual governance known as Chhosi, which he borrowed from Tibet known as *Cho-sid-nyi*. Being a strictly Lamaist religious society, Bhutanese people never maintained a distinction between the social, political and religious aspects. Accordingly, Shabdrung designed a governmental system in which he made both the aspects of secular and religious. This unique theocratic political system was based on reincarnation process, both in religious and political systems. Under the system of Chhosi, the King appointed two Monks one was Je Khenpo (Dharma Raja) and the second was Druk Desi (Deb Raja) who were entitled to observe the spiritual and civil administration respectively. The term of office for the Druk Desi was for three years but in some cases they hold the power for successive terms in the future. In the beginning the post of Deb raja was held by monks and later bye laymen. The civil administration consists of the Druk Desi, Penlops of the provinces, the Dzongpos of the Dzong or districts and their subordinate alone with the village headmen.

He also divided the nation in to small administrative units for better governance of the country and appointed a local governor for each unit known as Penlop. He divided the nation into three main administrative regions and three Dzongs as shown in the tables below:[2]

Table 2.1
Administrative Regions

Regions	*Head of Region/Governor*
West and South West	Paro Penlop
East and South East	Tongsa Penlop
South and Central Region	Daga Penlop

Table 2.2
Dzongs

Dzongs	*Head of Dzongs/ District Administration*
Punakha	Punakha Dzongpon
Thimphu	Thimphu Dzongpon
Wangdi Phondrang	Wangdi Phondrang Dzongpon

The King Namgyal also introduced a council consisting of the Deb Raja, Dharma Raja, Penlops and heads of all the administrative units and other high ranking religious and secular officers to guide and help the affairs of state administration. Deb Raja included six ordinary members known as Lenchen and three extraordinary members collectively known as Chenlah(Penlops of Paro, Tongsa and Daga) and the Dharma Raja had twelve Principal Gyolongs or Priests.[3] (See Figure 2.1)

FIGURE 2.1
The Structure of the Council under Shabdrung Ngawang Namgyal (1651)

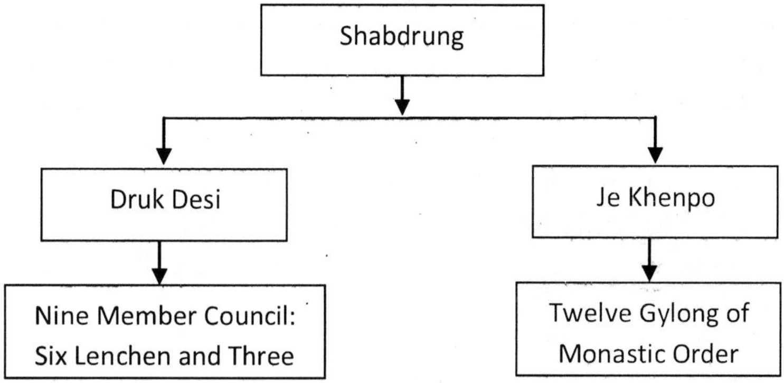

Foreign Relations

Shabdrung Ngwang Namgyal followed an open ended policy towards foreign relations. He wanted to build up relations with neighbouring areas like Coach Bhiar, Ladhak, Sikkim, Gorkha ad Nepal. As a powerful ruler to the nation he maintained a good relation with them and used to receive gifts. It was under Ngwang Namgyal's reign, that first foreigners, two Jesuit Portuguese priests came to Bhutan in the year 1629.[4]

Collapse of the System of Druk Desi

When the Shabdrung Namgyal decided to functionalise the system of spiritual and civil administration in Bhutan, he failed to make this system fully materialised and structured so that his followers or successors can also maintain this without any further change. He died at the age of 57 in the year 1651, but the Monks deliberately kept this secret for more than fifty years to ensure the political stability and problems of succession in the country.[5] However, as any of the monarchical nation, Bhutan also plunged in to inter-military civil war after the death of Namgyal. Being a Theocratic political system, the high post of religio-political was basically determined under the principle of re-incarnation or re-birth, many Druk Desis and Penlops claim to be the re-incarnation of the Previous Shabdrung. The institution of Shabdrung was lasted for around 250 years after the death of Shabdrung Ngwang Namgyal from 19651 to 1907. About fifty-five Druk Desis (Table 2.3)[6] ruled the nation till the establishment of the hereditary monarchical system in 1907 under Wangchuk Dynasty.

Table 2.3
Druk Desis in Bhutan from 1650 to 1905

Sl. No.	*Name of the Druk Desi*	*Ruling Period*
1	Tenzin Drukgye	1650–1655
2	Tenzin Drukdra	1655–1667
3	Chhogyal Mingyur Tempa	1667–1680
4	Tenzin Rabgye	1680–1694
5	Gedun Chomphel (d. 1701)	1695–1701
6	Ngawang Tshering	1701–1704
7	Umze Peljor	1704–1707
8	Druk Rabgye (d. 1729)	1707–1719
9	Ngawang Gyamtsho (d. 1729)	1719–1729
10	Mipham Wangpo	1729–1736
11	Khuwo Peljor	1736–1739
12	Ngawang Gyaltshen	1739–1744
13	Sherab Wangchuck	1744–1763
14	Druk Phuntsho	1763–1765
15	Druk Tendzin I	1765–1768
16	Donam Lhundub (d. 1773)	1768–1773

17	Kunga Rinchen	1773–1776
18	Jigme Singye (1742–1789)	1776–1788
19	Druk Tendzin II	1788–1792
20	Tashi Namgyal	1792–1799
21	Druk Namgyal	1799–1803
22	Tashi Namgyal (2nd reign)	1803–1805
23	Sangye Tendzin	1805–1806
24	Umdze Parpop	1806–1808
25	Bop Choda	1807–1808
26	Tsulthrim Drayga (1790–1820)	1809–1810
27	Jigme Dragpa II	1810–1811
28	Yeshey Gyaltshen (1781–1830)	1811–1815
29	Tshaphu Dorji	1815
30	Sonam Drugyal	1815–1819
31	Tendzin Drugdra	1819–1823
32	Choki Gyaltshen	1823–1831
33	Dorji Namgyal	1831–1832
34	Adap Thrinley	1832–1835
35	Choki Gyaltshen (2nd reign)	1835–1838
36	Dorji Norbu	1838–1847
37	Tashi Dorji	1847–1850
38	Wangchuk Gyalpo	1850
39	Jigme Norbu (in Thimphu)	1850–1852
40	Chagpa Sangye (in Punakha)	1851–1852
41	Damcho Lhundrup	1852–1856
42	Kunga Palden (in Punakha)	1856–1861
43	Sherab Tharchin (in Thimphu)	1856–1861
44	Phuntsho Namgyal	1861–1864

45	Tshewang Sithub	1864
46	Tsulthrim Yonten	1864
47	Kagyu Wangchuk	1864
48	Tshewang Sithub (2nd reign)	1864–1866
49	Tsondru Pekar	1866–1870
50	Jigme Namgyal (1825–1881)	1870–1873
51	Kitsep Dorji Namgyal	1873–1877
52	Jigme Namgyal (2nd reign)	1877–1878
53	Kitsep Dorji Namgyal (2nd reign)	1878–1879
54	Chogyal Zangpo (d. 1880)	March 1879 – June 1880
55	Jigme Namgyal (3rd reign)	June 1880 – July 1881
56	Lam Tshewang (1836–1883)	July 1881 – May 1883
57	Gawa Zangpo	May 16, 1883 – August 23, 1885
58	Yanglob Sangye Dorji (d. 1901)	1885–1901
59	Choley Yeshe Ngodub (1851–1917)	1903-1905

The Penlops and the Dzongpons gained more powerful and sometimes stood against the Druk Desi. Many of the Shabdrungs were assassinated, dismissed or made to resign from the post by the rivals. By the 19th century the institution of Penlop made monopoly under the Wangchuk dynasty in both spiritual and temporal administration. In the middle-ages, the spiritual power was becoming more and more powerful in Bhutan and superior to the temporal power as in the middle ages of Europe.[7] The system of Chhosi proved to be unstable and disintegrating force as the coordination and harmony between the spiritual and temporal powers was lost, and kept them under disputes over the re-incarnation and fight between local Penlops for political power.

Political Developments under Wangchuk Dynasty

When the institution of monarchy was replaced with the system of democracy in many parts of the world, the tiny Himalayan Kingdom saw the birth of a new hereditary monarchical system under Wangchuk dynasty in the early 20th century. Undergoing a system of Shabdrung Ngwang Namgyal, by the time totally decentralised and unstable due to conflicts and civil war, which made the nation again divide under Penlops and Je Kenpo, the nation saw the rise of Ugyen Wangchuk, a Tongsa Penlop in the early 1900s. The political situation has changed by 1903 in Bhutan, as both the Shabdrung and Druk Desi Yanglob Sangye Dorji (1883-1903) and the then Je Kenpo took over both the civil and spiritual administration of the country.[8] Being a feeble or weak Desi, Ugyen Wangchuk, the then Penlop of Trongsa, in 1907 took over both the spiritual and temporal administration of Bhutan who was externally supported by British India. He defeated all his rivals in the nation and once again reunified the nation under one ruler and in 1907. He was unanimously chosen as the hereditary monarch of the country by the people, clergy and governors at Punakha, the then capital of Bhutan. Both the first two Kings in the Wangchuk dynasty followed almost similar administrative and government systems and kept the policy of isolation from outside world.

Governance of Ugyen Wangchuk (1907-1926) and Jigme Wangchuk (1926-1952)

The new political change in the history of Bhutan made a number of changes in the nation. The Kings of Bhutan with the establishment of the Wangchuk dynasty began to be called as Druk Gyalpo meaning *Dragon King,* as the country is called as the Dragon Kingdom in Dzongkha language. The first ever Druk Gyalpo became the King Ugyen Wangchuk once he ascended to the throne of Bhutan. The nation maintained its political independence and kept isolated to avoid much social or structural transformation in the country. The monarchical system replaced the history of bloodsheds and struggle for political power by the Penlops, Deb Rajas and reincarnations of Shabdrung to provide a strong central authority in Bhutan. A *modus vivendi* between the monarchy and the Drukpa monastic system in Bhutan helped in preventing a direct conflict between these two institutions. In the year 1926, Jigme Wangchuk succeeded his father Ugyen Wangchuk and was able to build a highly centralized political system under a solid platform which his father provided. Under his reign, the institution of monarchy became the absolute and high court of appeal in all matters as in any monarchical system of governance. In course of time, the Dzongpons and other officials were either the members of royal family or personally selected by the Druk Gyalpo.[9]

The central administration of Bhutan became more strong and structuralised under the reign of Ugyen Wangchuk and Jigme Wangchuk. The power of the district officers, the monastic order and the nobility to influence the decision making procedure that had existed prior to 1907 was diminished after the establishment of a hereditary monarchical rule. A strong shift towards the centralization of administration was visible in the post 1907 political development as the powers of district level officers were made subject to supervision and control by the monarch. The district and village administrations were under the supervision of Dzongpon and Gups respectively under the first two Kings. There were eleven Dzongs in Bhutan's

Eastern, Central and Western regions headed by Dzongpons. The southern region was governed under the jurisdictions of Dorji Family in the early 1890s. The relations between the Wangchuk families and the Dorji Families had a significant role in the post 1907 era of Bhutan's administrative changes. The powers of the district officers were comprehensive as they were responsible for the law and order functions and serving as the head of the then police force and the Judge at the district courts, while in village level the central administrative control was less. The village headmen or Gups were assisted by Pipon in the local level. Under the reign of Jigme Wangchuk, the officers at the district level were subject to transfer from one district to other in order to deprive an oppertunity from gaining local support and thus going against the central authority.

The economic condition of Bhutan was pastoral and non-monetised featured barter system. No central budgeting system prevailed in Bhutan under the first two Kings. The King appointed a revenue officer called *Nyerchin* in each district to collect the rent in kind from farmers.

Judicial System

During the reign of Shabdrung and the first two Druk Gyalpos, the concept of an independent judiciary was absent. Till the end of 1952, the government officials were enjoying the power of judicial functions at various levels. The *Gups* or mandals in the village level were enjoying the original jurisdiction on minor crimes where as the major crimes were heard by the district officials as the district judge. At the top, the Druk Gyalpo himself served as the final court of appeal and he had the sole power to sentence criminals. The organization of the judicial system under the first two Kings is figured as below:

Figure 2.2
Judicial System under the Wangchuk Reign Till 1952

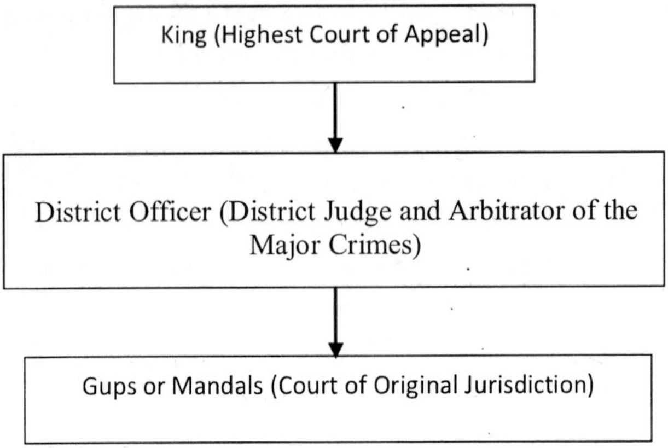

Source: Royal Court of Justice, Bhutan

Foreign Relations Under the First Two Kings

Ugyen Wangchuk had started a policy of isolation and he maintained foreign relations only with its neighbouring nations, which was later followed by his successor Jigme Wangchuk. Bhutan's foreign relations were constrained to a limited number of neighbouring nations in South Asia. Bhutan kept its policy of isolation until they opened their boundaries to the outside world in 1960s. The geo-political situation of Bhutan in the region marked a major factor in the foreign relations. The pressure from Tibet influenced by China and the British rule in the north eastern parts of India made the nation to keep a friendly relations with these nations to survive as an independent country in the region. Under the first two rules of Wangchuk dynasty, the nation established foreign relations with British India, Tibet, China, Nepal, Sikkim and Arunachal Pradesh in India.

The administration under the first two Kings was simple as to keep the law and order stable and collection of revenue in kind for the payment to the royal family and clergy. The system of administration was not much developed under Ugyen Wangchuk and Jigme Wangchuk was ruthless as it revolved around the royal family and clergy and made the ruler and ruled in different poles. The nation was showing a tendency of moving towards dictatorship as all the powers were controlled by the ruler and the appointment of officers was done by the Druk Gyalpo. Most of the central, district and village officers were from the royal family only or from the Dorji family thus monopolizing the major positions in administration.

Political Developments under Jigme Dorji Wangchuk (1952-1972)

A new era in the political history of Bhutan as a distinct polity has begun after 1952. The political leadership underwent a change when King Jigme Wangchuk died on March 24, 1952 and his son Jigme Dorji Wangchuk succeeded him in October 27, 1952. This period witnessed significant changes in the South Asian region with an independent India and creation of Pakistan and Bangladesh, Tibet was taken over by China and the War between India and China in 1962 and the end of colonial rule by British partially all over the world. When the world saw the end of almost all monarchical rule and dictatorship giving way for democracy and participatory governance, Bhutan was still under its hereditary monarchical system. The change in the political situation of the neighbouring countries and Western nations made Bhutan to think of a new approach to its political development. Thus the nation began to open its borders and began to give-up the policy of isolation and started to change its political structure for carving out a place in the comity of nations. Slowly and steadily, Bhutan began to move to the contemporary world and international political stream from its totally isolated status.

The third King Jigme Dorji Wangchuk is known as the father of modern Bhutan as he put the nation on the path of Modernisation. The nation being sandwiched between the two fast changing India and China and the structural political change in the rest of the world, wanted to get an independent status of a Modernised country. Parmanand (1992) observes this matter and notes:

> *"The geopolitical and geo-strategic importance of Bhutan is enhanced by the fact that it is a buffer state between two Asian giants- the People's Republic of China and India. On this count, Bhutan's smallness in terms of size and population becomes irrelevant."*[10]

The King with his foresight realized the need of Modernisation with a gradual change in its social, economic and political development while upholding the unique culture of the nation. The nation was always under a fear that the process of Modernisation might endanger the culture of Bhutanese society.

Till the reign of the Second King, the public policy in Bhutan was simple, straight-forward and consistent internally as the primary objective of the Kings were to make the political power centralized, maintain the economic status quo and keep the nation under the policy of isolation to establish a unique social identity in the region. In the year 1952, the Third King Jigme Dorji Wangchuk initiated the change in the policies that his predecessors followed. The change was slow in the beginning but became more comprehensive and specific by 1960s, when the nation opened its borders to the outside world. The King had realized that the country could no longer shut its eyes closed to what is happening in the outside world.[11] The nation's administrative system was in an imperfect beginning of something undeveloped stage under his reign till 1960s which was not able to handle the challenges engendered by the internal and external factors. Being an economic oriented nation, the King Druk Gyalpo Jigme Dorji Wangchuk decided to Modernise the administrative system for the economic, political and social progress and stated that:

> *"Limited reforms introduced over an extended period under non-crisis conditions were preferable to radical change that would tear apart the social and political fabric of Bhutan's traditional system and leads perhaps to national disintegration."*[12]

Thus the King began to transform both the theocratic and dynamic rule to a Bhutanese nation-state inorder to gain an independent identity and self sufficiency. He adopted a strategy of the mixed Economic Development for the planning and designing the administrative structure in Bhutan. The King organised a well planned and modernised governing system in the country to begin a new era in the political development of Bhutan's administrative structure.

Organization of Government under the Third King

During the third King's reign, many efforts have been initiated to reshape and modernise the political system which was prevailed under the first two Kings of Wangchuk dynasty. Though Bhutan had neither a written constitution nor any documents regarding the duties and functions of the political institutions, the King was the Head of the State and in real sense the Head of the Government. During the period of the Third King (1952-1972) the monarch retained remained centre of the administration but shared some of his powers with other political and administrative institutions in the country.[13] Since 1907 1952, the organization of government changed to take a new look from the previous rulers. The Bhutanese political system introduced a number of sub-divisions and institutions in the discharge of the central administration and functions. As Geoffery K. Robert (1971) describes about the political system of any country like:

> *"A political system is a combination of structure, process and institutions, which interact with each other and across the boundaries of the system, with the environment. It mostly functions on system approach perspectives. It is those social interaction and institutions through which a society makes decision considered binding by most members of society most of the time. It is regarded as open system involved in exchanges with its environment and an adaptive system capable of adaptation to changing circumstances, regulation of its own components, response to stress and though feedback mechanism able to adjust to output to input conditions."*[14]

As such Bhutanese political system also has numerous divisions and parts to administer the nation. The organizations of government under the monarch to manage the state administrative affairs can be divided as follows:

1. The Central Administration including the Executive and the Legislature.
2. The Local Administration of the Districts and Villages
3. The Judiciary
4. The Armed Forces and the Civil Services

Thus any of the modern democratic nations Bhutan also structured their government under a well defined administrative system under the Third King Druk Gyalpo Jigme Dorji Wangchuk.

1. The Central Administration

With the introduction of an ambitious economic and political development in the future, the third Druk Gyalpo started an expansionist policy in size and functions of the central government. The strengthening of the central government structure was comparatively elabourated in post 1960s and a new permanent secretariat has been established at Thimphu. The city from 1961 onwards began to function as a centre of administration and the nation's capital. The central administration of Bhutan included the executives, legislature, Royal Advisory Council and the cabinet. Both the executive and legislature was developed in the nation as in any other developing states in the world, characterised with the unique and distinct Bhutanese culture.

1.1 The Executive

The executive branch of Bhutan's administrative system was headed by the Druk Gyalpo himself. The King represented the nation in all internal and external aspects. He is established himself as the apex of the political system of Bhutan. After reunifying the nation by rejoining rest of the provinces, the Third King became the greatest and real cementing force in Bhutan. He managed to control a multi-ethnic, multi-lingual and multi-religious society in the nation under a paternalistic rule. He became the fountainhead of the new administrative structure and began to change the nation's basic governing system without ignoring the culture and traditions of the nation. Being the Chief Executive, the Druk Gyalpo became the head of the state and government, commander-in-chief of the armed forces, the highest court of appeal and a commanding force in the religious and spiritual matters.

1.2 The Legislature: The Tshogdu (National Assembly)

Even before the establishment of any organised administrative structure the significant decisions were taken by consensus which was a result of a long debate in the people's gatherings in which officials and non-officials participated. Such gatherings are called Jomdu/ Jombu in Bhutanese language. The gathering of the higher officials is called as the Tshogdu. The establishment of a legislature is necessary in any modern nation to legislate laws for the people. The Third King, Druk Gyalpo Jigme Dorji Wangchuk, who began the Modernisation of the political structure of Bhutan, set the first and important step in the political reform under the royal order of 1953. Following the royal order, the King established the nation's first ever legislature in the nation known as the Tshogdu or National Assembly in 1953 at Punakha. At the time of the accession to the throne itself, the Third King announced the intension to establish a national assembly including the representatives of the people, monasteries and the government. The Third King introduced a traditional and modern political requirement of the nation for the composition of the Tshogdu. The members of the national assembly include mainly three types of representatives as:

- The People's Representatives,
- The Monastic Representatives, and
- The Government Representatives.

The number of members in the National Assembly varies as in 1953, 10 members were from the monastic bodies, 10 from the government officials and 110 were the representatives' of the people, thus making the total number of 130 members. Later in 1960 the total number was raised to 150. Under the Third King, the total number varied from 110 to 150.[15]

The people's representatives were elected by an indirect method in this period as the villager by consensus selected a representative and nominated them to the National Assembly. Under this system the district level officials call for a meeting in each village to which the headmen or Gups of the villages and selected members of the village community who are normally the heads of household and other adult males participate. The number of representatives is based on the number of villagers in each district and was not based on population size. The term of this members are for three years and any Bhutanese, non-convicted or those who have served a term in prison, of 25 years and above can be a member of the National Assembly. The Tshogdu members have the freedom of speech in the assembly on any of the matters of the Bhutanese life. All these resolutions require two-third majority in the Assembly and the final seal from the Monarch. The National Assembly if empowered to do a number of functions such as (i) enacting laws for the nation, (ii) approve senior appointments in the Government and (iii) advise the King on all the important matters on national importance.[16]

The Monastic Representatives are nominated by the various Drukpa monastic bodies located in different Dzongs of the country such as Thimphu, Tongsa, Paro, Daga, Wangdiphodrang, Lhuntshi, Mongar, Shemgang and Tashigang. Under the electoral procedure the Central Monk Body elects one member and the eight other major regional monk bodies elect six representatives. The large regional monk bodies of Paro, Tongsa, Daga and Wangdiphodrang elect one representative each while the others- Tashigang, Lhuntsi, Mongar and Shemfang elect two members. The Dorji Lopen, who is the second in command to the Je Khempo from the Central Monk Body and the two monk body representatives on the Royal Advisory Council are the other three representatives from the monastic order in the Tshogdu.[17]

The government representatives to the Tshogdu are mainly nominated by the Druk Gyalpo on their functional basis. The government officers included Ministers, members of the Royal Advisory Council, senior Civil Servants. The term of these officers were not limited as long as they hold their posts they enjoy being the members of the Tshogdu. It was a unique case in Bhutan as the civil servants were permitted to contest elections as against any of the other parliamentary democracy.

Under the Third King, there was no election commission as the government was not democratically elected. But one could see limited democratic practices in Bhutan though there was neither the concept of direct election nor universal suffrage. In the southern region of Bhutan, the election to the Tshogdu was made under a system in which each household gets one vote, which usually used by the head or elder member of that family and in other regions, the selection was made by a system of consensus. The basic drawback of this process was that the popular participation of the common people were absent as the posts normally goes to the traditional leaders, elites and the officials. The members of the Tshogdu are popularly known as *Chhimis* and this assembly meets twice a year chaired by the speaker of the house. The speaker of the house is elected among the members of the assembly for a term of three years. The Druk Gyalpo has the power to dissolve the National Assembly. This indeed became a basic structural reform innovated by the Third King for the Modernisation of the political system of Bhutan.

1.3 Royal Advisory Council (Lodey Tshogdey)

Under the administrative reorganization program of the Third Druk Gyalpo of Bhutan, revived the concept of a formal consultative institution in the country to advise the King and the government in all important and domestic matters for better governance. The King had taken its first step by establishing the Lodey Tsokde informally 1950s and instituted it as a formal government structure on 1965. This council functions as an advisory board of Bhutanese government and was in session throughout the year. The

Royal Advisory Council consisted of six representatives of the people, two elected representatives of the clergy and a representative of the government normally appointed by the Druk Gyalpo who is known as the chairman or Kaylon. It acts as a bridge between the government and people and oversees the execution of government policies and programmes. According to Dasho Rinzin Dorji, the main functions of the Royal Advisory Council can be summarized as below:

- To make its advice available to the Druk Gyalpo and council of ministers on all matters of national importance.
- To promote the welfare of the people and the national interest of the Kingdom.
- To develop friendly and harmonious relations between the government and the people; and
- To ensure that the laws and resolutions passed by the National Assembly are faithfully implemented by the government and the people.[18]

The Royal Advisory Council served as supervisory body over the council of ministers and became a unique organisation established under the Third King.

1.4 Council of Ministers (Lhengyel Tsok)

During the reign of the Third King, Bhutan underwent a major development in the modernisation of administrative system in 1968 when the Tshogdu approved the formation of a Lhengyel Tsok (Council of Ministers). The first council of minister was established in 1968 with only three ministries such as home affairs, trade, commerce and industry and finance. The Lhengyel Tsok was presided over by the Druk Gyalpo and included the ministers and members of Royal Advisory Council. This council of ministers began to function as an important decision making body in which the ministers are responsible to the King directly. There was no principle of collective responsibility as visible in other governments throughout the world as Bhutanese council of ministers had no leader. This new organ of government was a revolutionary change in the nation for crating the administrative infrastructure required in an increased and challenging modern needs of the nation.[19]

1.5 The Lhengyel Shungstog

The Lhengyel Shungstog was established in the year 1968. It included representatives of the King, all ministers and deputy ministers, a representative of the Army and all members of the Lodey Tshogdu representing the Tshogdu. This became a major policy making body during the early 1970's.[20]

2. Local Administration

In 1952, the Third King introduced a programme for administrative modernisation in local level which he functionalises in 1955 and in early 1960s for the creation of more suitable organisations and agencies for the implementation of the economic development programmes. The Regional administration in Bhutan is a major part of the central administration as the King decided to deal directly with the district officials. Local Administration became the basic backbone of the Bhutanese administration. For any government the local level administration and participation is unavoidable as the centre may remain unsuccessful in its governance. As defined by the Oxford Concise Dictionary; ***"As a territory marked for special Administrative purpose."***[21]

2.1 District Administration

The local administration reflects the objectives and success of a government and aspirations of the people in the nation. In Bhutanese context, district administration has been defined as "the sum total of administrative process and activities to maintain law and order to plan and implement the development projects and to make people's cooperation available for development purpose in the district."[22]

For the purpose of administration, Bhutan has been divided in to four regions or ***dzongdey*** under the Third King such as the Western Region, Eastern Region, Central Region and Southern Region. Each region was again divided in two districts or Dzongs as listed in table 2.4.[23]

Table 2.4
Distribution of Dzongs by Regions in Bhutan

Regions	*No. of the Dzongs (Districts)*
Western	7
Eastern	3
Central	5
Southern	3
Total	18

The Dzong was administrated directly by the Home Ministry through Dzongda or District Administrator who are appointed by the Druk Gyalpo. Their primary duty is to maintain law and order in the district and enforcement of the central policies. In every Dzong, there is other senior officer called Ramjam, who was responsible for collection of revenue and district finance. The large Dzongs are further divided in to sub-districts or *Dungkhag* for the betterment of the administration. Being a representative of the Druk Gyalpo, the Dzongda has very comprehensive power in the district. They were functioned as the head of the local militia-the only police force, and as the judge in the district courts.

2.2 Village Administration

The villages or Gewogs are the basic units of administration in Bhutan. Being a scattered populated nation with the absence of adequate transport and communication, the village administrative system is necessary for the central administration to execute the policies legislated by the National Assembly. Every village is governed by a village headman called Mandal in south Regions and Gup in other parts. The Gup and Mandals are responsible for functionalising the orders and policy directions from the district authority or Zimpon. There was a relationship established between the central administration and the village administration for a smooth functioning of the modernised government. The elections and administration in the village level was semi-democratic as the Gup is elected by the head of the household and rules for three years. Most important decisions regarding the village administration was taken by the village headman in consultation with the head of households in the village. Thus the power and authority of the central bureaucracy did not have much influence in the village administration.

3. Judicial administration

The concept of separation of powers and an independent judiciary in Bhutan was realised in 1968 when the Third King began a major reorganisation of the political structure and institutions. In the year 1969, the same principle was enforced in districts and the original judicial powers given to the district officials were taken away from them and assigned all this power to a district court (Thimkhang). Under Jigme Dorji Wangchuk, the Druk Gyalpo was considered as the highest court of appeal. In the year 1968, the King established a High Court (*Thimkhang Gongma)* and empowers it to review the King's decisions and the appeals from the district courts.

Legal code: Being a traditional theocratic political system, Bhutan had a religious legal code. The Third King in 1965 modified this making the legal system modernised and made all citizens equal in the eyes of the laws regardless of status and positions providing integrity to the Kingdom.[24]

4. Armed Forces

Bhutan in the pre-1950s had no organised army or police force except some local militia. The Third King under the policy of modernising the nation's political structure decided to create a new army and police force in the nation to look after the law and order in the state. Like any other nation in the world Bhutan had no such circumstances that forced the government to form an armed force in the country. His majesty Jigme Dorji Wangchuk, wanted to create such force for obtaining an independent national identity as he realized the importance of the nation in the South Asian region that stood between the mighty powers of India and China, established such forces.

4.1 The Bhutan Army

With the succession of the Third Druk Gyalpo in the year 1952, the government decided to create a regular army in the country. In the beginning, Bhutan sent its people to India for the training under the Assam Rifles, a paramilitary force in the Indian Army. In 1955, the country organised the Royal Bhutanese Army as a regular military force due to a number of reasons such as the Chinese invasion in Tibet and controlling the Tibet-Bhutan border regions, train the local militia in guerrilla tactics and defend internal and external aggression. Though the Royal Bhutanese Army was a small force with many organisational and operational problems, it was entrusted with major responsibilities. Due to the involvement of the two high officers of army in 1964-65 political crises, the King himself was apprehensive about the loyalty of the army. Following the political struggle, the King abolished the rank of Dozin (Brigadier) and Maski Ogma (Colonel) became the highest rank in the Bhutanese Army till 1968 and later reinstalled the rank but no one has been promoted in his reign.[25]

4.2 *Police*

As any of the developed or modern nation, Bhutan had no organised police force till 1965. The law and order were kept functionalised by the local militia on temporary basis. On 1st September, 1965, following a political crises of 1964-65, the King decided to establish a separate fully functioning police force in the country. The force was headed by the Home ministry and fully responsible of it in all operations. A Royal Bhutan Police Training School was set up in the nation and requested India to send an advisory team to assist the training. The Gakpen was the official in the home ministry who serves as the administrative head of the police in his headquarters at Phuntshonling, assisted by two Yongzim. The nation under the police administration was divided in to three areas such as western, eastern and southern headed by Dechaps who was in-charge of a number of police stations under his jurisdiction. Kempon commanded the police force in the district level.[26]

Lamaist Church

The Third King followed a concrete step and established an independent weak national church in Bhutan. During the reign of the third Druk Gyalpo, a compromise was achieved between the royal family and the Drukpa monastic sect for preventing a direct confrontation between these two institutions. Understanding the potential influence of the religious establishment on Bhutanese society and politics the chance of accommodating themselves to the monarchical system and polity has been restricted. In 1969, the government abolished the process of collecting rent-in-kind from the cultivators and replaced it with a new system under which the monasteries are directly subsidized by the government. The King of Bhutan was not directly involved in religious affairs thus constituting a serious gap in their authority structure.

Foreign Affairs under Third King

During the reign of the Third King, Bhutan's vulnerable geo political location between India and China forced the country go for relations with its neighbours for surviving independently and for maintaining peace in internal politics. Since 1750s, the external relations of Bhutan were mostly related to India. Due to closed political, economic and socio-cultural aspects, Bhutan always kept aloof from the politics of the big powers. In 1971, the first ever diplomatic mission was opened in India at New Delhi.[27] With the help of India, Bhutan became a member of the Universal Postal Union in 1969, UN in 1971, Colombo Plan in 1962 and Economic and Social Commission for Asia and the Pacific (ESCAP) in 1972. Adopting a process towards modernisation and development, Bhutan has terminated the policy of isolation that kept the nation from the outside world and accepted the policy of opening its boarders for development.

Financial Administration Under Third King

Financial administration is vital to any nation as it is the food and fuel of the administration. Sound fiscal management is therefore very important in Bhutanese administration as it was entering in to a modernised development under the Third King. The income of the nation was variously estimated on a rough basis till 1960s as there was no finance department to look after it. In 1971, there began a formal budget allocation of funds to the various departments on regular basis was introduced with a planned fiscal management. The King introduced a planned economic development based on the Indian model. The nation embarked the first planned economic development in 1961 which is called as the First Five Year Plan for the period from 1961/62 to 1965/66. The priority was given to end the nation's geopolitical isolation under this plan. The second five year plan was begun in 1966/67 till 1970/71, which was fully funded by the Government of India. This gave importance to the improvement of agriculture and education. The introduction of a finance ministry was a new beginning in Bhutanese administrative system, which controlled the allocation of funds.

Political Developments under Jigme Singye Wangchuk (1972-2008)

The year 1972 witnessed a new era in Bhutanese politics with a full flow of modernisation of the administrative system. After the death of the third Druk Gyalpo Jigme Dorji Wangchuk, his son Jigme Singye Wangchuk became the Fourth King of Bhutan. He was formally crowned as the King on 2nd June 1974. Under his reign, he stressed to achieve the following objectives;

1. To achieve an economic-self-reliance and welfare of rural areas;
2. To create essential infrastructures in the nation;
3. To develop human resources in the country;
4. Modernisation and development of the nation without ignoring the cultural heritage;
5. To create a single harmonious society and integration; and
6. To achieve the participation of the people in the development programmes of the government.

Being educated in India, he had absorbed western liberal values and believed in democracy. He wanted to internationalise the organisations of government and project the nation in all international field.[28] He was successful in this matter as when he introduced a unique ideology of Gross National Happiness instead of Gross National Products in 1972. During his period he successfully put this in to practice by modernising the organisations of government in Bhutan and giving more power to the people and National Assembly.

Gross National Happiness (GNH)

His majesty the Druk Gyalpo began his period with the introduction of a unique philosophical idea of Gross National Happiness in 1972, which made the entire world economies to think on the basis of happiness rather Gross National Product. He introduced this philosophical phrase to mention his commitment in building an economic system that would serve Bhutan's unique culture and spiritual values based on Buddhism. This was somewhat easier to state than to define with mathematical precision like Gross Domestic Product (GDP) or Gross National Product (GNP). This idea of GNH served as a unifying vision for Bhutan's five-year planning process and other development plans in the nation. Under this ideology the King provides four major pillars of GNH such as sustainable development, preservation and promotion of cultural values, conservation of the natural environment, and establishment of good governance. In the year 1971, the late King Jigme Dorji Wangchuk constituted the Planning Commission, an independent body consisting of 13 members for the development progress. The fourth Druk Gyalpo strengthened the functioning of this Planning Commission in order to formulate and functionalize the idea GNH. The King stated that the GNH is more important than the Gross National Product. According to his ideology this program was focused mainly on socio-economic revision towards the promotion of happiness as its primary value. Under this theory equal importance is given to the social, economic, spiritual, cultural and environmental need of the Bhutanese people. The concept of GNH has become the philosophical foundation for the entire policy making process in the country.

Organisation of the Government

The Fourth King followed his father's model of administration and policies and initiated some vibrant and effective developments. The basic administrative systems of Bhutan can be divided in to a three-tier governing system such as, Central Administration, regional administration, district administration and village administration. The Druk Gyalpo still continues to play an important role in the executive arch.

The Lodey Tshogdey

His Majesty the Druk Gyalpo Jigme Singye Wangchuk continued with the same model of the Royal Advisory

Council established by his late father Jigme Dorji Wangchuk in 1965. However, he introduced some new changes and developments in the functions, powers and composition of the advisory council during his reign. In 1975, the Royal Advisory Council consisted of a total of ten members such as, a Chairman (Shung Kalon) who is appointed by the Druk Gyalpo, two representatives of the monk body, five people's representatives, a representative for the Nepali Bhutanese community, and a women's representative.[29] The term of office was five years in the 70's and 80's which later changed in to three years in 1998.[30] This council mainly give advice to the national Assembly and to the Druk Gyalpo on matters related to national importance and it looks after the law passed by the assembly is been implemented faithfully by the government. The functions of the council was further strengthened by the fourth Druk Gyalpo by introducing a clause in the provision where the council was empowered to bring in to the notice of the King, council of ministers and the national assembly if any person including His majesty does anything harmful to the interest of the nation and the people.[31] The members of the council mostly are from the Tshogdu and in the 2007 December election it began to function as the upper house in the parliament.

Lhengyal Shungtshog

The nation underwent an important and vital change in the year 1968, when the late King established Lhengyal Tsok as a major administrative organ of the government. The council of ministers were comprises all Ministers, Deputy Ministers and all Royal Advisory Councillors and preside over by the King himself as the head of the government till 1998. There were seven ministries such as Foreign Affairs, Trade and Industry, Finance Home Affairs,

Social Services, Agriculture and Communication and four commissions such as Royal Civil Service Commission, The Special Commission of Cultural Affairs, Planning Commission and the Dzongkha Development Commission. The Druk Gyalpo in the year 1998 addressing the 181st sessions of the Lhengyal Shungtshog (Cabinet) announced the dissolution of the Lhengyal Shungtshog on June 26th and he declared himself as the head of the state alone and give-up his post of head of the government to the chairman of the cabinet. Under the new system introduced by the King, the Tshogdu will elect members of the cabinet for a period of five years and chairman who is elected from the cabinet will serve as the head of the government for one year. Thou the King is no more the head of the government, the cabinet has to seek his guidance from time to time.[32] This new system worked as a forum for discussion on issues related to national interest, national security and sovereignty and run the day-to-day affairs of the government.

The Tshogdu

The system of National Assembly became unchanged under the reign of the Fourth King. However, he initiated several measures to reform the system to consolidate the power in Bhutanese political system. He empowered the Tshogdu to vote of confidence over the Druk Gyalpo in July 1999. The distribution of the seats in Tshogdu in 1973 was based on the census of 1969. Accordance with the census of 1969 the western and central Bhutan with 28 percent of population were given 37 percent of seats, eastern Bhutan with 57 percent population was given 48 percent of seats in the Tshogdu and in southern Bhutan with 15 percent of population had 15 percent of seats.[33] Though the National Assembly in 1973 changed the system of election making it a directly elected boy of the people, the representatives were mostly appointed by consensus. The Fourth King in the late 2000's began to introduce a number of changes in the system. He thus initiated for the creation of a constitution for the nation by 2008. In the process of modernisation of the political system he introduced a new parliament which will be fully elected by the people.

The Elections of 2007 and 2008

In the year 2007 the Fourth King made an important change in the parliamentary system of Bhutan. He changed the system in to a bicameral parliament by constituting an upper house – the National council and a lower house- the national Assembly. The royal advisory council changed to become the national council and a national assembly was elected through universal adult suffrage.

National Council of Bhutan (*Gyelyong Tshogde*) is the upper house or the house of review in the legislature according to the Article 11 of the Constitution of Bhutan. It consisted of 25 members in which 20 were directly elected from each of the 20 districts (Dzongkhag), who are not allowed to hold affiliation with any political parties, and 5 were appointed by the King. The council meets twice a year and evaluate and advice the Tshogdu and Druk Gyalpo. The council elects a chairperson and deputy chairperson for themselves. Twenty members of the first National Council was elected in the first ever democratic elections held on December 31, 2007 and January 29, 2008 in the nation. The candidates to be elected to the national council should have the minimum qualification of a graduation from a recognised university and thus the first national Council members are generally young.

National Assembly (*Gyelyong Tshogdu*) is the new lower house of the parliament in Bhutan since 2007 The

Tshogdu, which was a unicameral legislature since 1951 came to an end in July 2007. Under the new democratic political system the King give most of his powers to the national assembly and empower it to enact and enforce the laws for the people. Under the new constitution of the nation the total number of seats in the assembly has been reduced to 55. In March 24, 2008 the new directly elected 47 representatives of the people began to rule the nation under political party system which was absent till then. There were only two political parties participated in the election of 2008, such as the Bhutan Peace and Prosperity Party (DPT, for *Druk Phuensum Tshogpa*) and the People's Democratic Party (PDP) and a total of around 80 percent people voted in the election. The nation has divided in to 47 constituencies in the general election of 2008 for electing 47 representatives. The total 20 districts were divided in to constituencies under the system of proportional representation. Table 2.5 gives a clear picture of the 47 constituencies divided between 20 districts in Bhutan. The national assembly became the ultimate law making authority in Bhutan after the general election on 2008.

Table 2.5
The 47 Constituencies of the National Assembly of Bhutan in 2008 General Election

Sl.No.	*Dzongkhag*	*Constituency*
1.	Bumthang	Choekhor Tang Chumey Ura
2.	Chhukha	Phuntsholing Bongo Chapcha
3.	Dagana	Drujeygang-Tseza Lhamoy Zingkha Trashiding
4.	Gasa	Goenkhatoe Laya Goenkhamey Lunana

5.	Haa	Bji-Katsho-Uesu Sombaykha
6.	Lhuentse	Gangzur Minjay Menbi Tshenkha
7.	Monggar	Monggar Dremitse Ngatshang Kengkhar Weringla
8.	Paro	Lamgong Wangchang Doga Shaba
9.	Pema Gatshel	Nganglam Khar Yurung Nanong Shumar
10.	Punakha	Lingmukha Toewang Kabji Talo
11.	Samdrup Jongkhar	Deothang Gomdar Jomotshangkha Martshala
12.	Samtse	Pagli Samtse Sipsu Dorakha Tading Ugentse Yoeseltse
13.	Sarpang	Shompangkha Gelephu
14.	Tashi Yangtse	Bumdeling Jamkhar Khamdang Ramjar
15.	Thimphu	North Thimphu South Thimphu
16.	Trashigang	Radhi Sakten Bartsham Shongphu Thrimshing Kanglung Samkhar Uzorong Wamrong
17.	Trongsa	Nubi-Tangsibji Drakteng Langthel
18.	Tsirang	Pataley Tsirangtoe Kikhorthang Mendrelgang

19.	Wangdue Phodrang	Nyisho Sephu Athang Thedtsho
20.	Zhemgang	Bardo Trong Panbang

Source: National Assembly of Bhutan, http://www.nab.gov.bt

Judicial Administration

The judicial system introduced by the third Druk Gyalpo continued to function till the introduction of the new constitution of Bhutan in 2008. By the new constitution, the Supreme Court became the highest appellate court in the country instead of the King, who enjoyed being the highest court of appeal till 2007. The Fourth King introduced a new concept of Jambis who are legal councillors experienced in terms of argument and negotiation. In contrast to the general criteria of sending civil servants to the judicial system, for the first time Bhutan send fresh graduates to study modern law. In 1974, there were nine district courts and four sub-district courts.[34] In the year 1975, a High Court was established with six judges out of whom four was directly appointed by the Druk Gyalpo for the Gazetted Officials, one representative of the Nepali Community and the last from the peoples representatives selected from the Tshogdu with the approval of the King. In present there are 20 district courts headed by Thrimpons and assisted by Thtimrabs, One High Court headed Chief Justice and a Supreme Court on the top. Under his reign, the legal staffs have been trained in India and overseas and the High Court conducted many workshops and training programmes for the Jambis. Though the system was working well, the independence of the judiciary is questionable as all the judges were appointed by the King and Cabinet and hold office at the pleasure of the King and fall under the administrative jurisdiction of the Home Ministry and later

Council of Ministers from 1998.[35]

Figure 2.3
Structure of the Judicial System in Bhutan under Jigme Singye Wangchuk

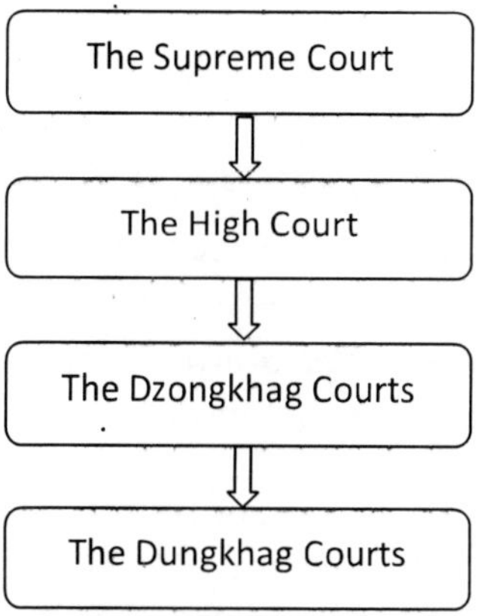

Source: Royal Court of Justice, Bhutan

Zonal (*Dzongdey*) Administration

His Majesty Druk Gyalpo Jigme Singye Wangchuk introduced the concept of Zonal administration in the Fifth Five Year Plan in the year 1981-1987. Though the country has been divided in to regions by the previous Kings, a structured administrative system was established by the Fourth King. Under the Zonal system of administration the country was divided in to four zones and setup headquarter for each zone. This new structure of local administration was introduced in 1987 and attached to the Ministry of Home Affairs. Tsirang and Chhuka zones began functioning from January 1989 and Trashigang and Gaylegphu zones commenced in September 1990. Under this administrative structure the nation was divided in to different Zones which cover different Dzongkhags. The western zone or zone I covers four districts such as Haa, Paro, Chukka and Samtse with headquarter at chukka. West-Central Zone or Zone II includes Punakha, Wangdi, Tsirang and Dagana districts and a Zonal headquarter at Tsirang. East-Central zone or Zone III covers Bumthang, Gaylegphu, Trongsa and Shemgang along with its headquarter at Gaylegphu. Eastern zone or Zone IV consists of five districts-Trashigang, Pemagatshel, Monger, Lhuntshi and Samdrupjonkar. The head office of zone IV is located at Trashigang. Under the initiative of fourth Druk Gyalpo King Jigme Singye Wangchuk, the process of decentralisation of local administration got a new face and structure. A detailed description of the *Dzongdey* administrative system under the Fourth King is given below in figure 2.4:

Figure 2.4
Zonal (*Dzongdey*) Administrative System before 2008

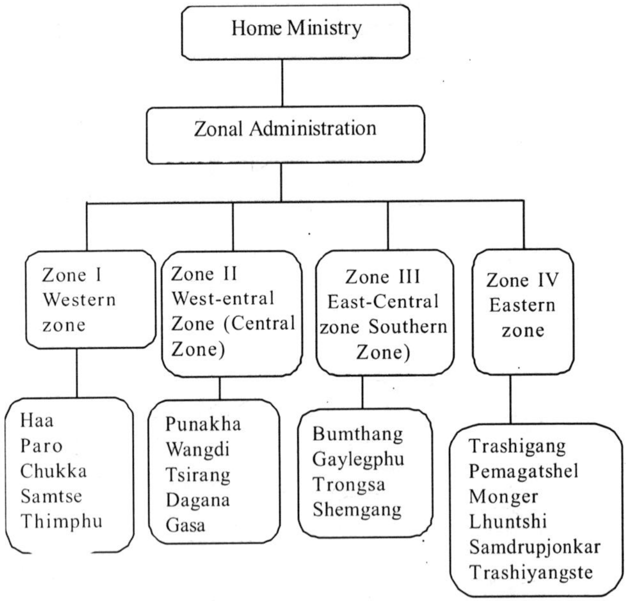

Source: Royal Government of Bhutan

Each *Dzongdey* is served by a Zonal administrator known as Dzongdep Chichhap who is directly appointed by the Druk Gyalpo and enjoy the power at his pleasure and he is assisted by a *Dzongrabs* (deputy district collectors). Under this system the Dzongdep Chichhaps are accountable to the Home Ministry. The Zonal administrators are responsible for following:

- Represent the King and the government
- Provide fair, just and efficient administration
- Ensuring socio-cultural and economic well being
- To look after the law and order and security of the Zone
- Coordination and implementation of Socio-economic development

Inorder to function and ensure the development of the zone, it has given various duties and responsibilities. The organisation of Zonal administrational has six main administrative divisions which are listed below:

1. Zonal affairs
2. Planning and Coordination
3. Social Service
4. Agriculture and Industry
5. Communication
6. Engineering

The basic purpose of this system of administration was to co-ordinate the development activities of the various districts under each zone which was divided on the basis of geo-physical and agro-climatic considerations. It is suppose to ensure the national objectives sufficiently account for local development and the requirements of each districts.[36]

District Administration

The district administration got a new realm of development under the reign of the fourth Druk Gyalpo. He initiated a number of structural changes and decentralisation measures to involve them in the decision making process. Under his decentralised administrative system he divided the nation in to twenty districts. He established three more new districts in the nation by the end of 20th century. In the year 1992 he created Trashiyangte district for Trashigang district. The King established the District Development Committees known as *Dzongkhag Yargey Tshogchung* (DYT) in every district between 1976-1981for good governance. It consists of *Dzongdha, Chimis* (National Assembly Representatives) of the district, the Gups and members elected by the people in blocks (*Mangmis*) to represent them in the DYT and it was chaired by the Dzongdha. The main function of the DYT is to discuss the development and policy matters related to the district and send this proposal to the National Assembly for final approval. All the responsibilities of the district administration were entrusted in the Dzongdha who act as a representative of the King in the District. They also come under the supervision of the Home Ministry as the Zonal Administration. The Dzongdha was empowered with a number of responsibilities under the Bhutanese Local Administrative structure such as Technical Administration, General Administration and Financial Administration. The introduction of the district level administration helped the nation to establish a well developed administrative system in the country.[37]

Village Administration

Villages continued to act as the basic unit of administration at the grass root level in the governing system of Bhutan. By the end of 2005 there were 205 villages in the nation. The Gup or village headmen act as the administrative head of the village governance, who enjoy quasi-democratic power. They are directly responsible to the Dzongdha. The Fourth King introduced a new policy of Block Development Committee known as Gewog Yargay Tshogchung (GYT) in 1991 to promote decentralisation in to the grass root level. This committee included the representatives of the village and this was headed by the Gup.

Foreign Relations

The foreign policy of Bhutan has entered in to a new phase under the Fourth King. The Royal Bhutan Mission in India was re-designed as the Royal Bhutanese Embassy on 8th August 1978. By the end of 20th century the nation had diplomatic relations with 21 countries including, India, Bangladesh, Nepal, Sri Lanka, the Netherlands, South Korea, Japan, Thailand, Switzerland and the countries of the European Community and 54 international agencies are involved in development projects in the country. In has joined a number of international organizations including the UN and SAARC. It has no diplomatic relations with the five permanent members of the UN Security Council. Under his reign Bhutan maintained a low profile in the international scene till the general election took place in 2008. The nation under its foreign policies tried to conciliate exclusive objectives such as;

- Sovereignty
- To achieve economic self reliance
- Peace and security of its nation and people
- Preservation of the cultural heritage
- Broadening of its foreign relations
- A special relation with India.[38]

Defence

The security sensitivities and imperatives of Bhutan had changed from that of the 60's. The main security concern of the nation today is to preserve the distinct national identity, political sovereignty, protection of culture and economic and political stability. The Royal Bhutanese Police force under the Fourth King confined to maintain law and order in the nation. The defence system of Bhutan is interlinked with the defence system of India for assistance and training. Being situated in a very important geo-political area between China and India, Bhutan's defence system became more important under the Fourth King. The insurgency problems of the North East Frontier of India, Assam, and Sikkim pose a vital treat to the military and police system in the nation.

Financial Administration

The financial administration of the country was not developed as in western world or even as in developing countries. Under the fourth Druk Gyalpo the nation began a very important structural and strategic change in the financial administration of Bhutan. Under his reign the Planning Commission had been given more powers and they were responsible for the formulation of overall development strategies, coordination of sectoral activities, policies and programmes and formulation of five year plans. This commission was also responsible for aid management and coordinating inter-ministerial development. It was also empowered to ensure the timely implementation of the five year Plans according to specified objectives and priorities.[39] He introduced the budget presentation in 1990s in the Tshogdu. The financial administration was responsible for raising, spending and keeping accounts of the funds received and collected and allocation of such funds to the public service. This works were mainly done by the Finance Ministry under the supervision of the King and cabinet. The Fourth King continued with the idea of five year plan in the nation. A planning commission was established in 1971 which was entrusted to prepare the third five year plan. The third five year plan was initiated in 1971to 1976 for which most of the funding came from India. The fourth five year plan which started in 1976 till 1981 was mostly concentrated on the agricultural field and animal husbandry to improve the economic stability of the nation. The fifth five year plan was introduced to make the economy of Bhutan self-reliant for the period 1981to 1986. A change in the economic system of Bhutan begins with the introduction of the sixth five year plan for the period from 1987 to 1992. It focused on industry, trade and commerce. The seventh five year plan which started in 1992-1997 provided major emphasis on internal resources mobilization and human development, privatisation and sustainable development. The total resources were diverted to improve the existing infrastructure for social services and industry during this period. The eighth five year plan (1997-2002) was focused at consolidation and improvement of all social infrastructures and its total outlay was Nu. 30,000 million. The main feature of this plan was the construction of Tala, Kurichu and Basochhu power projects and Dungsum cement project in Bhutan. This plan provides main emphasize on private sector, financial sector development and revenue mobilization. The ninth five year plan was started in 2002 to 2007, which was the last economic development plan in Bhutan before the general election. The development has got a new speed and flow under the Fourth King. The nation's economy began to strengthen so as to plan its development projects without much financial assistance from India or other nations. Thus economic development in Bhutan saw a gradual change in the structure of production and expenditure.

Political Developments under Jigme Khesar Namgyel Wangchuck (2008-present)

Jigme Khesar Namgyel Wangchuck, the son of Jigme Singye Wangchuk succeeded his father to become the fifth Dragon King (Druk Gyalpo) of the Kingdom of Bhutan. Though he became king on 14th December 2006, his coronation took place on 6th November 2008 during the auspicious year that marked 100 years of Monarchical rule in the Kingdom of Bhutan. He began his political life by accompanying his father in his tours and meetings throughout the Kingdom to interact with people and speak to them. He also officially represented the Kingdom on several international events even before becoming the Druk Gyalpo. On May 2002, he represented Bhutan at the 7th United Nations General Assembly and made his first speech to the UN where he addressed issues related to the welfare of the millions of children around the world. He also represented Bhutan in the Thai King Bhumibol Adulyadej's 60th Anniversary Celebrations in Bangkok on June 2006.

His political carrier began on October 31, 2004 as he was installed as the Trongsa Penlop in Trongsa Dzong. The appointment of Khesar as the Trongsa Penlop was a continuation of tradition that was started by Zhabrung Ngawang Namgyal in 1647 signifying the ture heritage of a person to the Bhutanese Thorne. The investiture ceremony of Khesar as the Trongsa Penlop was the formal declaration of his status as the Crown Prince and next heir to the Bhutanese Thorne.

Political Accomplishments

The new King began his reign in a changing phase of the country's political structure. He started his political activity by presiding over the last sessions of the parliament where electoral laws, land reforms and other important issues were deliberated. He emphasised the need for and responsibility of the people towards ensuring the success of democracy in the kingdom. He took a major initiative in encouraging the participation of the youths of Bhutan in the upcoming democratic exercises and to strive for greater standards of education, business, civil service and the need for the people to cooperate with the state to work hard for better future. He signed a new treaty of friendship with India in February 2007, replacing the old treaty of 1949. Many initiatives were taken by the new King to strengthen the system in preparation for the democratic government and the elections that took place in 2008 and later.

After the formal coronation, King Jigme Khesar's first political landmark project was the launching of the National Cadastral Resurvey in March 2009 which aimed at resolving the long standing land issues of excess land that affects every citizens of the country. The King through this project also provided land to landless farmers around the country. Another major political accomplishment of the fifth King Jigme Khesar was his presents and supervision of the rebuilding efforts of the areas following a major earthquakes and floods in 2009. Recently, he was invited by the Government of India to be the Chief Guest for the 64th Indian Republic Day Celebrations in New Delhi on 26th January 2013.

Conclusion

The administrative history of Bhutan gives a clear

picture of the nation's intention be a Modernised political entity. The Wangchuk dynasty brought the nation to a new realm by introducing a number of modern political structures and development plans. In the year 2008, when the nation faced a general election the nation began to known to the world as the youngest democracy in the world with a evolutionary shift in power from the absolute monarchy to the democratically elected parliament without any revolution or political crisis. Though the nation faces a number of challenges to the successful functioning of the democratic system, the monarchs in the nation becomes the spiritual and moral supporters in strengthening and developing the political structure of the country. The introduction of the National Assembly, Planning Commission, Cabinet, the unique ideology of Gross National Happiness, the policies of isolation which later changed to opening up of its borders to the world and the development programs based on five year planning were some of the major features of the hereditary monarchical system in Bhutan. The nation witnessed a change from its traditional based economy and society in to a Modernised one without losing or ignoring its culture and religious values.

NOTES

1. Fort, which served as the Centre of Administration.
2. Rizal, Dhurba, (2002) *Administrative System in Bhutan*, Adroit Publishers, New Delhi. p. 26-27.
3. Ibid. p.28.
4. Aris, Micheal, (1980) *Bhutan: The Early History of Himalayan Kingdom*, Vikas Publications, New Delhi. p.217.
5. Dhurba Rizal, (2002), n.2, p.31.
6. Petech, Luciano, (1972) *"The Rulers of Bhutan c. 1650–1750". Oriens Extremus. Zeitschrift für Sprache,Kunst und Kultur der Länder des Fernen Ostens*, vol. 19, Hamburg. p. 203-213.
7. Dhurba Rizal, (2002), n.2, p.35.

8. Ibid, p.39.
9. Rose, Leo E., (1977) *The Politics of Bhutan*, Cornell University Press, New York. p. 149-150
10. Parmanand, (1992) *The Politics of Bhutan: Retrospect and Prospect*, Pragati Publications, Delhi.p.166.
11. Dhurba Rizal, (2002), n.2, p.62.
12. Leo E. Rose, (1977), n.9, p. 126.
13. Ibid, p. 144.
14. Robert, Geoffrey K. (1971) *A Dictionary of Political Analysis*, Longman, London. p. 167.
15. Sinha, A.C. (1991) *Bhutan: Ethnic Identity and national Dilemma*, Reliance Publishing House, New Delhi. pp. 201-202
16. A.C. Sinha, (2001), *Himalayan Kingdom Bhutan:Ttraditions, Transition and Transformation*, Indus Publishing Company, New Delhi. pp. 87-88.
17. Leo E. Rose, (1977), n.9, pp. 158-159.
18. Dasho Rinzin Dorji, (1989) *A Brief Religious, Cultural and Secular History of Bhutan*, The Asia Society Galleries, New York. p.13.
19. Dhurba Rizal, (2002), n.2, pp. 68-69.
20. Ibid, p. 70.
21. The Oxford Concise Dictionary.
22. Dhurba Rizal, (2002), n.2, pp. 68-69.
23. Ibid, p.77.
24. Ibid, p. 89.
25. Ibid, p. 94.
26. Leo E. Rose, (1977), n.9, p. 205.
27. Ravi Verma (1988) *India's Role in the Emergence of Contemporary Bhutan*, Capital Publishing House, New Delhi. p.57.
28. Dhurba Rizal, (2002), n.2, pp.108-109.
29. Leo E. Rose, (1977), n.9, pp. 166-167.
30. 76th Session of National Assembly, Proceedings and Resolutions, 29th June to 30th July 1998.
31. Dhurba Rizal, (2002), n.2, p. 118.
32. Ibid, p. 122.
33. Leo E. Rose, (1977), n.9, p. 161.
34. Ibid, p. 207.
35. Dhurba Rizal, (2002), n.2, pp. 133-134.
36. Ibid, pp. 110-115.
37. Ibid, pp. 115-117.
38. Ibid, pp. 138-139.
39. Gross Natioanl Happiness Commisssion. Available at: http://www.gnhc.gov.bt/

CHAPTER 3

Analysing the Trends towards Modernisation in Bhutanese Politics

Introduction

The process of Modernisation plays an important role in the transformation of political situation in the developing nations. Adopting the principles of globalisation and Modernisation of the society requires a change in the political structure to cope with the new issues and challenges of the country and lead the nation in the right direction on the road to development. Being a traditional Buddhist society and nation, Bhutan always had wanted to embrace Modernisation of its political structure while adopting the principles of Modernisation. The process of Modernisation had in a way forced the rulers to opt for a new government structure based on democracy that upholds the status of an independent Bhutanese state among the developed and developing nations in the world. Political Modernisation is a delicate concept to delve with, as there are number of actions and elements such as political parties, ideologies, political culture, system and charismatic leaders that bring changes during the transformation towards Modernisation and political development. In this chapter, an effort will be made to understand and examine the Modernisation process in the political structure in Bhutan. Emphasis will be given to the importance of the effect of Modernisation on various aspects such as political structure, public administration, human rights, good governance and sustainable development.

Political Modernisation of Bhutan can be viewed from its historical, typological and evolutionary perspectives. The changes in the political structure began as the nation started to move towards Modernisation under the Third King from 1928 onwards. The political changes in any country can be divided in to three; Historical, Typological and Evolutionary. Historically, political Modernisation in a nation refers to the changes in the political structure and culture due to commercialization, urbanization and industrialisation. Typologically, the change refers to the process of transformation of the pre-modern or traditional polity in the nation with the post modern polity that's the democratic form of polity with a democratic government at the centre and local levels. Evolutionary political Modernisation refers to an open-ended increase in the capacity of political system to develop so as to cope with or resolve problems to absorb and adapt continuous changes in the nation. These perspectives helped Bhutan in its political Modernisation to develop the nation towards a standardized modern polity. The nature of political structure in Bhutan around the mid-20th century was almost undifferentiated and unspecialized as the Kings retained all the executive, legislative and judicial powers to himself. Buddhist religion also played a vital role in the political culture characterizing a theocratic political structure in the state.[1]

Historical Development in the Political Structure

The traditional political development of Bhutan began from the middle of 17th century onwards when the nation was unified under Shabdrung Ngwang Namgyal. He introduced the first ever political structure known as Chhosi- the *dual system of government*, in the nation for administrative purposes. Under this system, he introduced two new administrative positions in the country known as Druk Desi or Deb Raja and Je Khenpo or Dharma Raja, to look after the temporal and spiritual aspects of the Bhutanese people respectively. During the period of Shabdrungs from 1616 till 1907, Bhutan was under a theocratic political structure. In the beginning of the 20th century the nation witnessed a change in its political structure with a Hereditary Monarchy, replacing the then administrative head who is selected on the basis of reincarnation of the Shabdrung. This change was a turning point in the political history of Bhutan that began the Modernising process with the help of British India. Though the First Druk Gyalpo His Majesty Ugyen Wangchuck insisted on the policy of isolation, much of Bhutan's modern development has been attributed and introduced during his reign. He introduced a number of internal reforms including the Western-style schools, internal communication, modifying the Buddhist monastic system and encouraging trade and commerce with India. The process of Modernisation effort was further continued by his successor Jigme Wangchuck who established more educational institutions, roads and other infrastructures in the nation. But still then Bhutan was not aware of the western model of political development and remained isolated from the international affairs.

Beginning of the Democratic Process

The nation began the move towards Modernisation in full flow under the Third Druk Gyalpo His Majesty Jigme Dorji Wangchuck in 1952. Bhutan, under his leadership, started to change the traditional theocratic political system with a Modernised western political system i.e. democratic government. Though in the beginning, the political system was not a perfect democracy as visible in the western nations or in the South Asian region, the process for such change was initiated by the introduction of a number of democratic institutions in the country. The nation's first ever move towards a modern political system was began in 1953, when the Third King established the Tshogdu (National Assembly), to involve people in the decision-making process of the country. Following the successful introduction of the Parliament, in 1965, the King introduced another institution known as the Lodey Tshogdey (the Royal Advisory Council) in order to establish a modern structured government combining the monarchical and democratic principles together. By the second half of 20th century, Bhutan made a number of radical changes in its political structure to modernise the system. He began to develop the political system by giving it a shape and picture of Western style polity by introducing different institutions such as executive, legislature, council of ministers, Military and the launching of foreign relations.

With the succession of the Fourth King, Bhutan began to move faster in its Modernising process by including more and more people in decision making process in a democratic way. He took important steps in administrative decentralisation process for involving the common people in decision making process. The Third Druk Gyalpo strengthened the process of Modernising the political system by establishing the Dzongkhag Yargey Tshogchung (DYT) and Gewog Yargay Tshogchung (GYT) in the district and bloc levels by the end of the 20th century. Under his reign, the political development was totally influenced by the western model political system and globalisation process. The King wanted to create a political system that upholds the unique status and statehood of Bhutan among the developed and developing nations. Under the Third Druk Gyalpo, the Modernisation process in the political system attained in its heights along with his unique philosophy of Gross National Happiness. The nation witnessed a dramatic change in the power sharing authority in 1998, when the King issued a Royal Edict (Kasho) stating that, the King will devote all his executive powers to an elected cabinet and will abide by the principle of political responsibility to the parliament.[2] In December 2007, the first ever National Council election transformed Bhutan's transitional political system in to a modern one following the first ever democratic general election to the National Assembly in March 2008 which was based on universal adult franchise.

Modernisation and the Political Structure of Bhutan

Modernisation has a bigger role in the framing of the new democratic political system and enacting a written constitution in Bhutan in 2008. The Western political ideologies and the influence of globalisation are clearly visible in the transformation of the nation's political system from a traditional political entity to a modern one. The development of political structure and modernisation process has a unique characteristic when one talks of Bhutan. Contrary to any developing nation's political change, which normally emanates from the peoples demand in the form of a revolution or bloodshed, Bhutan's change was fully and formally initiated and implemented by the Kings. The modernisation process initiated in the mid-1950s by the Third King Jigme Dorji Wangchuk, who is known as the architect of modern Bhutan, had a different strategy and pattern that surprised the close observers of Bhutan's modern history. After the end of its *self-imposed isolation* in 1961, the progress in modernising the political structure of Bhutan had a tremendous improvement in all its spheres. The nation has been getting its inspirations from the ideological influences of west and implementing it in Bhutan without endangering its tradition and culture. Though the influence comes from the West, the political behaviour in Bhutan has been different from the predetermined patterns of western political theories. However, given the fact that the influence of western style of development pattern towards modernity is visible in almost all the developing third world countries, it is impossible for a small nation like Bhutan to remain immune from the happenings around for long. As such the progress of development led the nation towards modernising its socio-economic and political spheres, the dilemma in this development process is how best the nation can adopt and accommodate the change and keep its functioning intact without losing its unique cultural and traditional identity. This pattern of development created a dilemma for the government and stands crucial for the Modernisation of Bhutan's polity in the coming future.[3]

The Election Commission

The democratisation of the political system witnessed new changes in the political sphere of Bhutan. The Election Commission of Bhutan (ECB) was a new beginning in the process of democratizing the nation and Modernising the political system of Bhutan. The ECB was established on 16th January 2006, under the leadership of the Fourth Druk Gyalpo His Majesty Jigme Singye Wangchuck. The main objective of establishing an Election Commission in Bhutan was to provide an environment for free and fair elections in the nation.[4] The Election Commission of Bhutan consists of a Chief Election Commissioner and two other election commissioners. According to the Election Act of the Kingdom of Bhutan, 2008, the Election Commission should be an independent body in the country. Under this Act, the Election Commissioner and two election commissioners are appointed by the Druk Gyalpo for a term of five years from the list of names recommended and submitted jointly by the prime Minister, the Chief Justice of Bhutan, the Speaker, the Chairperson of the National Council and the Leader of the Opposition Party.[5] According to the Election Act of 2008, the Election Commission shall be responsible for the direction and control of the preparation of electoral Rolls for all elections to Parliament and Local Governments and the superintendence. This act also provides the following responsibilities to the Election Commission, such as:

a. Register political parties;
b. Promote public awareness on electoral matters by conducting education and information dissemination programmes or by any other means;
c. Provide information and advice on referendums and electoral matters to Parliament and the Government;
d. Facilitate coverage of elections by the media in accordance with the Rules framed for that purpose;
e. Make Rules for carrying out the purposes of this Act, without prejudice to the provisions of this Act, and such Rules be issued by notification;
f. Provide in the cases approved by the Ministry of Foreign Affairs, assistance in matters relating to elections and referendums to authorities of

g. foreign countries or foreign organizations; and
h. Perform any other functions as authorized under this Act or any other law in force.

The Election Commission also reviews the electoral system, conduct researches, and introduce any device or system for the electoral purpose and posses the summoning, inspection, and adjudication powers of a court. The Election Commission of Bhutan is supported by a Secretariat to which it may delegate its authority by order or any resolution. The decisions and actions of the Election Commission of Bhutan are not reviewable by any court in Bhutan except in cases of election petitions or election appeals.[6]

The Election Commission organizes a serious of activities in the nation to ensure the success of elections at the national and local level. They conduct meetings all around the nation to brief on the importance of electing the right candidates and how to cast votes. The participants who get educated on the election meetings should educate their respective villagers once back in their villages.[7] The ECB organizes Functional Literacy and Possession of Skills Tests for the candidates who are aspiring to contest in the elections. They have to sit for both the written and viva test in Dzongkha, except for Thrompons who has to have at least a formal university degree as minimum qualification. The test ensures that the local government representatives have basic reading and writing skills in Dzongkha in order to discharge their responsibilities for social and economic welfare of the people. The ECB encourages more and more women candidates to participate in the Functional Literacy and Possession of Skills Tests so that their representation percentage increases in the decision making process of the nation.[8]

Introduction of Political Parties

The need of democracy in the present century is one or more political parties in the state with a strong ideological backup. Article 15 of the Constitution of Bhutan clearly states about the objectives and duties of a political party in Bhutan. All political parties in Bhutan are regulated by the Constitution of 2008. Under the provision of the constitution, there must be a multi-party system under which two parties at a time occupy either ruling or oppositions in government. Until now, only two parties are registered with the Election Commission of Bhutan. Most of the other political parties are regarded as extremist, terrorist or militant groups as they are involved in blasts and violence in the nation. They are

- Bhutan Communist Party (Marxist-Leninist-Maoist)
- Bhutan Peoples' Party
- Druk National Congress
- Bhutan National Democratic Party
- Bhutan Democratic Socialist Party
- Bhutan Gorkha National Liberation Front
- Bhutan National Congress
- Bhutan National Party

People's Democratic Party (PDP)

The people's Democratic Party was established on March 24, 2007, by the former Prime Minister and Agriculture Minister of Royal Government of Bhutan, Sangay Ngedup. The PDP is the first political party in the nation to get registered under the Election Commission of Bhutan. On August 6, 2007, it applied for registration and on September 1, 2007, the Election Commission of Bhutan registered the party. The main objectives of the party for the 2008 General Election was:

- Safeguard the sovereignty, peace, security and unity of Bhutan;
- Transform the ideals of Gross National Happiness into everyday reality for every Bhutanese;
- Work for political, social, cultural and sustainable economic advancement of all Bhutanese;
- Adhere to the ideals and principles of the Constitution of the Kingdom of Bhutan, in spirit and in action;
- Build a flourishing, effective and functional democracy;
- Establish exemplary governance, whether in the Government or in the Opposition; and
- Serve with humility, integrity, and compassion to fulfil our stated policy priorities.[9]

The PDP presented its candidates in all 47 constituencies for the National Assembly election of 2008. In this election the party could win only two of the 47 seats and just one third of the votes cast.

Druk Phuensum Tshogpa or Bhutan Peace and Prosperity Party (DPT)

The Bhutan Peace and Prosperity Party is the other major political party in Bhutan. It was formed on July 25, 2007 as a merger of the All People's Party and the Bhutan people's United Party. On August 15, 2007 Jigmi Yoezer Thinley, who was the former Prime Minister and the Home Minister of Bhutan, was elected as the president of the party. The Party applied for a formal registration on August 15, under the Election Commission of Bhutan and became the second political party in the nation after the Commission accepted the registration on October 2, 2007. In the first ever general election of Bhutan, on March 24, 2008, the party won 45 seats out of 47 seats to the National Assembly. The party is conservative in nature and Royalist in its outlook.

The Vision and Mission of the Party

According to the party leaders, the vision of the DPT is to establish a sovereign and prosperous nation of enlightened citizens who are committed to the pursuit of Gross National Happiness through growth with equity and justice, encompassing economic self reliance, social harmony, environment integrity and political justice in the country.

The party also put forward the following objectives for the betterment of the nation;

1. To realize the vision of His Majesty the King for a truly vibrant and rogressive democracy wherein sovereign power will lie with the people and the purpose of government shall be to fulfil their hopes and aspirations.
2. To always strive to ensure that national unity, security, justice, fundamental rights and freedom are never compromised.
3. To abide by the Constitution and uphold the Rule of Law.
4. To persevere with endeavours to build and strengthen conditions for the happiness of the Bhutanese people.
5. To ensure stability and serve as a standard of constancy and trustworthiness amid the vagaries of party politics and the ever changing political landscape.
6. To establish standards and norms for party politics and behaviour by way of example so that parties

and individuals choose to follow them or be so inspired, as to give all voters true and comparative choice.

7. To be guided, demonstrably, by the highest management and social ethics and principles so that the party shall be worthy of the loyalty of its own members and the trust and confidence of the people.
8. To recognize and give opportunity to potential leaders to rise to positions of political office irrespective of their social standing or economic status.
9. To govern, when given the mandate, with transparency, accountability and compassion in keeping with the ideals and purposes enshrined in the Constitution of our country.[10]

Emergence of New Political Parties, 2013

The year 2013 witnessed a new development in the political system of Bhutan with the introduction of three more new political parties to contest the 2013 election. They are Bhutan Kuen-Nyam Party (BKP), Druk Chirwang Tshogpa (DCT) and Druk Nyamrup Tshogpa (DNT).

Bhutan Kuen-Nyam Party (BKP)

Bhutan Kuen-Nyam Party (BKP) is the new political party in Bhutan symbolized by the *Kuen-Nyam Khorlo*. They were registered as a political party in the Kingdom of Bhutan on the Twenty-First Day of the Eleventh Month of Water Male Dragon Year of the Bhutanese Calendar corresponding to 3rd of January 2013.[11] This party focuses on equality. Rup Narayan Adhikari, is the declared party leader who is an engineer by profession and an old veteran in the private and public sector.

The party symbol *Kuen-Nyam Khorlo* represents a

number of ideas. The yellow circle symbolizes the rich and unique culture that values allegiance to the Constitution of the Kingdom of Bhutan. The green circle in the symbol signifies sustainable management and utilization of natural resources for green economic development for the benefit of all Bhutanese people. The brown circle symbolizes the efforts to sustain broad-based and regionally balanced economic development and growth, reinforcing social development through equal opportunities to avoid exclusion and overcome socially divisive disparities, while respecting diversity as part of the enabling environment for socio-economic development. The red circle signifies the nation's united conviction towards equitable social development as an important factor for the eradication of poverty and enhancing human wellbeing and the quality of life of all Bhutanese people. The symbol further represents the compassionate responsibility for reducing inequalities, pursuit of people empowerment, rule of law, provision of safety nets, and participation in a democratic and pluralistic system respectful of all human rights and individual respect. Finally, the blue centre circle symbolizes good governance that will be critical for the health of the socio-economy, the environment and the nation's unique culture. The white colour in the background symbolizes Bhutan Kuen-Nyam Party's purity of heart and mind in the service of *Tsawa-Sum*. All five circles are interdependent in nature and will interact in coordinated spheres as represented by the outer five rings with the center circle maintaining close harmony in the overall pursuit of Gross National Happiness.

Aims and Objectives of the Party

The Party put forward a number of aims and objectives for which they stand. They are listed below:

1. To preserve and protect the independence,

sovereignty and territorial integrity of the Kingdom of Bhutan.

2. To safeguard the freedom and advance the wellbeing of all Bhutanese through equal representation and democratic governance by exhibiting and sowing the seeds of genuine participatory democracy and nurturing democratic principles within all segments of society.
3. To promote the rich and unique culture and tradition of the country expressing a deepest allegiance to Constitution of the Kingdom of Bhutan.
4. To promote an egalitarian society, free from upper or lower orders, without class distinctions, segregation or ethnic divisions, a cohesive society without prejudices and discrimination and where there is equal opportunity for all citizens of the country.
5. To promote and ensure social order where each person in their capacity as a citizen, a farmer, wage earner, student, pensioner or a salaried worker can influence the laws, policies and programs of the organization and conditions of working life positively.
6. To create enabling conditions for the people to enjoy all civil rights and shoulder their individual and collective responsibilities to their families, communities and the nation.
7. To eradicate poverty and enhance human wellbeing and the quality of life of all Bhutanese people in a just and humane society where those who cannot provide for themselves can live in dignity.
8. To reduce inequalities, pursuit of people

empowerment, rule of law, provision of safety nets and participation in a democratic and pluralistic system respectful of all human rights and individual respect.

9. To guarantee social and political rights, responsibilities and freedoms for all Bhutanese including adequate food, shelter and health care, good and continuing education from early childhood, meaningful employment and being treated with equal dignity and respect regardless of gender, physical, geographical and cultural differences.
10. To strive towards the conservation and sustainable utilization and management of the natural resources for the benefit of all Bhutanese people for the present and the future generations.
11. To work towards sustaining broad-based and regionally balanced economic development and growth, reinforcing social development through equal opportunities to avoid exclusion and to overcome socially divisive disparities, while respecting diversity as part of the enabling environment for socio-economic development.
12. To promote greater participation of women in the political arena by providing an enabling environment in recognizing their contribution towards nation building.
13. To promote socially responsible private sector development and growth as the main determinant of the country's socio-economic prosperity.
14. To enable a future for the youth in which they can achieve their aspirations and be responsibly involved in defining the country's future and take pride in its past.

15. To continue pursuing a foreign policy of national interest as envisioned by the wise monarchs.
16. To promote and foster greater ties that exists with India.
17. To promote open, transparent and responsive governance at all levels guaranteeing freedom of speech, free media and independent institutions.
18. To set social, cultural, economic and political conditions and enhance systems to treat corruption at source.
19. To promote national unity and progressive socio-economic development to ensure the well being of the nation.

The Party Ideology and Principles

Bhutan Kuen-Nyam Party (BKP) stands for the realization of a compassionate and democratic social order and political system based on the universal ideals of justice, liberty, equality and fraternity as enshrined in the Constitution of the Kingdom of Bhutan. The new Party is founded on the philosophy of Gross National Happiness encompassing the following principles:

a) *Tha-Damtse Ley-Jumdre*
b) Equality – respect for each individual, people empowerment, human rights and rule of law
c) Inclusivity – participatory and inclusive political and governance processes to the advancement of social, cultural and economic growth of the nation; and
d) Cultural Value – safeguarding and promoting the special and unique Bhutanese way of life and setting.[12]

Druk Chirwang Tshogpa (DCT)

Druk Chirwang Tshogpa or Druk Democratic Socialist Party is the fifth political party registered in Bhutan to compete in the 2013 general elections. The party was registered under the Election Commission of Bhutan on 28th December 2012. Ms Lily Wangchuk is the declared leader of the party who is a well-known career diplomat and social activist. The party has chosen its candidates with more than five years of professional experience and no corruption case. The candidates are also those that are known in their constituency and are acceptable to their constituencies.

The election symbol of the Party is a Swan (Ngangpa), surging skyward from a lotus mount that is sprouting on a body of water with a Norbu (Precious Gem) as a backdrop flanked on either side by green leaves. The Water Body represents people and stability; the Lotus symbolizes purity and harmony; the Swan represents the rising glory of Bhutan with unity, equity and positive transformation; the Norbu or the Precious Gem represents Tsa Wa Sum or the Triple Gem, vitality with endurance and prosperity; the Green Leaves signifies GNH, spreading of prosperity and happiness; the Sharp Lines of the Wings means definitive, goal oriented, principled, integrity, direction and security of the nation that the Party will work towards. Overall, the election symbol of Druk Chirwang Tshogpa Party signifies Unity, Prosperity and Happiness for the people and country while, for the Party, it is symbolic of its principles of social democracy. The Blue and Black colours signify democracy, people, unity, peace, stability, equity and justice. The Pink colour represents democratic socialism on which the ideology of the Party is based. The Green colour symbolizes happiness, prosperity and GNH.

Vision and Mission:

The vision of Druk Chirwang Tshogpa Party is a peaceful and prosperous Kingdom of Bhutan with strengthened sovereignty, transparent and accountable democratic governance, politically united, active citizenry, inclusive and equitable growth, sustainable and people-centric development, economic prosperity, environmental conservation, cultural cohesion, social harmony and with the enabling conditions for the people of Bhutan to pursue Happiness.

The Mission of the Druk Chirwang Tshogpa Party is inspired by the unique development philosophy of Gross National Happiness and the Constitution of the Kingdom of Bhutan. The Party's mission is to serve Tsa Wa Sum with absolute loyalty and dedication in promoting Unity, Prosperity and Happiness.

The Objectives of the Party:

The official charter of the Druk Chirwang Tshogpa Party states the following objectives:

1. To bear true faith and allegiance to the Constitution of the Kingdom of Bhutan;
2. To safeguard the independence, sovereignty, security and territorial integrity of the Kingdom of Bhutan;
3. To build a strong and responsive Party with broad based membership and balanced participation from all sections of the society representing different regions, generation and gender.
4. To establish and advance transparent and accountable governance with active citizenry;
5. To promote inclusive growth with people centric development approach;

6. To endeavour to develop and execute policies that will address the socio- economic gap between regions, Dzongkhags and people;
7. To minimize inequalities of income, concentration of wealth, and promote equitable distribution of public facilities among individuals and people living in different regions of the country;
8. To promote vibrant democracy with strong, independent media and civil society;
9. To promote enabling conditions for people to pursue happiness by ensuring that all have access to basic necessities such as clean water, food, shelter, accessible healthcare and education, safeguarding the rights and freedom of the people, addressing varied social issues and disabled-friendly policies;
10. To ensure a good quality of life for the people of Bhutan by addressing the root causes of growing social issues (rape, domestic violence, murder, robbery, divorce, alcoholism, drug addiction, suicide, orphans, destitution and homelessness) with policy interventions, targeted programmes and care for those in need;
11. To address the needs of the rural population through infrastructure development programmes, better connectivity, rural employment, enhancement of economic opportunities and targeted interventions for alleviating poverty and addressing human wildlife conflict (HWC) by promoting and supporting research into effective HWC solutions;
12. To create more gender sensitive vocational training programmes and targeted interventions to address higher employment amongst youth and to prevent mismatch of jobs and skills.

13. To create and provide gainful employment opportunities for the youth;
14. To promote greater participation of women in all spheres with gender responsive policies;
15. To promote economic growth and self-reliance while ensuring equity, balanced regional development, and the sustainable use of natural resources;
16. To encourage and foster private sector development through fair market competition and prevent commercial monopolies.
17. To foster professionalism at the workplace, and the efficient and responsive delivery of public services by every government organization;
18. To encourage excellence in civil service delivery with implementation of systematic performance appraisals and efficient management systems;
19. To promote social justice, cultural harmony and equality to all the people, regardless of ethnicity, religion, region, gender, social origin, disabilities or language;
20. To strive to create conditions that will enable the sustainable development of a good and compassionate society with universal human values;
21. To protect and conserve the pristine environment and pursue renewable natural resources projects that promise sustainability;
22. To preserve and promote the rich traditional, cultural, religious and spiritual heritage as the essential basis of national identity;
23. To expand and improve education services with emphasis on standards, quality and accessibility, values and skills for full development of the human

personality;

24. To improve the delivery of health services with an emphasis on quality of service and preventive measures;
25. To institute a food safety programme with an emphasis on reduction of the importation of pesticide-laden vegetables and subsidies to encourage more organic farming;
26. To promote friendly relations and goodwill with the international community on the basis of peace, cooperation and the sovereign equality of states; foster respect for international law and treaty obligations, and encourage settlement of international disputes by peaceful means in order to promote international peace and security;
27. To play a responsible and constructive role in regional and global affairs; and in particular to further strengthen the close and collaborative relationship and economic cooperation with India; and
28. To conduct strictly in accordance with the Code of Conduct for Political Parties in all Party affairs.[13]

Druk Nyamrup Tshogpa (DNT)

Druk Nyamrup Tshogpa (DNT) is the another party which was registered under the Election Commission of Bhutan as the official political party in the country. It focuses on freedom, justice and solidarity as its motto. The Election Symbol of the party is a peach blossom flower with stalk and leaves. The Peach blossom is known as *Khamshing Meto* in Dzongkha. The blossom paints the first colour of spring and it represents hope, the essence of the human spirit that embraces the virtuous aspiration of peace, happiness and prosperity. For the Druk Nyamrup Tshogpa party it is the symbol of purity and beauty that shows their pledge to serve the King, the Country and the People. The other notion of the symbol is that the nation's wealth, peace and happiness must take all the direction of the country as the sweet fragrance of the blossom.

Vision and Principles of the Party:

The vision of the Druk Nyamrup Tshogpa Party is a prosperous, progressive, equitable and just nation based on the rule of law where social justice, individual freedom, popular participation and sustainable development are guaranteed.

The main principles of the party are as follows:

a) The Party should follow the principles of social democracy, as suited to Bhutan.
b) The Party should commit itself to promote and nurture the needed institutions to ensure that the overarching principles of justice, freedom and solidarity are strongly protected.
c) The Party shall protect individual rights and promote individual duties, as enshrined in the Constitution, both de jure (in law) and de facto (in practice).
d) It shall endeavour to promote the philosophy of Gross National Happiness (GNH) and individual wellbeing in keeping with national values and principles of good governance.
e) The Party shall respect the principles of market economy which have proven in advancing human creativity and enterprise development and contributing to economic growth and social progress
f) The Party shall make public policies and enact laws

for the maximum benefit of all the Bhutanese people as the shareholders of State resources.

g) The Party shall endeavour to develop and execute public policies to minimize inequalities of income and concentration of wealth, and promote equitable distribution of public facilities among individuals and people living in different parts of the Kingdom.

Objectives of the Party:

Druk Nyamrup Tshogpa (DNT) strives to fulfil the following objectives:

a. To pursue social and economic development while promoting the culture and values of the country.
b. To strengthen national unity, social cohesion and patriotism through justice and fairness where all persons are equal before the law.
a. To pursue the goal of inclusive, equitable and sustainable economic growth by harnessing natural resources justifiably so that the state of natural environment and eco-system is not compromised.
b. To follow a path of balanced regional development to address the problems of poverty, inequality and underdevelopment.
c. To create favourable conditions for enhancing the growth and contribution of the private sector through fiscal and monetary policies, incentives and measures.
d. To foster regional and global peace, security and cooperation and develop friendly relations with all members of the international community.
e. To maintain close and harmonious relations with all the nation's neighbours, especially safeguarding and nurturing Indo-Bhutan friendship, in keeping with Bhutan's historical tradition.[14]

The New Constitution of Bhutan

One of the important aspects of modernising the political system took place in the year 2005, when the government unveiled the proposed constitution in which the absolute monarchy was transformed to a constitutional monarchy by establishing a parliamentary democracy in the country. In July 2008, Bhutan enacted its first ever written constitution which is the basic requirement of any modern democratic political system. The process for the drafting of a new constitution began from 2001 onwards. The official meetings for the drafting of the constitution took place in Bhutan and India respectively. A detailed program of the drafting of the constitution is given below in table 3.1

The drafting committee for the constitution of Bhutan consisted of a total of 39 members who were represented by all sections of Bhutanese society. The members included the Chief Justice of Bhutan, the Speaker of the National Assembly, two representatives from the monastic body, one elected member from each of the twenty Dzongkhags, the Zhung Kalyon and all the people's representatives of the Royal Advisory Council, five representatives of the Government, two lawyers from the Judiciary and the member Secretary from the Office of the Legal Affairs. The Chief Justice of Bhutan is the Chairman of the Committee.[15] A detailed list of the members of the drafting committee is given below in Table 3.2.

On March 23, 2005, the King of Bhutan His Majesty Jigme Singye Wangchuk announced the drafting of the new constitution. On 6 September 2005, the Druk Gyalpo of Bhutan informed the Cabinet that the Constitution of Bhutan should be adopted in 2008. A nation-wide consultation was held in Bhutan for the creation of a draft constitution. The Druk National Congress has been ardently

Table 3.1
Meetings Took Place for the Drafting of the Constitution

Period	*Place*	*Details*
30/11/2001	Throne Room, Tashichhodzong Thimphu.	His Majesty the Druk Gyalpo inaugurated the drafting of the written Constitution for the Kingdom of Bhutan with Zhugdrel Phuensum Tsokpai Tendrel ceremony.
30/11/2001 to 14/12/2001	Royal Banquet hall, Thimphu	The First meeting was convened
4/2/2002 to 08/02/2002	Zangdo Pelri Hotel, Punakha	The Second Meeting was convened.
27/03/2002 to 11/04/2002	Royal Banquet hall, Thimphu	The First Draft was discussed and debated in the Third meeting.
10/06/2002 to 19/06/2002	Royal Banquet Hall, Thimphu	Further discussion held on the Draft Constitution. This is the Fourth meeting of the Constitution Drafting Committee.
09/10/2002 to 18/10/2002	Kurje, Bumthang	The 39-member Committee deliberated on the principles and instruments that are critical to a Constitutional Government. They also studied different forms of democratic governments within the perspective of Bhutanese traditions and values. This was the Fifth meeting of the

		Constitution Drafting Committee.
23/11/2002 to 25/11/2002	Royal Banquet hall, Thimphu	Finalised the First Draft Constitution. This is the Sixth meeting of the Constitution Drafting Committee.
09/12/2003	Throne Room, Tashichhodzong, Thimphu	Submission of the First Draft Constitution to His Majesty, the Druk Gyalpo.
13/10/2003 to 17/06/2004	New Delhi &Goa, India	Review Meeting with Mr. K.K Venugopal.

Source: http://www.constitution.bt

Table 3.2
The Detailed List of the Members of the Constitution Drafting Committee

Sl. No.	*Name*	*Designation*	*Changes of Name (New)*	*Members Present Address*
1	Lyonpo Sonam Tobgye	Hon'ble Chairman		Royal Court of Justice,High Court
2	Dasho Ugen Dorji	Member		National Assembly of Bhutan
3	Ven. Drabi Lopon Kuenlay Gyeltshen	Member		Central Monastic Body
4	Ven. Yangbi Lopon Chimmi	Member		Central Monastic Body
5	Dasho Rinzin Gyaltshen	Member		Royal Advisory Council
6	Dasho Jamyang	Member		Royal Advisory Council
7	Dasho Chador Wangdi	Member		Royal Advisory Council
8	Dasho Gyeltshen	Member		Royal Advisory Council
9	Dasho Sonam Wangchuk	Member		Royal Advisory Council
10	Dasho Adap Passang	Member		Royal Advisory Council
11	Dasho Leki Pem	Member		Royal Advisory Council
12	Dasho Tashi Phuntsog	Member		Ministry of Information & Communications
13	Dasho Meghraj Gurung	Member		Bhutan Post & Telegraph

14	Lopen Lungtaen Gyatso	Member		Institute of Language & Cultural Studies, Semtokha
15	Karma Ura	Member		Central for Bhutan Studies
16	Dr. Dechen Tsering	Member		National Environment Commission
17	Dasho Lungten Dubgyur, LL.M (Edinburg)	Member		Royal Court of Justice, District Court, Chukha
18	Pasang Wangmo, LLB	Member		Royal Court of Justice, District Court, Thimphu
19	Jampel	Member		Bumthang
20	Palden Dorji	Member		Chukha
21	Dorji	Member		Dagana
22	Lhakpa Tshering	Member	Ugyen	Gasa
23	Lhaba	Member		Haa
24	Khamtula	Member		Lhuntse
25	Pedma Dorji	Member		Mongar
26	Wangdi	Member		Paro
27	Guchu Wangdi	Member		Pema Gatshel
28	Namgyal Phuntsho	Member		Punakha

29	Dechen Wangchuk	Member	Yonten Thinley	Samdrup Jongkhar
30	Chandra Bahadur Ghaley	Member	Talay Drukpa	Samtse
31	Thakur Prasad Homagai	Member		Sarpang
32	Thinley Dorji	Member	Dorji Bidha	Thimphu
33	Jangchub Dorji	Member		Trashigang
34	Lobzang Tshering	Member		Trashi Yangtsi
35	Dophu Tashi	Member	Chophel	Trongsa
36	Phurgye Drukpa	Member		Tsirang
37	Sigay Dorji	Member	Kuenga Namgyal	Wangdue Phodrang
38	Dechen Wangdi	Member	Sonam Gyeltshen	Zhemgang
39	Dasho Kuenlay Tshering, LL. M (Leiden)	Member Secretary		Office of Legal Affairs

Source: http://www.constitution.bt

campaigning for the establishment of a democratic government and drafting of a new constitution since 1994 in order to modernise the political structure of Bhutan. The drafting of a new constitution realized the need for a democratic, vibrant, responsible and accountable socio-economic and political society by providing its people with equal opportunity respect for rule of law, special care for minorities and underprivileged, preserve the nation's rich cultural heritage and protect the security and sovereignty of the nation. The unveiling of a draft constitution was an irretrievable step towards Modernisation of the political structure of Bhutan and encouraging the Bhutanese to collectively pursue the well-being of the nation. The Druk National Congress suggested for a constitution that was to be placed above all, including the Tsa-Wa Sum (the King, Country and People) and it must safeguard the rights of the people as well as the King and the institutions of monarchy. The constitution must be respected by both the King and the people irrespective of position and status to ensure peace, stability and safeguard the sovereignty and integrity of the nation. The path of Modernisation in Bhutan is likely to witness a new era of development and prosperity under the new codified law of the nation drawn from the Constitution.[16]

Modernising the Public Administration in Bhutan

The public administrative structure of Bhutan has been influenced by the principles of Modernisation during the reign of Third Druk Gyalpo itself. The administrative structure of Bhutan made a number of changes in the process of modernising the country. Beginning from the National Assembly to the Local Administrative units, one can clearly view a bigger role of Modernisation and globalisation in this change. Bhutan as a new born child in the adoption of globalisation and Modernisation, grown in its developmental aspects with regards to the policies initiated for public-private partnership and a well developed e-governance system. The nation now moves ahead of other South Asian countries in maintaining a well developed public administration system and implementation of its policies. The influence of globalisation and Modernisation has given a new life in the country's public administrative structures. The New Constitution of Bhutan now provides a well defined procedure and process of administrative policies and a clear cut division and powers of the three branches of government. The constitution provides for a better local administrative structure and defines its functions and importance in the nation. Figure 3.1 gives an overview of the administrative system in Bhutan.

1. The Legislature

According to Article 10.1 of the constitution of Bhutan, the Legislature consists of the Druk Gyalpo and a Bicameral Legislature including the National Assembly and the National Council. In the year 2007 and 2008, the nation went for a fresh democratic election to both the National Assembly and National Council in a democratic way. During the reign of the Fourth King, the entire structure of legislature has been changed and a new western model legislature was introduced. The progress towards Modernisation helped the nation to uphold an independent statehood status in the world. The peaceful change towards a parliamentary democracy was a unique process in contrast to the other South Asian nations which followed a revolutionary movement to achieve democracy. The first joint sitting of the democratically elected parliament of Bhutan was held from 8th May to 30th May, 2008.

FIGURE 3.1
Administrative Systems of Bhutan's Democratic Government

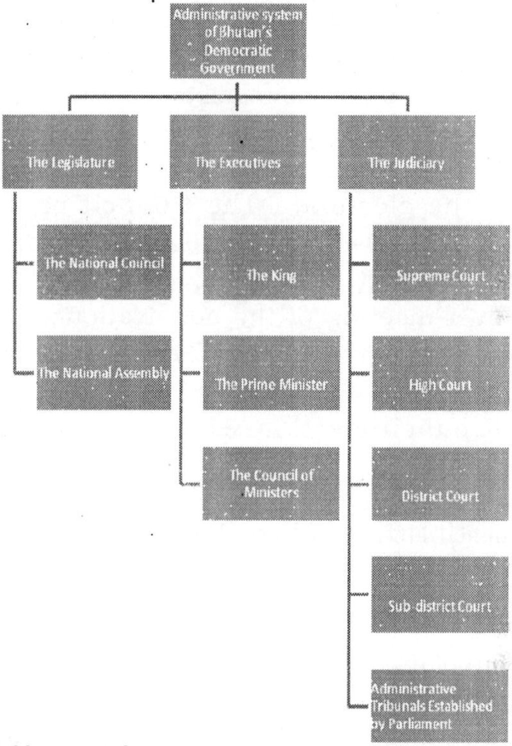

Source: www.bhutan.gov.bt

a. National Council

The National Council, which consists of 25 members, is the upper house of Bhutan's parliament. Besides, this body functions as a subordinate house creating and reviewing the legislation, the National Council review matters affecting the security, sovereignty and national interest of Bhutan that needs an immediate attention for law enforcement. According to the provisions of the Constitution of Bhutan, the council assembles at least twice a year. The National Council of Bhutan was established and its 20 members were elected in a democratic way by the electorates of 20 *Dzongkhags* on December 31, 2007 and January 29, 2008. The rest five members of the Council are nominated by the Druk Gyalpo. According to the new Constitution of Bhutan, the members should not belong to any political parties and should hold a graduate degree from a recognized university as the minimum qualification to contest the election.[17] The Council must elect a Chairperson and Deputy Chairperson from among its members at the first sitting after the general election.[18] The first ever meeting of the new National Council of Bhutan was held from June 17 to July 24, 2008. The Election Commission of Bhutan has declared the next National Council election which will take place in December 2011.

National Council Election of December 2007 and January 2008

The first ever election for the National Council took place in 31 December 2007 and 29 January 2008. 15 members out of the 20 total seats were elected on December 2007 in the 15 districts of Bhutan. Elections to the remaining 5 seats took place on January 2008. In contrast to the National Assembly election held on March 2008, the election to the National Council was not on a party based one. According to the Election Commission, the minimum qualification for a candidate to contest in the election to the National Assembly was graduation from a university. A total of 43 candidates contested in 15 Dzongkhags in the election held on 31 December 2007. A detailed list of members who are elected to the National Council of Bhutan in the elections held on 31 December 2007 and 29 January 2008 are given in table 3.3 and table 3.4.

Table 3.3
Elected Members to the National Council on 31st December, 2007

Dzongkhag	*Winner*
Bumthang	Tshewang Jurmin
Chukha	Tshewang Lhamo
Dagana	Sonam Dorji
Mongar	Naichu
Paro	Ugyen Tshering
Pema Gatshel	Jigme Rinzin
Punakha	Namgay Penjore
Samdrup Jongkhar	Jigme Wangchuk
Samtse	Mani Kumar Rai
Sarpang	Karma Donnen Wangdi
Trashigang	Sonam Kuenga
Trongsa	Jagar Dorji
Tsirang	Justin Gurung
Wangdue Phodrang	Sonam Yangchen
Zhemgang	Pema Lhamo

Source: http://www.kuenselonline.com/ncelections/index.php

Table 3.4
Elected Members to the National Council on 29 January 2008

Dzongkhag	*Winner*
Gasa	Sangay Khandu*
Haa	Tshering Dorji*
Lhuentse	Rinzin Dorji*
Thimphu	Sangay Zam
Trashiyangtse	Kezang Namgyal

* elected unopposed
Source: http://www.kuenselonline.com/ncelections/index.php

a. National Assembly

The Tshogdu or National Assembly was originally decreed in 1953 by the Third King Jigme Dorji Wangchuck, who initiated the process of Modernisation in the nation. Under his reign, the National Assembly consists of 150 members, functioned as a unicameral legislature within the Monarch's framework for administration of the political system. Later, the National Assembly of Bhutan, under the 2008 Constitution, restructured it by reducing its membership to a maximum of 55 members who were elected on the basis of universal adult franchise in a democratic voting system by the citizens of constituencies within each Dzongkhag (District).[19] On March 24, 2008, the first ever general election based on universal adult franchise was held to elect 47 members to the National Assembly. According to the new constitution of the nation, the National Assembly should meet at least twice a year and elect a Speaker and Deputy Speaker from among its members. The democratic transformations of the political system took place from a tradition of nominating or do so by consensus changed in to providing voting power to all the adult citizens in the nation, was a new beginning of Modernisation in the nation in its political sphere. The main functions of the National Assembly given under the Constitution of Bhutan are enacting laws for the country, approve senior government appointments and advise the King on matters of national importance. According to Article 13.2, money bills or financial bills shall originate only in the National Assembly and all the bills passed by the assembly should get the assent of the Druk Gyalpo for enforcement. The King formally does not hold the power of veto, but he can return the bills for further amendments or considerations. The National Assembly has the power to remove government officials from the post by a two-thirds vote of no confidence and also has the power to remove any minister whom the King appoints, but none of the above said prerogatives of the Assembly has been exercised by the National Assembly.[20]

Details about 2008 General Election

There were only two political parties registered by the Election Commission of Bhutan to contest the election in 2008, such as the Bhutanese Peace and Prosperity Party (DPT, for Druk Phuensum Tshogpa) led by the former Prime Minister, Minster of Foreign Affairs and Minster of Home and Cultural Affairs Jigme Y. Thinley and the second party was the People's Democratic Party (PDP) led by another former Prime Minister and Agriculture Minister of the Royal Government of Bhutan Sangay Ngedup (Table 3.5). The election witnessed a dramatic victory for Jigme Y. Thinley's Bhutanese Peace and Prosperity Party by winning 45 seats out of 47 seats.

Second General Election 2013

The Second General election to the National Assembly was held 31 May and 13 July 2013. The election was taken place in two rounds. In the first round, all the four political parties registered contested in all the 20 Dzongkhas (the administrative and judicial districts of Bhutan) for the Primary Round of elections to the National Assembly 2013. After the primary round, the first two parties with the highest vote tallies progressed to the second round, in which they put forward candidates in each of the 47 National Assembly constituencies. In the first round of the elections, out of the four parties contested, the Bhutan Peace and Prosperity Party, or Druk Phuensum Tshogpa (DPT) and People's Democratic Party (PDP) came first and second respectively receiving the highest number of valid votes casted. The other two new parties, Druk Nymrub Tshogpa

Table 3.5
List of Elected Members to the National Assembly in the 2008 General Election

Sl. No.	*Name*	*Constituency*	*Position*
1	Hon. Lyonpo Jigme Tshultim	Radhi-Sakteng	Speaker
2	Hon. Lyonchhen Jigme Y. Thinley	Nanong-Shumar	Prime Minister
3	Hon. LyonpoTshering Tobgay	Sombaykha	Opposition Leader
4	Hon. Lyonpo Yeshy Zimba	South Thimphu	MoWHS
5	Hon. Lyonpo Khandu Wangchuk	Lamgong-Wangchang	MoEA
6	Hon. Lyonpo Wangdi Norbu	Bartsham-Shongphu	MoF
7	Hon. Lyonpo Ugyen Tshering	North-Thimphu	MoFA
8	Hon. Lyonpo Zangley Drukpa	Khar-Yurung	MoH
9	Hon. Lyonpo Minjur Dorji	Kanglung-Uzorong	MoHCA
10	Hon. Lyonpo Thakur S. Powdyel	Dorokha-Tading	MoE
11	Hon. Lyonpo Pema Gyamtsho	Tang-Chhoekor	MoA
12	Hon. Lyonpo N. L. Rai	Shompangkha	MoIC
13	Hon. Lyonpo Dorji Wangdi	Panbang	MoLHR
14	Hon. Yangkhu Tshering Sherpa	Kikhorthang-Mendrelgang	Dy. Speaker

15	Hon. Karma Wangchuk	Chumey-Ura	Member
16	Hon. Chencho Dorji	Phuntsholing	Member
17	Hon. Ugay Tshering	Bongo-Chapcha	Member
18	Hon. Sonam Jamtsho	Drujeygang-Tseza	Member
19	Hon. Hemant Gurung	Lhamoy-Zingkha-Trashiding	Member
20	Hon. Damcho Dorji	Goenkhatoe-Laya	Member
21	Hon. Kinley Dorji	Goenkhamey-Lunan	Member
22	Hon. Ugyen Tenzin	Bji-Katsho-Uesu	Member
23	Hon. Karma Rangdol	Gangzur-Minjay	Member
24	Hon. Tshering Tenzin	Menbi-Tshenkhar	Member
25	Hon. Karma Lhamo	Mongar	Member
26	Hon. Ugyen Wangdi	Dremitse-Ngatshang	Member
27	Hon. Sonam Penjore	Kengkhar-Weringla	Member
28	Hon. Chencho Dorji	Doga-Shaba	Member
29	Hon. Choida Jamtsho	Nganglam	Member
30	Hon. Namgay Wangchuk	Lingmukha-Toewang	Member
31	Hon. Tshering Penjor	Kabji-Talo	Member

32	Hon. Ugyen Dorji	Dewathang-Gomdar	Member
33	Hon. Norbu Wangzom	Jomotshangkha-Martshala	Member
34	Hon. Prahlad Gurung	Pugli-Samtse	Member
35	Hon. Durga Prashad Chhetri	Sipsu	Member
36	Hon. Lila Pradhan	Ugentse-Yoeseltse	Member
37	Hon. Prem Kumar Gurung	Gelephu	Member
38	Hon. Dupthob	Bumdeling-Jamkhar	Member
39	Hon. Kesang Wangdi	Khamdang-Ramjar	Member
40	Hon. Choeki Wangmo	Thrimshing	Member
41	Hon. Lhatu	Wamrong	Member
42	Hon. Nidup Zangpo	Nubi-Tangsibji	Member
43	Hon. Rinchen Dorji	Drakteng-Langthel	Member
44	Hon. Narbahadur Gurung	Patala-Tsirangtoe	Member
45	Hon. Gyem Dorji	Nyisho-Sephu	Member
46	Hon. Passang Thrinlee	Athang-Thedtsho	Member
47	Hon. Tshering Dorji	Bardo-Trong	Member

Source: http://www.nab.gov.bt

and Druck Chirwang Tshogpa, received lesser number of votes resulting their elimination from the final round of election. A fifth party, the Bhutan Kuen-Nyam Party, attempted to participate in the election, but failed to field a university-educated candidate in Gasa District in the northern part of the country. Consequently, the Bhutanese Elections Commission disqualified the party, even though each of the four other parties had made official requests to the commission to allow the Bhutan Kuen-Nyam Party to participate.

Result of the preliminary election 2013, the total votes received and the percentage are given in the following table.

Table 3.6
First Round Election to the National Assembly 2013

Sl. No	*Political Parties*	*Total Votes*	*%*
1	Druk Phuensum Tshogpa (DPT)	93949	44.52%
2	People's Democratic Party (PDP)	68650	32.53%
3	Druk Nyamrup Tshogpa (DNT)	35962	17.0%
4	Druk Chirwang Tshogpa (DCT)	12457	05.9%

Source: Election Commission of Bhutan

A total of 381,790 voters were registered under the election commission for the general election 2013 out of which 211018 people turn out for the preliminary election which is around 55.27%. due to the mountainous terrain, the voting process in bhutan was a challenging practice as the officials as well as the voters had to trek for several days and hours respectively to reach the polling stations. The participating Political Parties campaigned keenly to inform, communicate and interact with the public. The State support to election campaign, as provided under the Constitution and the Electoral Laws, ensured that the electorate had access to information on each Party's ideology and campaign manifesto, leadership and Candidate-designates.

In the second round of election, both Bhutan Peace and Prosperity Party and People's Democratic Party contested in the 47 constituencies to take the place of honour in Second Parliament of the Kingdom of Bhutan either as the Ruling Party or the Opposition Party. In the second round of election, out of the total number of registered voters, 66.23% voters turnout for the election. In this round, the People's Democratic Party (PDP) won the election with 54.88 % vote to defeat Bhutan Peace and Prosperity Party which managed to get only 45.12% of votes. The details of the second round of election is given below:

Table 3.7
Second Round Election to the National Assembly 2013

Sl. No.	*Political Parties*	*Total Votes*	*%*	*Seats Won*	*+/-*
1	People's Democratic Party (PDP)	138,760	54.88	32	+30
2	Druk Phuensum Tshogpa (DPT)	114,093	54.12	15	-30

Source: Election Commission of Bhutan

The result of the second general election was a turning point in Bhutan's political history as the first government Druk Phuensum Tshogpa could manage to get only 15 seats in the parliament who secured a total of 45 seats out of 47 in the first general election. The then opposition party People's Democratic Party (PDP) manage to secure a total of 32 seats in the 2013 election with respect to their 2 seats in the 2008 election. In 30 July 2013, Tshering Tobgay sworn in as the second Prime Minister of Bhutan since the nation transformed itself into a parliamentary democracy.

2. The Executives

The new democratic government brings forth a new system of executives in the country which is totally different to that of the previous system. According to the new constitution and the democratic system, the executive branch of the government acquired a modern style and became a developed system. Under the new system, the executive powers are divided between three different positions- the Head of the State, Head of the Government and the Council of Ministers. The influence of western model democracy and political ideologies and the fast growing globalisation process had a bigger role in the transformation of government structure of Bhutan.

a. The King

The Head of the State is referred to a person or post which represents the state at official and ceremonial functions but may not be involved in the day-to-day activities of the government.[21] The Druk Gyalpo is known as the Head of the State under the new Constitution of Bhutan. Bhutan shifted from an absolute monarchy to a Constitutional Monarchy in 2008 and the King does not poses any original powers that he enjoyed in the past years. Though the position of King is hereditary, as per the new Constitution of Bhutan, he must retire at the age of 65 and hand over his powers to the Crown Prince or Princess, provided the Royal Heir has come of age. The King can be removed from the post if both houses of the parliament pass a non-confidence motion against him with a two-third majority. According to the Article 15 of the Constitution of Bhutan, the Druk Gyalpo shall not be answerable in any court of law for His actions and His person shall be sacrosanct. The Constitution vests various powers on the

Druk Gyalpo such as promoting goodwill and good relations with other nations, receiving state guests, visit to other countries, protect and uphold the constitution of the country in the best interest of the people of Bhutan. The King of Bhutan also poses some prerogative powers like the King or Queen of Great Britain like:

(a) Award titles, decorations, *dar* for Lhengye and *Nyi-Kyelma* in accordance with tradition and custom;
(b) Grant citizenship, land *kidu* and other *kidus*;
(c) Grant amnesty, pardon and reduction of sentences;
(d) Command Bills and other measures to be introduced in Parliament; and
(e) Exercise powers relating to matters which are not provided for under this Constitution or other laws.

The constitution of Bhutan also gives a number of executive, legislative and judicial powers to the King in appointing various posts in the nation such as:

(a) The Chief Justice of Bhutan in accordance with section 4 of Article 21;
(b) The Drangpons of the Supreme Court in accordance with section 5 of Article 21;
(c) The Chief Justice of the High Court in accordance with section 11 of Article 21;
(d) The Drangpons of the High Court in accordance with section 12 of Article 21;
(e) The Chief Election Commissioner and Election Commissioners in accordance with section 2 of Article 24;
(f) The Auditor General in accordance with section 2 of Article 25;
(g) The Chairperson and members of the Royal Civil Service Commission in accordance with section 2 of Article 26;

(h) The Chairperson and members of the Anti-Corruption Commission in accordance with section 2 of Article 27;

(i) The heads of the Defence Forces from a list of names recommended by the Service Promotion Board;

(j) The Attorney General in accordance with section 2 of Article 29;

(k) The Governor of the Central Bank of Bhutan on the recommendation of the Prime Minister;

(l) The Chairperson of the Pay Commission in accordance with section 1 of Article 30;

(m) The Cabinet Secretary on the recommendation of the Prime Minister;

(n) The Secretary General of the respective Houses on the recommendation of the Royal Civil Service Commission;

(o) Ambassadors and Consuls on the recommendation of the Prime Minister;

(p) The Secretaries to the Government on the recommendation of the Prime Minister who shall obtain nominations from the Royal Civil Service Commission on the basis of merit and seniority and in accordance with other relevant rules and regulations; and

(q) Dzongdags on the recommendation of the Prime Minister who shall obtain nominations from the Royal Civil Service Commission.[22]

b. Prime Minister

The Head of Government is the top administrative leader who is designed to manage the day-to-day activities of the government. The Head of the Government is empowered to protect and strengthen the sovereignty of the Kingdom, providing good governance and ensuring peace and security in the nation. The Prime Minister is responsible to keep the Druk Gyalpo informed from time to time about the affairs of the state, international affairs of the nation, etc. He is the head of the cabinet and individually accountable to the Druk Gyalpo. Lyonchhen Jigme Y. Thinley became the first Prime Minister of the democratic government of Bhutan in 2008.

c. Council of Ministers (Lhengye Zhungtshog)

Under Article 20.2 of the Constitution of Bhutan, the executive power is vested in the Lhengye Zhungtshog, which consists of the Ministers and the Prime Minister on top, who leads them. The Ministers are appointed on the basis of the required people for providing good governance to the people. Until 1999, the Cabinet of Bhutan consisted of Council of Ministers led by the King himself, but the entire picture changed after 1999 when the nation took a major step towards democratization. The King dissolved the existing cabinet and withdrew his role in the decision-making in day-to-day governance. All this occurred after July 26, 1999, when the National Assembly enacted the *Lhengye Zhungtsho* Act on advice of the King which was the first codification of the modern Council of Ministers. According to the Constitution, the ministers must be a citizen of Bhutan, must not be married to a foreign national and must have already held senior government posts at the rank of Secretary to the Royal Government or above. Candidates were nominated by the King and elected indirectly through the National Assembly. The Council of Ministers are collectively responsible to the King and to the parliament and cannot issue any executive order, circular, rule or notification inconsistent with, modifying, varying or superseding the laws of Bhutan. Table 3.6 gives a detailed information regarding the ministries and its departments

Table 3.8
Ministries and Departments under the Democratic Government of Bhutan

Sl. No.	*Ministry*	*Departments*
1	**Ministry of Agriculture**	• Council for RNR Research of Bhutan • Department of Agriculture • Department of Forest • Department of Livestock • Department of Survey and Land Records • Druk Seed Corporation • Food Corporation of Bhutan • Forestry Development Corporation Limited • National Biodiversity Centre
2	**Ministry of Economic Affairs**	• Department of Energy • Department of Geology and Mines • Department of Industry • Department of Tourism • Department of Trade
3	**Ministry of Education**	• Department of Adult and Higher Education • Department of School Education • Department of Youth, Culture and Sports • Dzongkha Development Authority

4	**Ministry of Finance**	• Department of Aid and Debt Management • Department of National Budget • Department of National Properties • Department of Public Accounts • Department of Revenue and Customs • Directorate of Lottery
5	**Ministry of Foreign Affairs**	• Department of Bilateral Affairs • Department of Multilateral Affairs • Department of Protocol
6	**Ministry of Health**	• Department of Public Health • Department of Public Services
7	**Ministry of Home and Cultural Affairs**	• Bureau of Law and Order • Department of Civil Registration and Census • Department of Culture and Heritage • Department of Immigration • Department of Local Governance • Office of the Census Commissioner
8	**Ministry of Information and Communications**	• Bhutan Infocomm and Media Authority • Department of Civil Aviation • Department of Information and Media • Department of Information Technology • Road Safety and Transport Authority

		• Bhutan Broadcasting Service • Bhutan Post • Bhutan Telecom • Druk Air • Kuensel Corporation
9	**Ministry of Labour and Human Resources**	• Department of Employment • Department of Human Resources • Department of Labour • Department of Occupational Standards
10	**Ministry of Works and Human Settlement**	• Department of Roads • Department of Urban Development & Engineering Services • Department of Urban Development and Eng. Services • Standard and Quality Control Authority

Source: www.bhutan.gov.bt

in the new democratic government which is totally framed in a modern-western way.

3. The Judiciary

Shabdrung Ngwang Namgyal introduced the first set of law in Bhutan which was finally codified in 1652. The law of Bhutan was mainly based on the Buddhist principles and violation of both Temporal and Spiritual laws. This new law codes specifically refer to the Ten Pious Acts known as Lhachoe Gyewa Chu and the Sixteen Virtuous Acts of social piety, referred to as the Michoe Tsangma Chudrug. The Shabdrung's Code is considered as the foundation of the present Bhutanese legal system. Though the original legal system amended several times over the years, the legal system continues to uphold the principles of Buddhist ideologies and reflect the culture and lifestyle of the Bhutanese people. The Modernisation in the legal system began in 1959 under the Third King Jigme Dorji Wangchuck, who enacted comprehensive codified law code known as the Thrimzhung Chhenmo or the Supreme Law. This new revised code of law covers almost all civil and criminal matters and includes laws regarding land, marriage, inheritance, weights and measures, theft and murder. The Thrimzhung Chhenmo is considered to be the basis for all the subsequent laws enacted in Bhutan.[23] Under the new constitution of Bhutan the judicial system got a modern style and shape by restructuring the entire system. According to article 21.2 of the constitution of Bhutan 2008, the judicial authority of Bhutan shall be vested in the Royal Courts of Justice comprising the Supreme Court, the High Court, the Dzongkhag Court, the Dungkhag Court and such other Courts and Tribunals as may be established from time to time by the Druk Gyalpo on the recommendation of the National Judicial Commission.

a. Supreme Court

The Supreme Court of Bhutan, which is the highest court of appeal under the new constitution, was setup in 2008. According to article 21.7, the Supreme Court must be comprised of the Chief Justice and four Drangpons or Associate Judges and shall have the power to review the judgments and orders by High Court. The Drangpons of the Supreme Court must be appointed from among the Drangpons of the High Court or from among eminent jurists by the Druk Gyalpo. The duties of Supreme Court include render advice to the Druk Gyalpo on matter of public importance and question of law. The Supreme Court has the power to withdraw any case pending before the High Court involving a substantial question of law of general importance relating to the interpretation of this Constitution on its own motion or on an application made by the Attorney General or by a party to a case.[24]

b. High Court

The High Court of Bhutan was established in the year 1968 under the Third King Jigme Dorji Wangchuk as a process of modernising the judicial system of Bhutan. Under the new Constitution of the nation, the High Court consists of a Chief Justice and eight Drangpons or Associate Judges appointed by the Druk Gyalpo among juniors, peers and eminent jurists in the nation. The term of office of the judges of the High Court is 10 years or until the age of 60. According to the Constitution the High Court shall be the court of appeal from the Dzongkhag Courts and Tribunals in all matters and shall exercise original jurisdiction in matters not within the jurisdiction of the Dzongkhag Courts and Tribunals.[25]

c. District and Sub-district Courts

The District or Dzongkhag Courts of Bhutan was established in 1960/61 under the Third Druk Gyalpo. There are 20 Dzongkhag Courts in Bhutan distributed among the 20 districts in the nation. The Dzongkhag Courts exercises original jurisdiction in all cases in its territorial jurisdiction and it hear the appeals from a Dungkhag Courts. These District Courts are presided over by a Dzongkhag Drangpon or Magistrate and assisted by one or more Drangpon Rabjams.

Sub-district Courts or Dungkhag Courts was established in 1978 under the Forth King His Majesty Jigme Singye Wangchuck while modernising and decentralising the judicial administration in Bhutan. These Sub-district Courts are presided over by a Dungkhag Drangpon. The minor civil disputes are adjudicated by the village head.

3. Local Administrative Structure

The effect of Modernisation is clearly visible in the local administrative system of Bhutan. The administrative structure of Bhutan changed from a centralized ruling authority to a decentralised rule making body by giving the common people the right to be involved in decision making process. The system of Chhosi, separating religious aspects from political administration, and the governors of the three provinces such as Trongsa, Paro and Dagana managed to form an initial, rudimentary central government of Bhutan. By the end of the 19th century, the historical system of administration gave way to a new system due to the weakening of decentralised Shabdrung system and the influence of British diplomacy. In the early 20th century, Ugyen Wangchuk put an end to the duel system of administration and introduced the hereditary monarchical system of administration with the help of the British. The highly praised duel system was replaced thereafter with a structurally and operationally centralised set of rudimentary institutions placing the King at its core. As the history moved forward, the Third King under his Modernisation initiatives in the early 1960s transformed the state in to a diversified bureaucracy with a centralized administration providing a starting point for a professional administration. The geographical terrain of Bhutan provided bigger challenges to the administrative control and a Modernised decentralisation process challenging. Under the Third and Fourth King, the nation adopted a modern bureaucratic setup by operating a decentralised administrative system in a three-tire format- Central, District and Block level.[26] The constitution of Bhutan clearly put forward a number of objectives that the Local Government should observe:

(a) Provide democratic and accountable government for local communities;
(b) Ensure the provision of services to communities in a sustainable manner;
(c) Encourage the involvement of communities and community organizations in matters of local governance; and
(d) Discharge any other responsibilities as may be prescribed by law made by Parliament.

According to the Local Governments Act of 2009, the local level governments shall comprise of the Dzongkhag Tshogdu, Gewog Tshogde and Thromde Tshogde. The Act clearly states that the local government is not a law-making body and thus do not posses any legislative powers, but can make rules and regulations consistent with the law enacted by the parliament at the centre.

a. District or Dzongkhag Administration

Under the Central Administrative System, the nation has been divided in to 20 districts or Dzongkags for making the decentralised administration easy and effective. The Dzongkags comes under the jurisdiction of the Home Ministry and is administrated by the Dzongdas. Under the Third and Fourth King the district administration got a new shape and flow as it began to get more and more autonomous powers which the centre used to enjoy. The initiatives for a master plan for political mobilization and devolution of power started from 1981 under the Fourth King who totally modernised the system of administration. In this year the King introduced a modern change in the district administration by establishing *Dzongkhag Yargye Tshogchung* (DYT- District Development Committee). The administrative activities of the Dzongkhag are done by the *Dzongkhag Tshogdu* or District Council. Under the new Local Government Act of 2009, this District Councils are a non-legislative executive body of the Dzongkhag and it is composed of the *Gup* and *Mangmi* (elected leaders) from each *Gewogs* (blocks), one representative from the Dzongkhag Thromde or Municipality in the district and one representative from the *Dxongkhag Yenlag Thromdes*.[27] The district administrative council is assigned with a number of general powers, regulatory functions, administrative functions and financial powers. The Dzongkhag Tshogdu is empowered with number of powers such as balancing of the socio-economic development, promoting business, protecting the consumers, coordinating government agency activities at the district level, reviewing Gewog regulations and ordinances and representing the Dzongkhag at the national level. Though the district assembly is not empowered to legislate any laws, they can enforce rules on health and public safety, regulating environmental pollution, advertising in regard to environmental aesthetics, regulating the broadcast media and gambling under every district. The assembly is also responsible for bearing their own finances, law and order and enforcing the *Driglam namzha* laws.[28]

b. Village or Block Administration

The block or Gewog is the lowest administrative level in Bhutan under the Local Government Act of 2009. The nation is divided into 206/205 Gewogs or Blocks for expanding the decentralised administrative program to the grassroots level. The establishment of block level administration to provide effective services to the people is a positive outcome of the modernisation process in Bhutan. The nation moved so fast in its modernising process to make a change from an unorganized village administration to an organized one in a short period. This Gewogs are made of a small group of villages in Bhutan and works like an intermediate geographic administrative unit between the Dzongkhag and villages. For the easiness of electoral purpose the block level administrative units are further divided in to Chewongs for election use and Thromdes or Municipalities for administrative purposes. The nation began to transform its local level administration from the ear 1991 by establishing the Geog Yargye Tshogchung (GYT, Block Development Committee). From there the nation moved towards a Modernised administrative system from a traditional one. The Parliament of Bhutan in the last one decade passed a number of legislation regarding the Gewogs administration, especially the Local Government Act of Bhutan 2002, 2007 and recently in 2009, providing a full and final structural and administrative nature to the local governance. The Gewog administration is comprised of the Gup, Mangmi (deputy), Tshogpa (village or village cluster representative) and the non-voting Chupon (village messenger) and Gewog Clerk. The office of the Gup and Mangmi is for three years while other representatives are for one year term. Every decision in the GYT is passed by a simple majority. In the beginning the Gewog headman who is called as the Gup was elected by a semi-democratic ways for a period of three years, but under the Local Government Act of 2002 the entire system of electing the Gup was changed and transformed the old system of semi-democratic style with fully democratic one. Under the autumn 2002, the Gups were elected directly by the people based on the principle of universal adult franchise. As the district administrative system, the GYT also enjoy regulatory functions, administrative powers and financial powers. Under the regulatory functions, the GYT is empowered with a wide range of activities such as,

(a) Frame and enforce rules for protecting the health, safety and well being of the people of the Gewog;
(b) Regulate and allocate safe and clean drinking water from water supply schemes;
(c) Regulate allocation of irrigation water in accordance with the provisions of the relevant laws;
(d) Monitor establishment and operation of mines and quarries in consultation with the concerned community;
(e) Regulate the creation and designation of local recreational areas around villages;
(f) Regulate the protection and harvesting of edible

forest products in the community forest in accordance with the Forest and Nature Conservation Act of Bhutan;

(g) Regulate the maintenance of traditional architectural designs of houses within the broad framework of set national codes;

(h) Control construction of structures within road right of way in accordance with the Road Act of the Kingdom of Bhutan, and rules and regulations made there under; and

(i) Prevent illegal construction and all other types of encroachment in community land as well as on government land and government reserved forest land.[29]

The Administrative Powers of the GYT

(a) Formulate five year plans of the Gewog for submission to the Royal Government;

(b) Approve Gewog annual plans within the budget ceiling provided by the Royal Government;

(c) Promote area-based development planning;

(d) Monitor, evaluate and ensure the implementation of the planned activities in accordance with the monitoring framework provided by the Royal Government;

(e) Be the custodian of community land, community forests, including sokshing, nyekhor tsamdro, and medicinal herbs and accordingly prevent illegal house construction and all other types of encroachments in such community land as well as on government land and forests;

(f) Conserve and protect water sources, lakes, springs, streams, and rivers;

(g) Protect and preserve ney, neykhang of yuelha and

zhidag, which are not part of custody of monastic body or central agencies;

(h) Prevent the depredation of crops by livestock and wildlife in accordance with the provisions of the Forest and Nature Conservation Act of Bhutan;

(i) Ensure collection and deposit of premiums for rural insurance and such schemes.

(j) Encourage setting up of economic enterprises within the Gewog;

(k) Accord approval for hiring and mobilization of labour for the upkeep of communal facilities in accordance with the rules made by the Royal Government;

(l) Submit motions arising from villages for consideration in Dzongkhag Tshogdu; and

(m) Perform any other functions as may be prescribed by law.[30]

The Financial Powers of the GYT

(a) Review and approve Gewog's annual budget based on ceilings for submission to the Ministry of Finance;

(b) Approve procurement in accordance with financial rules and regulations;

(c) Carry out re-appropriations within the Gewog budget as may be required, as per financial rules and regulations;

(d) Review accounts of all expenditures of Gewog and ratify in accordance with financial rules and regulations; and

(e) Approve the maintenance of development infrastructures, the expenses for which shall be met from the retained local taxes and other funds. Provided that a detailed plan for the use of such funds, along with a work plan for the implementation of the activities are prepared.

(f) Gewog Tshogde may mobilize, spend, and invest money for the support of its functions in accordance with the Royal Government's policies and rules and regulations.

(g) Gewog Tshogdes shall, at such rates as may be approved by Parliament, levy following taxes:

   (i) Land tax;
   (ii) Building tax;
   (iii) Cattle tax;
   (iv) Grazing tax;
   (v) Entertainment Tax;
   (vi) Advertisement tax other than advertisement in newspapers, print, radio and internet;

(h) Such other taxes as may be determined by Parliament from time to time;

   (a) Gewog Tshogde shall appropriate and ensure collection of taxes specified in this Act.
   (b) Gewog Tshogde may levy and vary rates of fees and charges on utilities in accordance with the existing law.[31]

All these powers and functions of the Block level administrative system is an outcome of the Modernisation process and globalisation effect, which happened in Bhutan after the nation decided to open its borders and welcome the western political ideologies for a better future.

c. Thromde or Municipality/ Corporation Administration

A Thromde is the third and last level administrative division in the decentralisation process in Bhutan. This level was legally acquired the status of an administrative body most recently under the Local Government Act of

2009 and the role of Thromdes in elections in the country was defined in the Election Act of 2008. The introduction of such a lower level administrative structure was the result of the Royal Government of Bhutan's program of decentralisation and devolution of power and authority. The administration in the Thromde is carried out by the Thromde Tshogde if the population of the Thromde is sufficient or it is administrated by the District Council or Block Council as decided by the central Government. The Parliament decides the total area of the Thromde in consultation with the National Land Commission Secretariat and Local Authorities. The Municipal Council or the Thromde Tshogde is composed of seven to ten elected members and headed by a Thrompon. The Local Government Act of 2009 put forth some administrative, regulative and financial powers to the Thromde Tshogde which is stated below.

Administrative or General Functions of the Thromde Tshogde

(a) Formulate policies and priorities in respect of the Dzongkhag Thromde;
(b) Preserve and promote cultural, architectural and aesthetic aspects of the Thromde;
(c) Provide civic and other services which are essential for the general well-being of the residents of a Dzongkhag Thromde;
(d) Ensure that development and other activities within a Thromde occur in a planned and harmonious manner;
(e) Approve land use and development plans in accordance with the laws made by Parliament and rules and regulations made thereunder;
(f) Approve local area plan including land pooling

schemes and any other relevant planning techniques;

(g) Administer and manage all government land falling within the jurisdiction of Thromde and register in the name of concerned Thromdes in accordance with the Land Act and approved local area plan;

(h) Purchase, lease, or otherwise acquire land and property or dispose it off in the interest of the Thromde in accordance with the policies of the Government; and

(i) Perform any other functions as may be prescribed by law.

The Regulatory Functions of Thromde

a. Frame and adopt rules and guidelines for enabling the Thromde to carry out its functions;
b. Frame and enforce rules for protecting the health, safety and well being of the residents, preserving and promoting the quality of the Thromde environment;
c. Regulate advertisements;
d. Prepare urban development plans or amend an approved urban development plan to regulate and enforce land use and building activity in the Dzongkhag Thromde;
e. Formulate guidelines for entertainment and recreational activities and venues;
f. Enforce all laws and rules pertaining to the urban sector;
g. Regulate and enforce appropriate land uses including nonconforming land uses and vehicle repair workshops, and building activities in the Thromde; and

h. Control squatter and illegal settlements, and regulate commercial activities.

Financial Powers of the Thromde

a. Review and approve the annual budget to be met from its resources and review and endorse budget proposals for submission to the Ministry of Finance for Royal Government funding where necessary;
b. Use its budget, grants, local fees, service charges, fines and taxes;
c. Approve purchase, lease, or otherwise acquire land and property or dispose it off in the interest of the Thromde in accordance with the policies of the Royal Government; and
d. Raise, borrow, spend, and invest money for the support of its functions in accordance with laws, Royal Government's policies and rules and regulations.
e. Thromde Tshogde may levy the following in a manner, and at such rates as maybe approved by it as per laws in force:

   (i) Land tax;
   (ii) Property tax;
   (iii) Property transfer tax;
   (iv) Betterment charges; and
   (v) Vacant land and underdevelopment tax.

f. Thromde Tshogde shall, in exercise of its power under section 64 of this Act,. ensure that the fees and charges are:

   i. Not excessive, oppressive, or confiscatory;
   ii. Not contrary to law, public policy, national economic policy, or in restraint of trade; and
   iii. Set at a level no higher than the cost of the most

efficient method of providing the service.[32]

Thus under the new Local Government Act of 2009 made the nation to move towards a decentralised and modern way of providing its people the opportunity to participate in the decision making process. But a number of challenges remain in the decentralisation process while increasing the local participation in the political process. First of all, while the principle of separation of powers are clear at the national level, the legislative and executive powers at the district and block level are intertwined. The other challenges arise from the Bhutanese with a Nepali background, who generally underrepresented in political organizations at both the national and local levels.[33]

4. Public Private Partnership (PPP) in Bhutan

The influence of globalisation and Modernisation forced the Royal Government of Bhutan to go for a Public Private Partnership in development programs, rather insisting on a fully government ownership in the economy. After the establishment of a democratic parliamentary government, the nation began to shift its development path from a traditional agrarian one to a modern globalised one. The Royal Government of Bhutan initiated private sector development in the nation from 2009 onwards by drafting three new investor-friendly policies. The Economic Development Policies (EDP) which was started in 2010 is intended to achieve some major goals such as, (i) achieving economic self-reliance, (ii) generating employment in the nation, (iii) harness and add value to natural resources in a sustainable manner, (iv) realizing the importance of import substitution, (v) promoting entrepreneurship among the Bhutanese people, (vi) diversifying the economic base and (vii) increasing the export ratio of the nation. The first ever Public Private Partnership agreement was signed in September 2009 to develop an Information Technology Park, which marked the government's commitment to leverage foreign private investment flows into Bhutan. The new democratic government in March 2010 approved a frame work for Private Partnership in the Infrastructure which will initiate an increase in the public private partnership policy of the nation. With the introduction of a Modernised development process, the Royal Government of Bhutan is now initiating further steps to drat new rules and regulations to operationalise these policies. The nation is now trying to encourage more and more Foreign Direct Investment (FDI) in the nation to broaden the employment opportunities and revenue earnings. According to the studies the FDI is likely to increase during the 10th Five Year Plan about 25 percent per annum. The country now seeks to encourage partnerships with foreign developed nations to increase its FDI and economic development possible.[34]

The International Finance Corporation (IFC), a member of the World Bank Group, initiated an ambitious development agenda between policymakers and the private sector players to increase the public-private partnerships. This event brought together specialists and experts from around the world and made the officials of ministries and public sector departments of energy, transportation, civil aviation, agriculture, water, sanitation, waste management and private sector members and other multilateral partners to come together and propose a development program for the nation. The public-private partnership is intent to improve the quality of services in Bhutan, gaining efficiencies and boosting economic growth in the social and physical infrastructure. Through public-private partnership the development of the nation's economy benefits from modern knowledge sharing and building awareness on designing, structuring and tendering sustainable projects. The Royal Government of Bhutan is trying to make important changes to spur growth through Public-Private Partnership while keeping in mind the principles of Gross National Happiness.[35] Under the principle of public private partnership, the nation started a project called the Dagachhu Project joining together the state-owned Druk Green Power and Tata Power for an increased FDI in energy development and a reduced state debt burden.

5. E-governance and Development in Administration

In order to provide for Good Governance and easy service delivery in the nation, the Royal Government of Bhutan began to change the governing system in to a modern one by introducing technological innovations and change. Though the nation shifted to democratic government with a participatory decision making process, the geographical structure and landscape is a formidable challenge to development in the nation. Thus the introduction and development of e-governance system play a crucial role in providing services from the government to the people, especially to the rural and hilly areas of Bhutan. The establishment of e-governance will ensure the nation's potentials for developing and Modernising local governance, democratic participation and effective public service delivery in the country. This will enhance transparency and accountability in government's daily to day work and promotes public awareness and engagement in public policy. Recognizing the significance and importance the Royal Government of Bhutan (RGoB) had encouraged and given high priority in the usage of e-governance system for a broader governance reform agenda by establishing Information and Communication Technology (ICT) units in each ministry. The introduction of e-governance system helps to develop and experiment e-based services in the nation and open a new world of Single Window System in all bureaucratic matters at central, district and Geog level. Currently, the government is in a primitive stage of introducing such e-based services to the people and training the new generation civil servants to produce hundred percent successes in it. The initiatives taken by the Royal Government of Bhutan will help providing support to the Department of Information Technology (DIT) in coordination with each ministry in developing and providing e-based application services.[36]

Under the e-governance program, the Dzongkha Development Commission (DDC) is planning to make the use of English-Dzongkha dictionary electronic so that the dictionary can be used in mobile phones which will be so convenient and faster to use by the Bhutanese people and foreigners. The availability of an electronic dictionary will promote the national language among the people and people no longer have to spend time flipping through pages to find meanings of words.[37] The electronic-platform will ensure the success of ICT goals in the country by providing useful measures to the government. With the introduction of e-governance, the people can now acquire their citizenship identity cards electronically for their passports. The e-platform which is developed by the Department of Information Technology (DIT) will help the government institutions to provide better governance through electronic mediums. Under this provision the officers in an office or organization using such e-platform will be able to monitor the service being processed. This service will provide the Bhutanese people much relief as they can check the status of an application online by saving the time and disappointment travelling to the government offices. The Modernisation of the IT sector in Bhutan helped the government to ensure both transparency and efficiency in administration and service delivery. The government has provided for IT personnel at different Community Information Centres (CICs) for providing a user friendly atmosphere to the local people who have no IT knowledge. Till date 35 CICs has been set up by the government in the country to provide for an e-platform to the common people. According to the National Replication Plan 2009, the implementation of e-governance is done in two phases as the first phase focuses on automating and digitizing existing services and procedures and the second phase will focus on integration and optimization of the services. This will enable the citizens to use a single number for multiple services provided by the same government by providing a single payment gateway.[38]

The Royal Government recognized the need of using ICT for poverty reduction and sustainable development in Bhutan. The ICT can assist the government to reduce poverty by created and transfer knowledge, improve the efficiency and transparency of institutions and by facilitating the participation and empowerment of the poor in the nation. The dissemination of ICT is crucial in accessing the information and avoiding the possibility of a division that could exacerbate the rural-urban disparity in the nation. The development of e-services will add efficiency to the governmental agencies and Modernisation of the political structure.[39] The e-governance has a tremendous potential as a modern mechanism for strengthening good governance, effective public service delivery and democratic participation among the people. The introduction of e-governance became a crucial element in providing services to the people, especially those who live in remote rural areas of Bhutan. The major outputs of the e-governance project in Bhutan are firstly, Standardized e-platform model for a Geog (block) Administration Office developed and experimented; secondly, Forestry and Dzongkhag (district)-Geog e-services developed and piloted as an integral part of One-Stop Shop Approach in a selected Dzongkhag at two rural Geogs and one urban area and lastly, The national replication plan on the local e-platform model and commonly used services developed.

Good Governance and Sustainable Development

The process of Modernisation has changed the existing traditional way of governance and developmental attitudes of the nation. Being a small land-locked nation, Bhutan was experiencing various societal and political transitions, especially in the last decade. The changing nature of the country's development from a rural economy based on subsistence farming to an economy with growing service and industrial sectors relies mainly on exports of hydro-energy and tourism. The transition from a closed centralized monarchy into a democratic constitutional monarchy with a decentralised local governance system strengthened the process of Good Governance and sustainable development. The nation occupies a special position in the international arena by explicitly adopting sustainable development and good governance as the main objectives of its development strategy.[40]

a. Civil Service and Bureaucracy

The Modernisation process changed the entire

structure of the civil service and bureaucracy in Bhutan, which was centred and driven by a strong centralized monarchical administration. The bureaucracy in Bhutan has acquired an accelerated diversification and rapid growth under the new modern democratic government. With the religious orders banned from the inner core of the political institutions, the political structure received a unique status among other South Asian regions. The late 2000s saw the peak of the expansion of bureaucracy in Bhutan encouraging nearly all better educated youngsters to join the governing system. In 2002, the Royal Government of Bhutan has revised the Civil Service Rules and Regulations of 1990 to reorganize the staffing structures and reshuffling of ministries and agencies in the government. Till 2003, the executive branch was controlling the Royal Civil Srvice Commission (RCSC) for recruiting personal in to services, but in mid-2003, the commission was re-constituted as an autonomous body which will be controlled by an independent commission appointed by the executive, the legislature and the judiciary branch for recruiting civil servants in the nation.[41] The Royal Civil Service upholds the promotion and progress of good governance and Gross National Happiness. Under the new RCSC the core values of a civil servant must be Professionalism, Accountability, Integrity, Loyalty, Impartiality, Honesty, Leadership, Openness and Selflessness. The Royal Civil Service got modernised like any other developing or developed nation's civil servant or bureaucrat.[42]

b. Civil Society

The rising of the civil society in Bhutan, the space outside the sphere of government, has contributed to the growth of Modernisation process in the country. Being a new phenomenon, none of the organized civil society in

Bhutan dedicated to governance issues or election observation. The Civil Society Act was passed in Bhutan on July 2007, and till now only a handful of organizations has registered in the country. Civil society in Bhutan is expected to play a greater role in contributing to the achievements of the objectives of good governance.[43] The passing of the Civil Society Act in 2007 clearly define about Civil Society Organizations (CSO) in chapter 2nd and in chapter 3, it clearly states the objectives of a CSO in Bhutan. According to the act, a Civil Society Organization should be referred to associations, societies, foundations, charitable trusts, not-for-profit organization or other entities that are not part of government. The act divide the CSO in to two types of organizations distinguished by their differing objectives such as Public Benefit Organizations (PBOs) which are established in order to benefit a section or the society as a whole and Mutual Benefit Organizations (MBOs) which are established to advance the shared interests of people or supporters. The principles and objectives of the Act are given below;

The objectives of this Act are to:

a) Facilitate the establishment and growth of PBOs and MBOs in order to strengthen civil society, promote social welfare and improve the conditions and quality of life for the people of Bhutan;
b) Ensure a system of public accountability by providing a framework for responsible and effective self-regulation of CSOs;
c) Protect national and public interest;
d) Facilitate a constructive partnership between the Government and CSOs in order to advance the public interest;

e) Provide opportunities for people to serve public interest;
f) Benefit the public at large or particular sections of the public;
g) Demonstrate and continue to increase CSO's value to the larger communities of which they form a part;
h) Promote compliance by CSOs with their legal obligations to exercise effective control and management over the administration of their activities and funding; and
i) Promote the delivery of emergency relief services and other types of public services by PBOs, and promote the effective use of public and private financial resources by PBOs for such purposes.

Under this act the PBOs shall serve to supplement or complement the efforts made by the Government to:

a. Protect human life and health;
b. Prevent and alleviate human suffering and poverty;
c. Disseminate knowledge and advance learning;
d. Develop the Country economically and culturally;
e. Assist in the protection and promotion of national culture and heritage;
f. Protect the natural environment; and
g. Promote social harmony and Gross National Happiness.[44]

Under section 4(b) of the Civil Society Organizations Act, a Mutual Benefit Organisation should protect the sharing interests of their members such as;

(a) Organisation advancing the shared interest of people working in a particular profession
(b) Business engaged in a particular industry

(c) Youths studying in universities, and
(d) People who are interested in particular cultural activity, sports or hobby.[45]

This act forbids every CSO from following:

a) Do anything to impair the sovereignty, security, unity and territorial integrity of Bhutan;
b) Engage in any activities that are directly related to public elections;
c) Do anything to destroy the peace, stability and well-being of the nation;
d) Be involved in any incitement to an offence on the grounds of race, sex, language, religion or region;
e) Be involved in political activity;
f) Violate the spiritual heritage of Bhutan as expressed in Article 3 of the Constitution;
g) Be involved in conducting activities or managing institutions whose primary purpose is public religious worship;
h) Compel any person to belong to another faith by providing reward or inducement for a person to belong to another faith; and
i) Be organized or operated exclusively for financial gain.[46]

Till now 13 Civil Society Organizations have registered in Bhutan under the Civil Society Organizations Act. These are given under in table 3.7

The Modernisation process in the political structure provide for more and more platforms and forums at national and local level for CSOs to participate in governance and parliament actions. Although the CSOs are in its infancy, the encouragement of government for such organizations will make the CSOs a decisive factor in the coming years. The power sharing between government and such NGOs will become more and more accurate in a Modernised social and political structure.[47]

c. Participatory Governance

The reign under the Third and Fourth King witnessed a historical change of governance from a centralized authoritarian rule making to a participatory decision making involving the common citizens of the nation. After the Modernisation of the political system the decision making has moved to the grass-root level in the country, thus making the political structure more participatory in nature. The voter turnout for the 2008 general election indicates that the Modernisation process of the governance system in the nation gradual increased the awareness among the Bhutanese in the political process of the nation. According to the election commission statistics most of the households ensured that at least one household member votes in the general election. The participatory planning process has introduced in the Geog level by the Gup to the GYT members. Under the new participatory governance system by including everyone in the decision making process, simple, open and transparent process do help to ensure the inclusion of lower income groups and women in the country.[48]

Gross National Happiness and Modernisation

GNH was a unique principle which introduced in Bhutan by its Fourth King, inorder to build an economy which is sustainable and protect and preserve its culture and tradition during the process of Modernisation of the nation. This was a principle that used to measure the well being of the people in the nation. This was a unique concept that included both material and spiritual development of the development of the human society. His Majesty the fifth

Table 3.9
Registered Civil Society Organizations in Bhutan

Sl. No	*CSO*	*Registered on (Date)*	*PBO/MBO*
1	BCMD (Bhutan Centre for Media & Democracy)	12/03/2010	PBO
2	The Loden Foundation	12/03/2010	PBO
3	RENEW (Respect, Educate, Nurture & Empower Women)	09/04/2010	PBO
4	BAOWE (Bhutan Association Of Women Entrepreneurs)	15/04/2010	PBO
5	Guide Association of Bhutan	29/06/2010	MBO
6	Bhutan youth Development Fund	20/07/2010	PBO
7	Royal Society for Protection of Nature	02/09/2010	PBO
8	Draktsho Vocational Centre for special children & Youth	26/11/2010	PBO
9	Tarayana Foundation	26/11/2010	PBO
10	The Disabled Persons' Association of Bhutan	26/11/2010	PBO
11	LHAK-SAM	26/11/2010	PBO
12	Royal Society for Senior Citizens	21/02/2011	PBO
13	Association of Bhutanese Tour Operators (ABTO)	03/03/2011	MBO

Source: Civil Society Organizations Authority, http://www.csoa.org.bt

King during his speech delivered on 7th November 2008 quoted;

> *"Yet we must always remember that as our country, in these changing times finds immense new challenges and opportunities, whatever work we do, whatever goals we have - and no matter how these may change in this changing world - ultimately without peace, security and happiness we have nothing. That is the essence of the philosophy of Gross National Happiness. Our most important goal is the peace and happiness of our people and the security and sovereignty of the nation".*[49]

Bhutan is unique in the Modernised world with preserving its tradition and culture unaffected by the evils of Modernisation and urbanization. Though there are some negative effects that visible in the nation, most of the traditional aspects and culture keep unchanged. The concept of GNH is much important principle in the development aspects of Bhutan as improvement of the happiness and satisfaction of the people is more valued than the growth of GNP or GDP. Thus GNH has been the overarching development philosophy of Bhutan by guiding the country's development policies and programs. Under the principles of GNH the development in the nation needs to be understood as a process that seeks to maximize the happiness than purely economic growth and profit. The rulers believe that a sustainable development of the individual and society is possible only when the economic, social, emotional, spiritual and cultural needs of the people achieved equally. This led a continuous process towards achieving a balance between the material and spiritual needs of the individual and society. According to the principle of GNH the development means must be considered in terms of the end and thus every step in material development and change must be measured and evaluated to ensure that it will lead to happiness and not just development or profit. Guided by the ideas of GNH, Bhutan has been making steady progress in very sector towards the goal of Modernisation throughout the years with an improvement in the development of human resources and the legal infrastructure.[50]

During the 2008 general election, GNH served as the guiding principle of both the political parties. Both the presidents of the party put forward GNH guided equity, Justice, good democratic politics and a small compact government. The new democratic government is now trying to provide good governance to the people with more emphasis on happiness of the Bhutanese.

Conclusion

The process of Modernisation has made significant impact to the political structure of Bhutan from the beginning of its adoption. Though this brought about a number of developmental changes and Modernised the socio-economical and political sphere, the nation is not free of any challenges that may arise in the near future which are visible in the neighbouring countries. These challenges are stated in Chapter five of this thesis. The new structure of government and its agencies, which acquired a modern structural style, will create a new status for the nation among other developing countries. The beginning of a responsible civil society and a participatory decision making process of the government is likely to provide for a developed and modern political structure for the nation with an ideological strength of Gross National Happiness. The culture and tradition of Bhutan is geared to guide the nation in its Modernisation process and development in the coming years.

NOTES

1. Kapileshwar Labh (1996) *Political Development of Bhutan: Emerging Trends*, in Ramkant and R.C. Mishra (ed), Bhutan: Society and Polity, Indus Publishing, New Delhi. p. 207.
2. Thierry Mathou, (1999) *Bhutan: The Political Reform in a Buddhist Monarchy*, Journal of Bhutan Studies,Volume 1, Number 1, Autumn. P. 114
3. Jai Prakash Sharma, (1996) *The Nature and Direction of Political Change in Bhutan*, in Ramkant and R.C. Mishra (ed), Bhutan: Society and Polity, Indus Publishers, New Delhi. p. 267.
4. United Nations Development Programme, *Strengthened Institutional Capacity of the Election Commission of Bhutan*. Available at: http://www.undp.org.bt/Strengthened-Institutional-Capacity-of-the-Election-Commission-of-Bhutan.htm
5. Royal Government of Bhutan, *Election Act of Bhutan 2008*. Available at: http://oag.gov.bt/wp- content/uploads/2010/05/Election-Act-of-Bhutan-2008both-Dzongkha-English.pdf
6. ibid.
7. Bhutan Broadcasting Service, *Election Commission Gears up for Local Government Elections*, March 4, 2011. Available at: http://www.bbs.com.bt/bbs/?p=4104
8. Bhutan Observer, *246 candidates register for functional test*, August 13, 2010. Available at: http://www.bhutanobserver.bt/246-candidates-register-for-functional-test/
9. People's Democratic Party of Bhutan. Available at: http://www.pdp.bt
10. Druk Phuensum Tshogpa (DPT). Available at: http://www.dpt.bt
11. Official website of Bhutan Kuen-Nyam Party, BKP receives Certificate of Registration from ECB. Available at: http://bkp.bt/bkp-receives-certificate-of-registration-from-ecb/
12. Election Commission of Bhutan: Charter of Bhutan Kuen-Nyam Party. Available at: www.election-bhutan.org.bt/REGISTEROFPOLITICALPARTY/BKP_Charter(Approved_by_ECB).pdf
13. The Election Commission of Bhutan, Charter of Druk Chirwang Tshogpa Party. available at: http://www.election-bhutan.org.bt/REGISTEROFPOLITICALPARTY/DCT_Charter(Approved_by_ECB).pdf
14. The Election Commission of Bhutan, Charter of Druk Nyamrup Tshogpa Party. Available at: http://www.election-bhutan.org.

bt/REGISTEROFPOLITICALPARTY/DNT_Charter (Approved_by_ECB).pdf
15. Constitution Drafting Committee of Bhutan. Available at: http://www.constitution.bt/html/members/members.htm
16. The Druk National Congress, *Draft Constitution of Bhutan: Suggestions for Better Future*. Available at: http://www.bhutandnc.com/constitution1.pdf
17. The Royal Government of Bhutan, *The Constitution of the Kingdom of Bhutan*. Available at: http://www.constitution.bt/
18. The Permanent Mission of Bhutan to the United Nations in New York. Available art: http://www.un.int/wcm/content/site/bhutan/cache/offonce/pid/4154
19. The Royal Government of Bhutan, n.13.
20. Division for Public Administration and Development Management, Department of Economic and Social Affairs, United Nations, *Kingdom of Bhutan: Public Administration Profile*, February 2005. Available at: http://unpan1.un.org/intradoc/groups/public/documents/un/unpan023230.pdf
21. Index Mundi, *Bhutan Executive Branch*. Available at: http://www.indexmundi.com/bhutan/executive_branch.html
22. Bisht, Medha, *Bhutan: Elections 2013*, e-International Relations, January 2, 2013. Available at: http://www.e-ir.info/2013/01/02/bhutan-elections-2013/
23. The Royal Government of Bhutan, n. 13.
24. Royal Court of Justice, *Judiciary of Bhutan*. Available at: www.judiciary.gov.bt
25. The Royal Government of Bhutan, n. 13.
26. Thomas Windrel, (2004) *Bhutan the Making of a Modern state*. Available at: http://www.winderl.net/countries/bhutan/Bhutan%20-%20Towards%20a%20Modern%20State.pdf.
27. Royal Government of Bhutan, Local Government Act of 2009. Available at: http://www.nab.gov.bt/downloadsact/Dzo74.pdf.
28. Ibid.
29. Ibid.
30. Ibid.
31. Ibid.
32. Ibid.

33. Thomas Windrel, (2004), n.22.
34. World Bank, *Bhutan Economic Update 2010*, April 2010. Available at: http://siteresources.worldbank.org/BHUTANEXTN/Resources/Bhutan_Brief_April_2010.pdf
35. International Finance Corporation, World Bank Group, *Bhutan Overview*. Available at: http://www.ifc.org/ifcext/southasia.nsf/Content/Bhutan
36. Royal Government of Bhutan, Department of Information Technology & Telecom. Available at: http://www.dit.gov.bt
37. Namgay Tshering, *DDC Plans Electronic English-Dzongkha Dictionary* in Bhutan Observer, March 18, 2011. Available at: http://www.bhutanobserver.bt/ddc-plans-electronic-english-dzongkha-dictionary/
38. Sonam Pelvar, *One up for e-governance* in Bhutan Times. Available at: http://www.bhutantimes.bt/index.php?option=com_content&task=view&id=1415&Itemid=94
39. Royal Government of Bhutan, *10th Five Year Plan 2008-2013*. Available at: http://www.educationfasttrack.org/media/library/Country_Documents/Bhutan/Bhutan_10th_Five-Year_Plan_2008-2013.pdf
40. Chhewang Rinzin, Walter J.V. Vermeulen and Pieter Glasbergen, (2006) *Public Perceptions of Bhutan's Approach to Sustainable Development in Practice*. Available at: http://www.geography.ryerson.ca/jmaurer/108BhutanGNH1.pdf
41. Thomas Winderl, (2004), n. 22.
42. Royal Government of Bhutan, *Royal Civil Service Commission of Bhutan*. Available at: http://www.rcsc.gov.bt/VisionMission.asp
43. Thierry Mathou, (2008) *How to Reform a Traditional Buddhist Monarchy- The Political Achievements of His Majesty Jigme Singye Wangchuck, the Fourth King of Bhutan (1972-2006)*, Centre for Bhutan Studies, Bhutan.
44. The Royal Government of Bhutan, *Civil Society Organizations Act of Bhutan*. Available at: http://www.judiciary.gov.bt/html/act/Civil%20Society%20Org%20Act.pdf
45. Civil Society organizations Authority of Bhutan. Available at: http://www.csoa.org.bt
46. Civil Society Organizations Act of Bhutan, available at: http://www.judiciary.gov.bt/html/act/Civil%20Society%20Org%20Act.pdf

47. Thierry Mathou, (2008), n.118.
48. Royal Governemnt of Bhutan, Decentralisation Outcome Evaluation Report. Available at: http://www.undp.org.bt/assets/files/publication/dec_OER.pdf
49. Tshering Dorji, Gross National Happiness in Bhutan, October 18, 2010. Available at: http://ezinearticles.com/?Gross-National-Happiness-in-Bhutan&id=5198079
50. Yana Expeditions Bhutan, Gross Natioanl happiness. Available at: http://jp.yanatravel.com/about-bhutan/gross-national-happiness

CHAPTER 4

Bhutan and The World
With Special Reference to India

Introduction

In the world of Globalisation and Modernisation, no country can remain isolated from the rest of the world for long, as every nation requires a helping hand from others. It is more true and visible in the case of the developing nations especially in the African and Asia continents. The growth of globalisation in the whole world created a condition in which every nation is dependent upon its neighbours or other nations. In such situation, the enemies becomes friends and some friends become unimportant as one sees in the case of India in the early 1990s when India looked more towards USA than USSR. Though Bhutan is a small nation and new to the process of globalisation and Modernisation, it generated a wide range of interest in International Relations, especially with Western and Eastern countries. Inaccessibility and the fear of being diverted and losing its unique culture and tradition were the main causes of the nation's isolation in the past. Geographical factors such as thick forests, high mountains ranges and adverse climatic conditions made Bhutan inaccessible from the East, West and the Northern nations in the present century.[1] With a mountainous terrain, Bhutan cannot go for railway lines and good road transportation across the nation thereby restricting its access to other nations or within Bhutan.

After the introduction of Modernisation under the Third Druk Gyalpo, Bhutan began to look towards the west for developmental programs. The nation was successful in getting a helping hand from around the world such as Canada, Switzerland, Denmark, UN and Japan along with its traditional financial partner-India. All these nations began developmental programs in Bhutan with a view to Modernise the country and assist in developing its socio-economic and political conditions.

In the late 1970s, the nation began to stand independent and move away from its reliance on India for its foreign affairs matters. Bhutan in the late 20th century joined a number of international organizations including the World Bank, the International Monetary Fund and the Asian Development Bank. In 1982, the nation joined world Health organizations and UNESCO. Currently, the nation is an active member of 45 international organizations. A major break happened in 1980 when the country established a direct diplomatic relations with Bangladesh. In the late 1990s, though fully controlled, Bhutan began to increase its contact with the rest of the world beyond India and its neighbours. The nation for the first time allowed non-Indian foreign institutions to purchase shares in the Bhutan National Bank in late 1998. In 1999, the nation entered into the world of global information highway and television broadcasts after long debates over its protection of tradition and culture.[2] Holding the SAARC meeting in Thimpu and Tamil- Sri Lankan talks has infused a new confidence in Bhutan's external relations and providing prestige and status in international relations.[3] Bhutan enhanced its status in international relations more developed after joining the UN in 1971.

In last decades, Bhutan established diplomatic relations with eight European nations such as Belgium, Switzerland, Denmark, Sweden, Norway, the Netherlands, Finland and Austria. All these nations contribute towards developmental programs in Bhutan. In the year 2011, Bhutan established diplomatic relations with Spain. The nation also maintains bilateral relations with South Korea, Canada, Brazil, Australia, Kuwait, Thailand, Bahrain, the Maldives, Sri Lanka, and Pakistan. However, USA and UK have no direct formal relations with Bhutan, but both this nations maintain an informal contact through their respective embassies in India.[4] Beginning with the bilateral relations with India, Bhutan began its race towards diversifying the relations in international community, thus projecting its status as an independent and sovereign nation. Table 4.1 gives a clear picture of Bhutan's diplomatic relations and missions across the globe.

Table 4.1
Bhutan's Diplomatic Relations and Missions

Sl. No	*Country*	*Year in which the Relations Established*
1.	Afghanistan	2010
2.	Argentina	2012
3.	Australia	2002
4.	Austria	1989
5.	Bahrain	1992

6.	Bangladesh	1973
7.	Belgium	2009
8.	Brazil	2009
9.	Canada	2003
10.	Denmark	1985
11.	European Union	1985
12.	Finland	1986
13.	India	1968
14.	Japan	1986
15.	Kuwait	1983
16.	Maldives	1984
17.	Nepal	1983
18.	Netherlands	1985
19.	Norway	1985
20.	Pakistan	1988
21.	Poland	2012
22.	Slovakia	2012
23.	Slovenia	2012
24.	South Korea	1987
25.	Singapore	2002
26.	Spain	2011
27.	Sri Lanka	1987
28.	Sweden	1985
29.	Switzerland	1985
30.	Tajikistan	2013
31.	Thailand	1989
32.	Turkey	2012
33.	United Arab Emirates	2012
34.	Vietnam	2012

Source: http://www.mfa.gov.bt/

Being an active partner in the international relations, Bhutan has legislated policies on extradition of criminals, both to and from the kingdom. A number of international organizations and foreign missions have started their offices in Bhutan in the past years. Table 4.2 gives a list of such organizations and missions in Bhutan.

Table 4.2
Foreign Missions in Bhutan

Sl. No	*Foreign Missions*
1	Embassy of India
2	Embassy of People's Republic of Bangladesh
3	Canadian Cooperation Office
4	Liaison Office of Denmark
5	JICA/JOCV Bhutan Office
6	SNV Bhutan
7	UNICEF
8	United Nations House
9	VSA Office
10	WWF Bhutan Program

Source: http://www.mfa.gov.bt/

Foreign Policy and Gross National Happiness in Bhutan

The small nations, which are politically, economically and militarily weak, are obvious to get influenced from the external forces, especially the stronger nations, as they does not bear much significance and capacity to play any significant role in the international politics. However, Bhutan's foreign policy was totally influenced and guided by the philosophy of Gross National Happiness from the beginning itself. The foreign policy of the nation was pursued with a limited interest to protect its national interest in the arena of international politics. Under the principles of GNH, the nation put forward two important aspects for the foreign policy of Bhutan. Firstly, to pursue the goals of development in a self-styled manner, suitable to the cultural, religious and geographical milieu of Bhutan and secondly, to preserve its traditional cultural identity, peace and stability. Being conscious about the fact that the nation is sandwiched between India and China, the rulers took the task to preserve its district identify as an independent nation in internal and external affairs. Thus, it is clear that the rulers of the nation believed that the preservation of the unique tradition and cultural identity is a must for survival and sustenance as a sovereign nation state in the international arena. By upholding the self-styled development process guided by the principles of GNH, Bhutan tries to attain its external dimensions through its foreign policy.[5] Bhutanese rulers clearly state that:

> *"The main challenge facing the nation as a whole is the maintenance of our identity, sovereignty and security as a nation – state. We must never lose right of the fact that we are a small nation state sandwiched between two of the world's giants. Our existence is not a historical accident. It is the result of conscious actions taken over several centuries that have some times compelled us to seek alliance without compromising our sovereignty. Nor must we ever lose sight of the fact that our nation is the last serving independent Mahayana Buddhist kingdom in the world. We are the sole serving custodians of a social and cultural system that extended beyond the eastern Himalayas to embrace a large part of eastern and south East Asia. The world has been impoverished by the loss of this social and cultural system, which is today unique to Bhutan where it both survives and flourishes".*[6]

The concept of GNH and the foreign policy orientation kept the nation's relations with a limited exposure to the outer world ever since the monarchical system of government established. From 1947 onwards, Bhutan followed a policy of close relations with independent India for the nation's internal and external matters. Though China also share the border of Bhutan, the nation kept silent and normal relations without any active involvement or engagement. Bhutan has not established diplomatic relations with any of the permanent members of the UN such as USA, Russia, Britain, France and China. It is clear that the nation is not going after modernising the country in the way most of the Asian-African countries have followed- the western paradigms of modernisation and development. Bhutan with a foreign policy guided by GNH, is trying to limit its foreign relations to avoid western cultural influences which may adversely affect the nation's unique socio-cultural fabric. The Bhutanese rulers believe that the western model of modernisation and development may invite destabilization and disturbance to the nation's cultural identity. The nation limited its foreign relations to those nations so as not to bring pulls and pressures in diplomatic relations. In fact, one can see that Bhutan's foreign policies have been simple and always come under the principles of GNH. Ultimately, the preservation of its cultural identity becomes the crucial issue of the Bhutanese foreign policy.[7]

India-Bhutan Relations

The relations between India and Bhutan can be traced back to the entry of Guru Rinpoche to Bhutan from India in 747 A.D. Under the Shabdrungs and first two Druk Gyalpos, who followed a policy of isolation from the rest of the world, Bhutan had relations only with India. A formal treaty based relation was begun in 1910, when the King signed a treaty with British India. Even during the periods of isolation, Bhutan had maintained good relationship with India, especially with the bordering states such as Ladakh, Lahul, Spiti and Kinnaur in the West and Sikkim, Cooch

Behar and Northern Assam in South-East. Under the treaty of 1910, the British Government agreed not to interfere in the internal affairs of Bhutan and the Bhutanese government agreed to be guided by the advice of the British government in regard to its external relations. After the independence in 1947, Indian government signed a new treaty with Bhutanese government on 8 August, 1949. Under this treaty, India played a major role in Bhutan's relations with the rest of the world. Though the treaty gives some sort of restrictions in the nation's foreign relations, India respected Bhutan's sovereignty and aspiration and in fact supported the nation for establishing diplomatic relations with other nations.[8]

Political Relations

The political scene in the entire Himalayan region and Indian sub-continent underwent great changes by the mid of 20th century. The takeover of Tibet by the People's Liberation Army in 1950 and the presence of Chinese troops near the border of Bhutan led to re-evaluate its traditional policy of isolation and looked for support from the Indian government, which became an immediate necessity. Such a relationship boosted the strategic interest of both the nations. Bhutan began its socio-economic development and Modernisation process mostly with the assistance of India. With the border conflict between India and Bhutan in 1962, Indo-Bhutan relations began to take on concrete form following state visits made by the Third King, His Majesty Jigme Dorji Wangchuk to India and by Prime Minister Jawaharlal Nehru between 1954 and 1961. A formal bilateral relation between Bhutan and India began in 1968, when a special officer of the Government of India is appointed to Bhutan. The Embassy of India in Bhutan known as the India House was established on May 14, 1968 and formal Resident Representatives were exchanged in 1971.[9]

The Treaty of Punakha 1910

By the turn of the century, continuing geopolitical developments raised the question of a new treaty with the British India. Ugyen Wangchuck signed a new treaty with British India on 8 January 1910, at Punakha Dzong between the Kingdom of Bhutan and British India known as The Treaty of Punakha 1910.

The main reason behind the signing of this treaty was the claim of Chinese over Bhutan and started interfering in its internal matters. This happened because of the growing relationship between British India and Bhutan made the Chinese furious and when they tried to stop the imperialist policy of British in the region. Thus, British India decided to revise the Treaty of 1865 to protect Bhutan from the Chinese influence. According to the new Treaty of 1910, Bhutan should consult British India on matters related to its foreign policy.[10]

The Treaty of Punakha, 1910, changed not only the political history of Bhutan but also the social and economic life in Bhutan. There were three major reasons which encouraged His Majesty King Ugyen Wangchuk to sign a new Treaty with British India. First, to protect Bhutan from the Chinese expansionist policies. Secondly, it was not possible for a tiny kingdom like Bhutan sandwiched between China and India to maintain a separate political entity without the help of British India. Thirdly, with this Treaty he wanted to modernise Bhutan and bring radical changes in the economic system of the country with the help of British India. However, he tried to preserve and ensured the autonomy of the country and kept if free from foreign influence.[11]

The Treaty of 1949

Aiming for peace and cooperation and non-interference in each other's internal affairs, India and Bhutan signed the Treaty of Friendship on August 8, 1949. However, updating the 1910's treaty with the British India, Bhutan agreed to let India "guide" its foreign policy and both the nations would consult each other closely on foreign and defence affairs. This treaty also established a free trade and extradition protocols between both the nations. The second half of the 20th century saw a major increase in India's economic, military and development aid to Bhutan that helped the Modernisation of its security. By the end of the 20th century, Bhutan began to express its dissatisfaction in being assisted by Indian Government in its foreign affairs. Though the relations between both the nations remained closer, the Royal Government of Bhutan expressed a need to amend some parts of the treaty to enhance the nation's sovereignty. Bhutan slowly gained its momentum of an independent actor in the international relations by joining the UN in 1971 and signing a new treaty with Bangladesh in 1972. The move towards being an independent actor in the international relations does not create any issues with the treaties signed with India in 1949. Both the nation's relations have not been affected by concerns over the treaty provisions.[12]

The Treaty of 2007

The 57 year old friendship between India and Bhutan opened a new era in their bilateral relationship in 2007 with the signing of the India-Bhutan Friendship Treaty of 2007. The Friendship Treaty of 1949 was renegotiated and amended between India and Bhutan and signed a new Treaty of Friendship in 2007, which gives Bhutan complete sovereign power in its foreign affairs. The new treaty replacing the provision of requiring guidance from the Indian Government was removed and granted complete freedom over arms import.

The Government of the Republic of India and the Government of the Kingdom of Bhutan signed a new treaty of friendship in New Delhi on February 8, 2007, updating the Treaty of 1949 by reaffirming their respect for each other's independence, sovereignty and territorial integrity, recalling the historical relations that have existed between our two countries and recognizing with deep satisfaction the manner in which these relations have evolved and matured over the years into a model of good neighbourly relations. With the new Treaty of 2007, both the countries committed to further strengthen the enduring and mutually beneficial relationship based on genuine goodwill and friendship, shared interests, and close understanding and cooperation. The Treaty of 2007 which was signed on February, came in to force on March 2, 2007 after the ratification between the governments in Thimphu.

The major feature of this Treaty is stated under Article 4 which states that the Government of India agrees that the Government of Bhutan shall be free to import, from or through India into Bhutan, whatever arms, ammunition, machinery, warlike material or stores as may be required or desired for the strength and welfare of Bhutan, and that this arrangement shall hold good for all time as long as the Government of India is satisfied that the intentions of the Government of Bhutan are friendly and that there is no danger to India from such importations. The Government of Bhutan under this article also agrees that there will be no export of such imported arms, ammunition and materials outside Bhutan either by the Government of Bhutan or by private individuals.

The revised treaty has rewritten Articles 2 and 6 of

the 1949 document and gives Bhutan more freedom to pursue its foreign policy and in the purchase of non-lethal military equipment as long as such decisions do not damage India's vital strategic interests.[13]

Indo-Bhutan Relations at Present

Since the establishment of a parliamentary democracy in 2008, the relationships between India and Bhutan reached to a new level of cooperation. The relationship between both countries further increased with the tradition of regular visits of the high-level officers. The State Visit of His Majesty the King Jigme Khesar Namgyel Wangchuck to India from 21st to 26th of December 2009 was his first such visit to a foreign country since his coronation as the King of Bhutan in 2008. Later from 5th to 7th October 2010, the King visited India during which University of Calcutta conferred upon him the Honorary Doctorate Degree of Law. His Majesty the King again visited India from 20-29 October 2010 for the National Defence College's (NDC) golden jubilee celebrations as Special Guest of Honour. His Majesty the King Jigme Khesar Namgyel Wangchuck and Her majesty the Queen Jetsun Pema Wangchuck paid a State Visit to India from October 23-31, 2011, the first foreign visit after the Royal Wedding on 13th October 2011. The King His Majesty the King Jigme Khesar Namgyel Wangchuck was the chief guest for the 64th Republic Day on 26th January 2013.

On January 14, 2013, the Indian External Affairs Minister, Salman Khurshid, was on an official visit to Thimpu strengthening the ties between both the nations. At present India is more concerned about the political issue of Bhutan's recent talks with China and the internal security concerns of both India and Bhutan. Another important matter of concern between India and Bhutan was the internal security issues that gained impotence at recent time as Bhutan witnessed occasional incidents of IED blasts in 2012 and increased activity of insurgent groups across the India-Bhutan border. A healthy relationship between both the nations is important at the present conditions and given its strategic importance, India cannot ignore the tiny kingdom and should always be sensitive to its relations to create a long-term relation.[14]

With the establishment of a new central government in India after the 16th Lok Sabha election, the world community in general and both Indian and Bhutan governments in particular are looking towards a better future for the bilateral relation between both the countries. Accompanied by the External Affairs Minister Smt. Sushma Swaraj, National Security Adviser Shri Ajit Doval, Foreign Secretary Smt. Sujatha Singh and other senior officials of the Government of India, the Prime Minister of the Republic of India Shri Narendra Modi paid a State Visit to Bhutan in June 2014. The visit of the Prime Minister to the tiny Himalayan Kingdom was significant, unlike any other previous ministers, as it is his first visit abroad after he was sworn-in as the Prime Minister of India on 26 May 2014 in New Delhi. The visit reinforced the tradition of regular high-level exchange between the two countries and it helped to uphold and strengthen the special and unique age-old friendship between Bhutan and India. The Prime Minister held official talks with His Majesty Jigme Khesar Namgyel Wangchuck, the King of Bhutan and His Majesty Jigme Singye Wangchuck, the Fourth Druk Gyalpo and the Prime Minister of Bhutan Lyonchhen Tshering Tobgay to discuss issues of mutual interests. Shri Shri Narendra Modi also addressed the Joint Sitting of the Parliament of Bhutan in the Gyalyong Tshogkhang on 16 June 2014 which helped to address various issues of mutual interests and a perspective for strong future relations.

The visit of the Prime Minister proposed new ideas for enhancing cooperation with Bhutan, while asserting that commitments made by the previous government will be fulfilled. The visit of Indian delegates proposed to hold a joint sports festival between Bhutan and the northeastern states of India, establish e-libraries in 20 districts in Bhutan and set up a university on Himalayan studies. India wanted to complete the power projects implemented both by the present as well as the previous UPA government would be completed speedily. The Foreign Affairs Minister Smt. Sushma Swaraj said that establishing e-libraries in 20 districts by GOI will help the nation as it make available around 2 million books to the youth of Bhutan. Both the countries leaders tried to resolve the concept that the Himalayas Divide, and stated that in fact the Himalayas are uniting as these region share a common legacy and need for development of the ecology of the region. The new government began a new era for India-Bhutan relations, strengthening the economy of both the countries and helping to develop the nations mutually. As a beginning, the Prime Minister unveiled the Foundation Stone of the 600 Megawatt Kholongchu Hydropower Project which is a Joint Venture project between the Indian and Bhutanese PSUs, SJVNL and Druk Green Power Corporation.[15]

Economic Relations

A planned development in Bhutan began in 1961 with the introduction of the Five Year Plans in the country. First two Five Year Plans were fully funded by the Government of India. Over the years, the assistance from the government of India has increased steadily from Rs. 107 million in the First Five year plan to Rs. 9000 million in the Eight five year plan. A detailed description of India's contribution to

Bhutan's Five Year Plans is given in Table 4.3. Though Bhutan began to get foreign aid from other nations after joining the UN, India continued to be the major donor of external aid to Bhutan. Over the last few decades, India has provided assistance to Bhutan mainly in the social sectors such as education and human resource development, health, hydropower development, agriculture and roads. Gradually, the economic relations between Bhutan and India collaborated on mutually beneficial projects like hydropower development and industrial projects. These projects are taken outside the Five Year Plan programs and considered beneficial to both the nations especially to the Indian companies. Such a mutual beneficiary projects will assure business opportunities in the manufacturing and other industries in both India and Bhutan.[16]

Today, India stands as the biggest development partner of Bhutan. In the year 2011, bilateral trade between India and Bhutan reached Rs. 61.6 billion which constituted 72 percent of Bhutan's total imports and 85 percent of its exports. Almost 70 percent of the kingdom's trade is with India and as of the statistics of 2011, a large amount of development budget of India's Ministry of External Affairs goes to Bhutan. For the year, 2010-2011 Bhutan received almost Rs. 1723 cores as loan from India in which most of the amount goes to development programmes. The recent visit of Salman Khurshid in 2013 was also a beginning process of Bhutan's "Eleventh Plan".[17]

India's Assistance to the Eleventh Five -Year Plan (2008-13)

Today, India stands as the biggest development partner of Bhutan. In the year 2011, bilateral trade between India and Bhutan reached Rs. 61.6 billion which constituted 72 percent of Bhutan's total imports and 85 percent of its

Table 4.3
India's Contribution to Bhutan's Five Year Plans

Five Year Plans	*Total Allocations*	*India's Contribution*	*% of India's Contribution*
1961-66 (1st Plan)	10.72	10.72	100%
1966-71 (2nd Plan)	20.22	20.22	100%
1971-76 (3rd Plan)	47.52	42.66	90%
1976-81 (4th Plan)	1,10.62	85.30	77%
1981-87 (5th Plan)	4,44.05	134.0	30.2%
1987-92 (6th Plan)	9,50.00	4,00.00	42.1%
1992-97 (7th Plan)	23,50.00	7,50.00	31.9%
1997-02 (8th Plan)	4000.00	1050.00	26%
2002-08 (9th Plan)	8900.00	2610.14	29.33%
2008-13 (10th Plan)	14800.00	3400.00	23%
2013-18 (11thPlan)	6600.00	4500.00	68%

[In Rs. crores]
Source: http://www.indianembassythimphu.bt/goi_assistance.html

exports. Almost 70 percent of the kingdom's trade is with India and as of the statistics of 2011, a large amount of development budget of India's Ministry of External Affairs goes to Bhutan. For the year, 2010-2011 Bhutan received almost Rs. 1723 cores as loan from India in which most of the amount goes to development programs. The visit of Salman Khurshid in 2013 was also a beginning process of India's help towards Bhutan's "Eleventh Five Year Plan".[18]

During the visit of the Prime Minister of Bhutan, Lyonchhen Tshering Tobgay to India in September, 2013, Government of India's Assistance Package for Bhutan's 11th Five Year Plan (July 2013 to June 2018), was decided . At Bhutan's request, India agreed to contribute Rs 4500 Crores. Additionally, GOI agreed to provide Rs. 500 Crore as

Economic Stimulus Package, to boost the Bhutanese economy and help RGOB overcome the problems arising out of the acute INR shortage.

Project Tied Assistance (PTA)

Out of the Rs. 4500 crore, Rs. 2800 Cr., will be provided as Project Tied Assistance (PTA) for funding 86 mutually agreed projects covering major priority sectors of socio-economic development like roads and bridges; education (schools); education (tertiary); health and construction of regional hospitals; engineering services; industries; energy; security; agriculture; livestock; judiciary; civil aviation; roads and urban transport; sports; culture; ICT & e-governance; scholarships and trainings, HRD etc.

Small Development Projects (SDP)

Rs. 850 Cr will be allocated for funding Small Development Projects (SDP). These projects are short gestation and community-oriented, focusing mainly on drinking water schemes, schools in rural areas, irrigation canals, farm roads, gewog connectivity roads, RNR centres, basic health units and staff quarters, market sheds, community meeting halls and other basic infrastructure in rural areas. Such projects are becoming increasingly popular with village communities actually identifying them, on the basis of their needs and requirements. Having a direct bearing on the lives of the grassroots people, these projects have become an effective tool for addressing rural poverty.

The remaining Rs. 850 Cr is provided as *Programme Grant* (Development Subsidy) to the RGOB. Programme Grant is released in quarterly installments of Rs. 42.5 cr.

In September 2014, the third round of the Bhutan-India Development Cooperation Talks or the Plan Talks for the 11th Five Year Plan of Bhutan was held in Thimphu. The Plan Talks are a regular feature of Bhutan-India Development Cooperation. India's commitment of Nu. 45 billion for the 11th Five Year Plan, excluding the Nu. 5 billion for the Economic Stimulus Plan, constitutes about 67% of the total external assistance Bhutan will be receiving during the Plan.[19]

Major Projects in Bhutan Funded by Government of India (GOI)

Besides the assistance for various Five Year Plans, India funds some major projects in Bhutan like the hydroelectric power projects, Penden and Dungsam cement projects, Hashimara-Phuentsholing Railway Line (the "Golden Jubilee Rail Line"), 'Total Solutions Project' (for capacity building in ICT sector and establishment of Bhutan Institute of Medical Sciences). In various agreements, Government of India has agreed to provide assistance to Bhutan in developing the hydropower sector and to purchase at least 10000 MW of power by 2020. In order to produce such huge amount of electricity, 10 hydropower projects have been agreed during the first Empowered Joint Group (EJG) Meeting held in Delhi on March 2009. Among these ten projects, the Punatsangchhu-I Hydro Electric Project was signed on 28th July 2007. The GOI had funded a number of projects under the cooperation between the two nations such as the Chhukha (336MW), Kurichhu (60MW), and Tala (1020MW) Hydro Power Projects; the Penden and Dungsam Cement Projects; and the Paro Airport Project.[17] Some of the completed or ongoing GOI funded Mega Projects are:

Chukha Hydro Electric Project (CHEP)

The Chukha Hydro Electric Project (CHEP) is a 336 MW project located on Wangchu River in Chukha district.

This was built by GOI at a low cost of Rs. 2460 million. This project has a significant share in the revenue generation of the Royal Government of Bhutan (RGOB) through export of electricity to India.. This project now is run by the Chukha Hydropower Corporation.

Kurichhu Hydro Electric Project (KHEP)

The Kurichhu Hydro Electric Project (KHEP) is a 60 MW project located on Kurichhu River in Mongar district. The project was established in April 2006, with the objective of providing enough and reliable power to eight eastern Dzongkhags to bring socio-economic development in the region. Under the KHE project, surplus power is exported to India which earned revenue to the RGOB.

Tala Hydro Electric Project (THEP)

This is a run-of-the-river 1020 MW project on the Wangchu River which was funded by the GOI with 60 percent of total expenditure as grant and 40 percent at low interest rate. This project comprises a 92 meter high concrete dam with a 22.2 km long water conductor system and an underground power house with 6 generating units and three single circuit transmission lines to the India-Bhutan border. All these six units were commissioned during the period of 2006-07.

Dungsam Cement Plant

Dungsam Cement Plant is a dry-process plant with an annual capacity of approximately 1 million ton per year. This plant is located at Nganglam in south-eastern region of Bhutan. the GOI provided funds and agreed to build required road and rail infrastructure for the plant which would commence its production from September, 2011.

Penden Cement Plant

Penden Cement Plant is located in Samtse District on Indo-Bhutan border. This plant was built with Indian assistance at a cost of Rs. 142 million with an initial capacity of 300 ton per day. The project went commercial in 1982. The cement factory has contributed to the total GDP of Bhutan.[20]

Ongoing Hydro-electric Projects in Bhutan funded by the Government of India.

1. Mangdechhu Hydroelectric Project

Mangdechhu Hydroelectric Project (720MW) is one amongst the ten hydroelectric Projects planned under the 10,000MW hydropower development by the year 2020 program of Royal Government of Bhutan supported by the Government of India. An agreement for execution of Mangdechhu Hydroelectric Project was signed between the two governments on 30th April 2010 at the approved cost of Nu./Rs. 33821.58 million (March 2008 price level) to be funded by GoI as 30% grant and 70% loan at 10% annual interest to be paid in thirty equated semiannual installments. NHPC Limited, a Central Public Sector Undertaking of GoI is the Design and Engineering consultant to the Project. The project is scheduled for commissioning by September, 2017.

2. Punatsangchhu-I

Punatsangchhu-I is the first Project of the 10,000 MW initiative taken by the Royal Government of Bhutan (RGoB) and the Government of India (GoI) in May 2008, for development by 2020. The Punatsangchhu-I Hydroelectric Project (1200 MW), a milestone in Indo-Bhutan relations, is presently the largest hydropower project undertaken in the Himalayan Kingdom of Bhutan by the RGoB and the

GoI. The Project, an environment-friendly run-of-the-river scheme, is located on the left bank of the Punatsangchhu in Wangduephodrang Dzongkhag in Western Bhutan. The Project will utilize 357m fall available in about 11 km river course.

WAPCOS Ltd. (Ministry of Water Resources, Government of India) is the engineering design consultants to the Authority. The premier organizations of Government of India, e.g.Central Electricity Authority, Central Water Commission, Central Water & Power Research Station, Central Soil & Materials Research Station, Geological Survey of Indiaand Survey of India make their valuable expertise available to the Project through WAPCOS.

3. Punatsangchhu-II

Punatsangchhu-II is the second Project of the 10,000 MW initiative taken by the Royal Government of Bhutan (RGoB) and the Government of India (GoI) in May 2008, for development by 2020. Agreement between the GoI and the RGoB for implementation of the Punatsangchhu-II Hydroelectric Project was signed on 30 April 2010 by H.E. Shri S.M. Krishna, Hon'ble Minister for External Affairs on behalf of the GoI and H.E. Lyonpo Khandu Wangchuk, Hon'ble Minister for Economic Affairs on behalf of the RGoB. On the same auspicious day, the foundation stone of the Project was laid jointly by H.E. Dr. Manmohan Singh, Hon'ble Prime Minister of India & H.E. Jigmi Y. Thinley, Hon'ble Lyonchhen of Bhutan.

Punatsangchhu-II Hydroelectric Project Authority (PHPA), an autonomous body was set-up for implementation of the Project on 08 June 2010. The project implementation started on 17 December 2010 with a completion schedule of 7 years including 2 years of infrastructure development.[21]

Trade Relations

Over the period of 1981-2001, the export to Indian accounted for an average of 86.5 percent of Bhutan's total export and the imports from India was around 79 percent of the total import of the country. Majority of the total trade relationship was with India and in the last decades, Bhutan began to receive import and export from and to the Western and Eastern nations. The major products for export to India are electricity, mineral products, product of chemical industries, base metals and products and wood and wood products. Imports from India to Bhutan include machinery, mechanical appliances, base metals, electronic items, foodstuff and other basic necessities and consumer items. Besides trade, Indian trade involvement was extended to other areas like private and public sector activities in Bhutan. Beyond such big companies operating in Bhutan, a number of small-scale trading and service activities are being operated by Indians. Existence of Indian investors in Bhutan is visible in the manufacturing and processing industries, construction, service, engineering, steel and electronic industries and consultancy in a large scale.[22]

Throughout the history of the country, India is the largest trading partner of Bhutan since the establishment of a formal relation between both the nations. The trade agreement between India and Bhutan, which expired on March 2005, has been renewed for a period of 10 years. This agreement also provides for a duty free transit of Bhutanese merchandise for trade with other countries. During the year 2005, imports from India were Rs. 12.80 billion that constituted around 75.1 percent of Bhutan's total imports and exports to India were Rs. 9.97 billion and constituted 87.5 percent of its total exports. In the year 2009, total imports from India were Rs. 23.3 billion and it constituted around 80 percent of the Bhutan's total imports and exports to India amounted to Rs. 20.5 billion which constituted 94 percent of the nation's total export.[23] A detailed data of the trade with India from 2000 to 2013 is given in Table 4.4.

Though Bhutan's economy is inextricably linked with India, an effort towards diversifying the import and export market and products are actively pursued by the Royal government of Bhutan during last decade. Besides the trade with India, imports of consumer goods from Bangladesh, Germany, Hong Kong, Singapore, Thailand, Japan and South Korea have increased in the last few years.[24]

Educational and Cultural Cooperation

Beyond trade relations there is close bilateral cooperation between India and Bhutan is visible in the education and cultural field. The Government of India is providing scholarships to the Bhutanese students both at undergraduate and postgraduate level. In the 10th Five Year Plan the scholarships have been increased from 50 to 85 in undergraduates and 77 for postgraduates. In order to strengthen the cultural ties between Bhutan and India, the India-Bhutan Foundation (IBF) was established in August 2003. This foundation focuses more on areas like education, cultural exchanges and environment preservation in the country. On 21st September 2010, Dr. Karan Singh, President of Indian Council for Cultural Relations (ICCR) and Lyonpo Minjur Dorji, Minister for Home and Cultural Affairs of Bhutan, jointly inaugurated the Nehru-Wangchuk Cultural Centre at Thimphu.[25]

India always remained committed to its support to Bhutan in its efforts towards economic, social and political development. The bilateral relations between the two countries gained momentum in the areas of hydropower development, information and communication technology,

Table 4.4
Trade Relations between India and Bhutan from 2000 to 2013

Year	*2000*	*2001*	*2002*	*2003*	*2004*	*2005*	*2006*	*2007*	*2008*	*2009*	*2010*	*2011*	*2012*	*2013*
Exports to Bhutan (Imports from India)	6.23	6.98	7.58	10.26	10.19	12.80	13.05	15.09	17.33	23.3	29.30	35.2	41.8	43.89
Imports from Bhutan (Exports to India)	4.37	4.70	5.13	5.92	7.76	9.97	14.48	22.72	21.48	20.5	26.00	26.4	27.8	28.98
[Rupees in Billion]														

Source: Royal Monetary Authority, RGoB

health, industry, education and culture. During the past decades, these relations were further consolidated with regular exchange of high-level visits and strengthening of bilateral cooperation between both the nations. On April, 2010, both the nations signed the Agreements for Punatsangchhu-II and Mangdechhu Hydro Electric Projects (HEPs) alone with the launch of Information Communication Technology Project "Chipen Rigphel" or "Total Solutions project". In the year 2009, Bhutan's total imports from India constituted 80% of the nation's total imports and exports to India constituted 94% of its total exports. Under the Small Development Projects Scheme, India initiated a total of 1259 projects in Bhutan which are at various stages of its implementation.[26]

Bilateral Relations between Switzerland and Bhutan

The beginning of a relation between Switzerland and Bhutan was based on a personal contact between King Jigme Dorji Wangchuk and Swiss industrialist Fritz von Schulthess Rechberg in 1950s. During 1960s and 70s, private aid organizations, especially Helvetas, financed the development projects in Bhutan. From 1978 onwards the Swiss government also became a partner in Bhutan's development projects. In the year 1980s and 1990s, Switzerland was one of the four major donors of Bhutan's development programs. A formal bilateral relation between Bhutan and Switzerland was begun in the year 1985.[27] Mr. Schulthess established the Foundation Pro Bhutan in 1972 to intensify assistance to Bhutan and raise fund in Switzerland. In July 1975, the programs of the Foundation was handed over to Helvetas, and in 1980, the Swiss Agency for Development and Cooperation (SDC)- a part of the Federal Department of Foreign Affairs of the government of Switzerland- began to support the programs of Helvetas.

As a result of the cooperation between the Royal government of Bhutan and Helvetas, several projects in Bumthang were expanded to national level, and many new projects were launched including the national Potato project, the construction of hospital at Bumthand and the Integrated Forestry Development Project in Bumthang. A new program to promote the development of farm-households in a more integrated way led the light to establish a Natural Resources Training Institute (NRTI) in Bhutan. The Helvetas began to support more activities in general education, civic education and building up the institutions, training and support in the field of culture and safeguarding of national heritage. In June 2008, the foreign secretary and Helvetas resident coordinator signed an agreement for increased cooperation in the RNR sector, rural infrastructure, decentralised governance, education and culture.[28]

Canada- Bhutan Relations

Canada and Bhutan have a long standing relationship and a history of close collaboration in the education sector since 1960s. In the year 1963, a Canadian Jesuit priest, Father William Mackey, came to Bhutan to establish a secular secondary school at the request of the royal Government of Bhutan. Since then, the Canadian government began to help the nation in its education sector and over 50 Canadians have taught in Bhutanese schools and more than 250 Bhutanese educators have studied in Canadian institutions. A formal diplomatic relationship between the Canadian government and the Royal Government of Bhutan began in June 2003. In recent years, the Canadian International Development Agency (CIDA) has provided support to a number of projects in areas such as curriculum development, teacher training and leadership capacity building. The official interaction between Canada and Bhutan is coordinated through the Canadian High Commission in New Delhi and the Bhutanese Permanent Mission to the United Nations in New York. Though education is the primary focus of Canada-Bhutan relation, both the nations also looked for strong cooperation in other areas of development. The International Development Research Centre (IDRC) has helped Bhutan in establishing its first ever link to the Internet, supported in enhancing food productivity and income generation in rural households through Community-based Natural Resource Management (CBNRM) and in establishing a web-based distance education delivery system in the country. In addition, over the past years, many Canadian private sector organizations have been collaborating with the Royal Government of Bhutan in the areas of education, construction, environment, hydro power projects and financial and public service management. The CIDA maintains a small Canadian Cooperation Office in Thimphu which manages aid programs and offers consular assistance to Canadians living in Bhutan.[29]

Japan- Bhutan Relations

Bhutan and Japan established bilateral diplomatic relations on March 28, 1986. By the end of 2009, a total number of 131 Japanese nationals reside in Bhutan and around 68 Bhutanese nationals reside in Japan. The trade relations between Bhutan and Japan by the end of 2009 showed tremendous growth by ending a total of 34 million yen from the export to Japan and 829 million yen from the import to Bhutan. Japan imports mainly vegetables and textiles from Bhutan, while Japan exports small excavators, automobile, products related to automobiles. On March 28, 2011, Bhutan and Japan commemorate their 25th year of establishment of the bilateral relations between the two countries.[30] Below in the table 4.5 and 4.6 gives a detailed list of diplomatic visits made by both the nations over the past years.

Table 4.5
Diplomatic Visit to Bhutan by the Japanese Delegates

Sl.No	Year and Month	Name of the Delegate
1	March 1987	H.I.H. Prince Naruhito
2	August 1992	Delegation of Socialist Party (headed by Makoto Taneda)
3	December 1993	President of JICA Kensuke Yanagiya
4	September 1994	Japan-Bhutan Parliamentary Friendship League (headed by Former Minister of Agriculture, Forestry and Fisheries Mutsuki Kato)
5	March 1997	T.I.H. Prince and Princess Akishino
6	October 1997	Ambassador Nobuo Matsunaga,the Envoy of the Japanese Government
7	April 1998	Former Prime Minister Toshiki Kaifu
8	January 2001	President of JICA Kimio Fujita
9	June 2005	Parliamentary Secretary for Foreign Affairs Katsuyuki Kawai
10	August 2006	Vice-Minister of Health, Labour and Welfare Kiyoshi Nakano
11	October 2006	Japan-Bhutan Friendship Parliamentarians League (headed by Former Minister for Foreign Affairs and chairman of the League, Nobutaka Machimura, 20th Anniversary of Diplomatic Relations)
12	April 2010	Parliamentary Vice-Minister for Foreign Affairs Chinami Nishimura

Source: www.mofa.go.jp

Table 4.6
Diplomatic Visit to Japan by the Bhutanese Delegates

Sl.No	*Month and Year*	*Name of the Delegates*
1	March 1986	Minister of Foreign Affairs Lyonpo Dawa Tsering (Establishment of Diplomatic Relations)
2	April 1987	Minister of Foreign Affairs Lyonpo Dawa Tsering
3	May 1988	Minister of Foreign Affairs Lyonpo Dawa Tsering
4	February 1989	H.M. King Jigme Singye Wangchuck (Imperial Funeral of Emperor Showa)
5	May 1990	Minister of Foreign Affairs Lyonpo Dawa Tsering (International Garden and Greenery Exposition, Osaka, Japan, 1990)
6	November 1990	H.M. King Jigme Singye Wangchuck (Enthronement Ceremony)
7	April 1991	Minister of Foreign Affairs Lyonpo Dawa Tsering
8	August 1993	Minister of Foreign Affairs Lyonpo Dawa Tsering
9	October 1993	Planning Minister Lyonpo C. Dorji
10	July 1994	Minister of Foreign Affairs Lyonpo Dawa Tsering
11	October 1996	Minister of Foreign Affairs Lyonpo Dawa Tsering
12	September 1997	H.M. Queen Mother Ashi Kesang Chodron
13	June 1999	Chairman of Council of Ministers, Head of Government and Minister of Foreign Affairs, Lyonchhen Jigmi Thinley
14	August 2000	Minister of Agriculture Lyonpo Kinzang Dorji

15	December 2001	Health and Education Minister Lyonpo Sangay Ngedup
16	June 2004	Finance Minister Lyonpo Yeshey Zimba
17	October 2004	H.M. Ashi Dorji Wangmo Wangchuck
18	June 2005	Minister of Home Affairs and Cultural Affiars Lyonpo Jigmi Thinley (2005 World Exposition, Aichi, Japan)
19	January 2006	Finance Minister Lyonpo Wangi Norbu
20	April 2006	Speaker of National Assembly Dasho Ugten Dorji
21	October 2006	Minister of Home and Cultural Affairs Lyonpo Jigmi Thinley
22	March 2007	Chief Justice of Bhutan Lyonpo Sonam Tobgye
23	March 2007	Attorney General of Bhutan Dasho Damcho Dorji
24	April 2007	Minister for Agriculture Lyonpo Sangay Ngedup
25	December 2007	Prime Minister Lyonpo Kinzang Dorji
26	August 2008	Chief Election Commissioner Dasho Kunzang Wangdi
27	June 2009	Additional Chief of Royal Bhutan Police Lt. Col. Tshewang Dendup
28	August 2009	Prime Minister Lyonchhen Jigmi Thinley
29	April 2010	Prime Minister Lyonchhen Jigmi Thinley
30	November 2010	Minister of Agriculture and Forests Lyonpo Dr. Pema Gyamtsho
31	February 2011	H.R.H. Ashi Kezang Choden Wangchuck

Source: www.mofa.go.jp

Japan had funded a number of projects in Bhutan over the past 25 years of their diplomatic relations. Japan provided Official Development Assistance (ODA) and Grant Assistance for Grassroots Projects (GGP) to Bhutan in the last few years. On June 2007, the Government of Japan and the UN extended assistance to Bhutan to the project entitled "Basic Education/Literacy, Income Security and Employment for Vulnerable People including Children and Women in Bhutan". In April 2007, Japan provided a loan of 3576 million yen to Bhutan to implement the "Rural Electrification Project" and in November, 2007, the Government of Japan provided an emergency grant aid of about 1.07 million dollars to Bhutan to support general elections through the UNDP. On October 2009, the Government of Japan extended an emergency assistance of 10 million JPY to the Royal Government of Bhutan for the damages of an earthquake.[31] Table 4.7 and table 4.8 give a brief description of the ODA and GGP grants to Bhutan from Japan in the year 2010 and 2011.

Bhutan-Denmark Bilateral Relations

Diplomatic relations between Bhutan and Denmark were established in 1985. The Danish development cooperation with Bhutan started in 1978 and the assistance was focused mainly on areas such as health, education, environment, urban development and good governance. The first country collaboration between Bhutan and Denmark was elaborated in 1997 covering the planning period 1998-2002. Denmark has been one of the largest donors of development assistance to Bhutan's Modernisation process. The Denmark Government also supports Bhutan with its programs of poverty reduction, education, health sector, environment sector, urban development and freedom of press movement.

Table 4.7
Official Development Assistance (ODA) and Grant Assistance for Grassroots Projects (GGP) in 2010

		Year 2010	
Sl.No	*Date and Year*	*Project/Projects*	*Amount*
1	January 19, 2010	The Project for Improvement of Machinery and Equipment for Construction of Rural Agricultural Road (Phase 2)	6 million US dollars
2	February 18, 2010	The River Training Works project at Hungrel,	US$91,867
3	July 8, 2010	"Grant Assistance for Underprivileged Farmers (2KR)" and "Non-Project Grant Aid (NPGA)"	3.8 million US dollars
4	July 8, 2010	"The project for improvement for the basic service of the Labour Room" to the National Referral Hospital, Bhutan	US$ 78,295
5	November 3, 2010	1. The Project for Improvement for Recycled Compactor Trucks in Thimpu City 2. The Project for Construction of Reinforce Cement Concrete Bridge at Choekhor	US $83,101 US$ 97,703

Source: www.in.emb-japan.go.jp

Table 4.8
Official Development Assistance (ODA) and Grant Assistance for Grassroots Projects (GGP) in 2010

		Year 2011	
Sl.No	*Date and Year*	*Project/Projects*	*Amount*
1	January 25, 2011	The Project for Replacement of Ambulances	1.9 million US dollars
2	January 31, 2011	The Project for the River Training Works at Hungrel, Paro Dzongkhag	US$91,867
3	March 3, 2011	Assistance to the Fire Service Division, Royal Bhutan Police Headquarters	US$80,309
4	March 7, 2011	The Project for Improvement of Machinery and Equipment for Construction of Rural Agricultural Road (Phase 2)	6 million US dollars
5	March 8, 2011	The Project for Construction of Reinforced Cement Concrete Bridge at Choekhor	US$97,703
6	March 21, 2011	The Food Security Project for Underprivileged Farmers 2010 (KR2-2010)	1.6 million US dollars
7	April 14, 2011	The Project for Construction of Bridges at Chumpa and Girina	US$70,702
8	April 16, 2011	The Project for Construction of Educational Facilities	13.3 million USD (1064 Million yen)

Source: www.in.emb-japan.go.jp

Danish-Bhutanese Co-operation 2003-2007

The main objectives of the Danish development policy were to promote sustainable development through economic development in Bhutan. The Danish assistance for the period of 2003- 2007 aimed to help the poor by ensuring crucial investments in education, health, women's participation in development process, promotion of human rights and establishing good governance in the country. This covered the period of 9th Five Year Plan of Bhutan. The programme had been characterised by strong Bhutanese ownership and execution. The small size of the country became a positive factor in creating visible and crucial results for the development of Bhutan. Thus, the Danish assistance to Bhutan had played a major role in the fields of health, environment and good governance and boosted the ongoing democratisation and public sector reform process in the country. The cooperation programme provided supports for areas with close consultation with the Royal Government of Bhutan so as to help reaching the Millennium Development Goals of the nation. Under the Danish-Bhutan cooperation, major attention was given to the objectives set for the longer term, towards the MDG.[32]

Danish-Bhutanese Cooperation 2008-2013

The experiences from the Danish support to Bhutan have been positive in the 2003-2007 Danish-Bhutan cooperation. This cooperation contributed to a number of important changes in the Bhutanese society including the poverty reduction, urban development, education and health sector. The Danish development assistance to Bhutan was aligned with public systems on reporting, monitoring, procurement and auditing during the period of 2003-2007. The new country strategy set for the period of 5 years from

July 2008 to June 2013 covering Bhutan's 10th Five Year Plan. The overall objective of this cooperation remained poverty reduction through sustainable economic development and democratic processes. Under this cooperation programme, the private sector will be strengthened through activities under the Mixed Credit Programme, the Public-Private Partnership facility and the Business-to-Business Programme. Table 4.9 provides with the sector allocation of the Danish Development Assistance during the period of 2008-2013.

Table 4.9
Sector Allocation of the Danish Development Assistance Tentative Distribution of Assistance During 2008-2013

Sl.No	*Sectors of cooperation*	*Percentage*
1.	Social Sectors (Health, Education, Vocational Training)	48%
2	Environment and Urban Development	24%
3	Good Governance	17%
4	Other	11%

Source: Strategy for Danish Development Co-operation with Bhutan 2008-2013

Over the past 10 years, the Danish- Bhutan cooperation has given emphasis to ensure the need of physical infrastructure in particular health and education. The Danish support programme will closely monitor developments in the education and health areas of special interest to the private sector to promote further private sector involvement in this sector. In the next 5 to 10 years, it is important for Bhutan and Denmark to give priority to enhance relations which can ensure continued cooperation after the development assistance has been phased out.[33]

Bangladesh-Bhutan Relations

Bhutan has a long history of relations with Bangladesh. Bilateral relations between both the nations were developed in 1971 and formal diplomatic relations were established in early 1973. Bangladesh is one of the first nations with whom Bhutan began its foreign relations. Besides India, Bangladesh and Bhutan opened its resident mission at Ambassadorial level in each other's capital from January, 1980 onwards. Since the establishment of diplomatic bilateral relations, both the countries have been actively engaged in strengthening bilateral relations through exchange of high level visits. In Table 4.10 a detailed description of the important visits made by Bhutan and Bangladesh Diplomats over the past years.

Table 4.10
Important Diplomatic Visits Between Bhutan and Bangladesh

Year	*Delegation Visited*
April 1972	The Foreign Minister of Bhutan Lyonpo Dawa Tshering paid an official visit to Bangladesh
August 1972	Mr. Shamsul Huq, the then Minister for local Government, Rural Development and Cooperatives of Bangladesh led a delegation to Bhutan.
June 1-5, 1974	The President of Bangladesh visited Thimphu
February 1984	The King of Bhutan paid a state visit to Bangladesh
June 1985	Princess Ashi Sonam C. Wangchuck, the eldest sister of the Bhutanese King, paid a short visit to Bangladesh soon after the cyclonic disaster in our coastal belt.
1985	The former Bangladesh Foreign Minister visited Bhutan to attend SAARC Foreign Ministers' Meeting

June 1986	The then Bangladesh President paid a state visit to Bhutan
October 1988	Bangladesh President also paid a working visit to Bhutan
February 1989	The King of Bhutan made a brief stopover at Zia International Airport en route to Tokyo to attend Emperor Hirohito's funeral service.
2- 4 August 1989	The former Foreign Minister of Bangladesh visited Bhutan
October 1990	The former Commerce Minister of Bangladesh visited Bhutan
April 1991	The Foreign Minister of Bhutan visited Dhaka
March 1992	The Bhutanese Minister of Trade and Industries visited Dhaka
April 1993	The King of Bhutan visited Bangladesh
July 1994	the Foreign Minister of Bhutan, Lyonpo Dawa Tshering visited Dhaka
November, 2002	The then Commerce Secretary of Bangladesh visited Thimphu in connection with the holding of a bilateral trade fair.
May 2003	The Trade and Industry Minister of Bhutan Mr. Khandu Wangchuk visited Dhaka
June 2004	The former State Minister of Forests and Environment of Bangladesh visited Bhutan
June 2004	A cultural team from Bangladesh Shishu Academy visited Bhutan and performed cultural shows in Thimphu, Punakha and Paro
24 May 2006	The Bhutanese Deputy Minister for National Environment Commission participated at the 7th SAARC Environment Ministers' Meeting held in Dhaka
August 2006	Mr. Khandu Wangchuk, Minister for Foreign Affairs of Bhutan participated at the 27th Session

	of the SAARC Council of Ministers' held in Dhaka
July 2008	The Finance Minister of Bhutan attended the BIMSTEC Ministerial meeting on Poverty Alleviation held in Dhaka
August, 2008	The Commerce Secretary of Bangladesh with a government delegation visited Bhutan
27 September to 5 October, 2009	Bhutanese Minister for Economic Affairs visited Bangladesh including Burimari land port
November 2009	The Hon'ble Prime Minister of Bangladesh Her Excellency Sheikh Hasina paid her first South Asian bilateral visit to Bhutan
March 24 to 29, 2011	The King His Majesty Khesar Namgyal Wangchuck visited Bangladesh and was the Guest of Honour at the celebrations of the 40th anniversary of Bangladesh's Independence Day.
14-18 February, 2013	The Fifth King of Bhutan Khesar Wangchuck and the Queen Jetsun Pema Visited Bangladesh.

Source: www.bangladeshembassy.bt

Trade Relations between Bhutan and Bangladesh

The trade volume is increasing rapidly based on mutually beneficial complementarities and strong economic growths in both the nations. Bangladesh offers quality and competitive products from wider basket of consumer goods, plastic, electrical and electronic products, software, pharmaceuticals, tea, etc. Besides, there is also large scope for expansion of trade between the two countries in the near future. Both the nations undertake joint ventures in manufacturing and service sectors of small and medium scale.[34] The relationship between the two countries was progressively diversifying both in material as well as less tangible forms encompassing the culture, trade and environmental areas in the past years. Bangladesh has become a very popular source for high quality products such as garments, cosmetics, household items and a wide range of consumables to Bhutan. Table 4.11 gives the details of Import and Export between both the nations from 2004 to 2010. The bilateral relations will also look in to possibilities of trade cooperation on fisheries and livestock, joint tourism packages, agriculture and agro-based processing industries. The Bangladeshi authorities are also hoping for importing electricity from Bhutan and involving Bangladesh in future hydropower projects in Bhutan.[35]

Table 4.11
The Trade Relations Between Bhutan and Bangladesh

Year	*Imports from Bhutan*	*Exports to Bhutan*
2004-2005	8.59	5.10
2005-06	12	1.72
2006-07	10	1.40
2007-08	13.74	1.35
2008-09	12	0.61
2009-10	25	3

(In Million US Dollar)
Source: www.bangladeshembassy.bt
Also see: www.bhutanobserver.bt
Other Areas of Cooperation

Over the past years, Bangladesh and Bhutan has maintained significant cooperation in the area of education. Many Bhutanese students completed their medicine and engineering studies in Bangladesh. Under the scholarship scheme, Bangladesh offers four seats every year to Bhutanese students to study medicine in the public medical collages in Bangladesh and Bangladesh University of Engineering and Technology also reserve seats for the Bhutanese students. Bangladesh offers one scholarship to Bhutanese Army for Staff Course in the Bangladesh Defence Service Command and Staff Collage. The bilateral relations in the field of cultural cooperation provide the institutional framework for the cultural exchanges between the two nations. Bhutan and Bangladesh share a potential beneficiary cooperation in the area of tourism, agriculture and environment and science and technology.[36] To sum up, Table 4.12 gives the important agreements and documents signed between Bhutan and Bangladesh.

Table 4.12
List of Important Agreements and Documents between the Government of People's Republic of Bangladesh and the Royal Government of Bhutan

No.	*Date*	*Agreement or Documents*
1	8 September, 1980	Agreement on Trade
2	8 September, 1980	Agreement on Transit
3	30 January, 1984	Memorandum of Understanding on Transit Arrangements to facilitate Commerce.
4	5 February, 1984	Protocol to the Agreement on Trade
5	5 February, 1984	Agreement on Economic and Technical Cooperation
6	4 June, 1986	Air Service Agreement
7	4 June, 1986	Agreement on Cultural Cooperation
8	7 November, 2009	Agreement on Trade

Source: www.bangladeshembassy.bt

Bhutan- Thailand Relations

The bilateral relations between the Kingdom of Bhutan and the Kingdom of Thailand began from 1989 onwards.

Both the nations maintained diplomatic relations for more than two decades. With social and political aspects in common, the relations grew stronger over the past years. Both the nations promote cooperation in the field of education, human resources, medicine and tourism in the recent years. On November 10, 2009, the Embassy of Thailand in Dhaka launched the creation of the "Bhutan-Thailand Friendship Park" in Thimpu to celebrate the 20th anniversary of the establishment of the bilateral relations between both the nations.[37] The tourism Authority of Thailand (TAT) and the tourism Council of Bhutan (TCB) in a joint meeting at Thimphu decided to increase the flow of tourists between the two countries. Both the nations have established a 'working committee' to boost the areas collaboration and to exchange ideas and formulate marketing strategies towards increasing tourist traffic between Bhutan and Thailand.[38]

Bhutan-China relations

Throughout history, the Kingdom of Bhutan had strong cultural, historical, religious and economic ties with Tibet. Bilateral relations between the Kingdom of Bhutan and the People's Republic of China have been tense and they never maintained an official diplomatic relations. Both the nations share a contiguous border of 4700 kilometres in the north. Since 1980's both countries have conducted regular talks on border and security issues aiming to reduce the tension between both. In the year 1998, Bhutan and China signed a bilateral agreement for maintaining peace on the border in which China affirmed its respect for Bhutan's sovereignty and territorial integrity. Under this agreement, both countries sought to build ties based on the Five Principles of Peaceful Coexistence. In 2002, China put forward its claims of evidence regarding ownership of disputed tracts of land.

On January 2010, with the nineteenth round of border talks between Bhutan and China a significant development was the focus on the disputed claim line in North Western Bhutan.[39] Though Bhutan has not made any official comments on establishing a diplomatic relations with China, the democratic opening has led to increased intension to benefits from formal relations with China. At present there are some domestic pressures to establish a limited economic tie with china as the process of democratisation takes root in Bhutan. The economic relations with China will reduce the high transactional cost of goods imported from the Kolkata port as the costs of some goods are cheaper if it import through the country's North-Western border via Tibet.[40] On 21 June 2012, Chinese Premier Wen Jiabao and Bhutan's Prime Minister Jigme Y. Thinley met at the sidelines of the Rio +20 summits. Both the leaders have discussed matters related to border issues and maintaining peace.[41] The bilateral relations between Bhutan and China will surely be a concern for the nation's closest friend India.

Conclusion

Historically, Bhutan's foreign policies were guided by Tibet, Britain and India till the nation started its Modernisation process and began to be independent in the international relations. Till 1860s, Bhutan acknowledged Tibet's influence in its foreign relations, as most of the Bhutanese elites were refugees from Tibet in the past. From 1865 to 1947, Britain guided Bhutan's foreign affairs and had a high influence in the nation's foreign policy formulation. After independence from the colonial rule of British, India guided Bhutan's foreign relations until the early 1970s. Coming out of its self-imposed isolation in 1970s,

Bhutan became a member of UN and its affiliated agencies, which boosted the nation to establish relations with other western and eastern nations independently. By the early 1990s, Bhutan's foreign relations were absolutely autonomous and began to establish embassies and diplomatic relations in many of the western and eastern nations. Till recently, only India and Bangladesh had a residential embassy in Thimphu. Most of the nations gave dual accreditation to their ambassadors in New Delhi to establish and enable their countries' interest in Bhutan.[42]

Since 1970s, Bhutan tried to conceptualize its developmental needs and efforts through its foreign relations under the frameworks of GNH and the nation's cultural identity and environment. Though foreign policy is important for the development of the nation, Bhutan established a balanced approach as in today's world no country can be isolated from outer world.[43]

NOTES

1. Kharat, Rajesh (2009), *Indo-Bhutan Relations: Strategic Perspective*, in Himalayan Frontiers of India: Historical, Geo-Political and Strategic Perspectives, K. Warikoo (ed), Taylor & Francis, New York, p. 137.
2. Encyclopedia of Nations, *Bhutan- Foreign Policy*. Available at: http://www.nationsencyclopedia.com/World-Leaders-2003/Bhutan-FOREIGN-POLICY.html
3. Jayapalan, N. (2000), *India and Her Neighbors*, Atlantic Publishers and Distributors, New Delhi. p. 249.
4. The Royal Government of Bhutan , Ministry of Foreign Affairs. Available at:
   http://www.mfa.gov.bt/
5. B.C. Upreti, (2005) *Gross National Happyness and Foreign Policy of Bhutan :Interlinkages and Imperatives*, Paper Presented at the The Second International Conference on Gross National Happiness, St. Francis Xavier University, Antigonish, Nova

Scotia, Canada on June 20 to June 24, 2005. Available at: http://www.gpiatlantic.org/conference/papers/upreti.pdf
6. Royal Government of Bhutan, (1998), *Bhutan 2020: A vision for Peace, Prosperity and Happiness*, Planning Commission, Thimpu. p. 26
7. Upreti, B.C. (2005), n.5.
8. Council on Foreign Relations, *Bhutan's Road to Democracy*, Interview with Prime Minsiter Jigme Y. Thinley by Jayshree Bajoria, September 25, 2008. Available at: http://www.cfr.org/publication/17331/bhutans_road_to_democracy.html
9. Choden, Tashi (2004), *Indo-Bhutan Relations Recent Trends*, Journal of Bhutan Studies, Volume 11, p. 115.
10. Labh, Kapileshwar 1974. *India and Bhutan*. New Delhi: Sindhu Publications, pp. 173-183
11. Rahul, Ram 1983. *Royal Bhutan*. New Delhi: A.B.C. Publishing House, p. 29
12. Embassy of India, Thimphu, *Treaty Between India and Bhutan 1949*. Available at: http://www.indianembassythimphu.bt/treaty.htm
13. Treaty between Indian and Bhutan, 2007. Available at: http://www.bhutandnc.com/Treaty.htm
14. Bisht, Medha (2013) Jigme Khesar Namgyel Wangchuk's Visit to India: Towards an Assuring Alliance, Institute for Defence Studies and Analysis, February 1, 2013. Available at: http://www.idsa.in/idsacomments/JigmeKhesarNamgyel WangchuksVisittoIndia_MedhaBisht_010213
15. Embassy of India, Thimphu, India's assistance to the Eleventh Five –Year Plan of Royal Government of Bhutan.
16. Choden, Tashi, (2004), n.9, p.115.
17. Bisht, Medha (2013). n.14.
18. Bisht, Medha (2013) Jigme Khesar Namgyel Wangchuk's Visit to India: Towards an Assuring Alliance, Institute for Defence Studies and Analysis, February 1, 2013. Available at: http://www.idsa.in/idsacomments/Jigme Khesar Namgyel Wang chuks VisittoIndia_MedhaBisht_010213
19. Embassy of India, Thimphu, India's assistance to the Eleventh Five –Year Plan of Royal Government of Bhutan. Available at: http://www.indianembassythimphu.bt/pages.php?id=33
20. Embassy of India, Thimphu, *Mega Projects*. Available at: http://www.indianembassythimphu.bt/mega.html
21. Embassy of India, Thimphu, Ongoing Hydropower projects in

Bhutan. Available at: http://www.indianembassy thimphu.bt/pages.php?id=36

22. Choden, Tashi, (2004), n.9, p. 115.
23. Ministry of External Affairs, India, *India-Bhutan Relations.* Available at: http://meaindia.nic.in/meaxpsite/foreignrelation/bhutan.pdf
24. Embassy of India,. Thimphu, *India-Bhutan Relatons.* Available at: http://www.indianembassythimphu.bt/indo.html#trade
25. Ministry of External Affairs, India, n.23.
26. Ministry of External Affairs, India, *Annual Report 2010-2011.* Available at: http://meaindia.nic.in/mystart.php?id=500417371
27. Council on Foreign Relations, *Bhutan's Road to Democracy,* Interview with Prime Minsiter Jigme Y. Thinley by Jayshree Bajoria, September 25, 2008. Available at: http://www.cfr.org/publication/17331/bhutans_road_to_democracy.html
28. Choden, Tashi (2004), *Indo-Bhutan Relations Recent Trends,* Journal of Bhutan Studies, Volume 11, p. 115.
29. Embassy of India, Thimphu, *Treaty Between India and Bhutan 1949.* Available at: http://www.indianembassythimphu.bt/treaty.htm
30. Treaty between Indian and Bhutan, 2007. Available at: http://www.bhutandnc.com/Treaty.htm
31. Bisht, Medha (2013) Jigme Khesar Namgyel Wangchuk's Visit to India: Towards an Assuring Alliance, Institute for Defence Studies and Analysis, February 1, 2013. Available at: http://www.idsa.in/idsacomments/JigmeKhesarNamgyelWangchuksVisittoIndia_MedhaBisht_010213
32. Choden, Tashi, (2004), n.9, p.115.
33. Bisht, Medha (2013), n.12.
34. Choden, Tashi (2004), n.9, p.115.
35. Embassy of India, Thimphu, *Mega Projects.* Available at: http://www.indianembassythimphu.bt/mega.html
36. Choden, Tashi, (2004), n.9, p. 115.
37. Ministry of External Affairs, India, *India-Bhutan Relations.* Available at: http://meaindia.nic.in/meaxpsite/foreignrelation/bhutan.pdf
38. Embassy of India, Thimphu, *India-Bhutan Relatons.* Available at:

http://www.indianembassythimphu.bt/indo.html#trade

39. Ministry of External Affairs, India, n.141.
40. Ministry of External Affairs, India, *Annual Report 2010-2011*. Available at: http://meaindia.nic.in/mystart.php?id=500417371
41. Federal Department of Foreign Affairs, Switzerland, *Bilateral Relations Between Switzerland and Bhutan*. Available at: http://www.eda.admin.ch/eda/en/home/reps/asia/vbtn/bilbhu.html
42. RA Online, *25 years of Bhutan- Swiss Cooperation, 2000*. Available at: http://www.raonline.ch/pages/bt/dev/btdev_swiss020.html
43. Government of Canada, *Canada-Bhutan Relations*. Available at: http://www.canadainternational.gc.ca/india-inde/bilateral_relations_bilaterales/canada _bhutan-bhoutan.aspx?lang=eng
44. Ministry of Foreign Affairs of Japan, *25th Anniversary of Establishment of Diplomatic Relations between Japan and the Kingdom of Bhutan*, Retrived on March 28, 2011. Available at: http://www.mofa.go.jp/announce/announce/2011/3/0328_01.html
45. ibid.
46. Royal Danish Ministry of Foreign Affairs, *Strategy for Danish Development Co-operation with Bhutan 2003-2007*, Denmark. Available at: http://www.um.dk/NR/rdonlyres/71E4DE11-7CA4-48F9-8B99-8A6DAAD3E3B5/0/BhutanDenmark_partnership.pdf
47. Royal Danish Government, *Strategy for Danish Development Co-operation with Bhutan 2008-2013*, Royal Danish Ministry of Foreign Affairs, Danida. Available at: http://www.netpublikationer.dk/um/9281/pdf/Bhutan-Denmark.pdf
48. Bangladesh Embassy, Thimphu, *Bangladesh-Bhutan Relations*, retrieved on June, 2011. Available at: http://www.bangladeshembassy.bt/index.php?option=com_content&view=article&id=14&Itemid=14
49. Chhetri, Pushkar (2011) *Bhutan-Bangladesh Trade Relations Get a Booster*, Bhutan Observer, 18 January, 2011. Available at: http://www.bhutanobserver.bt/bhutan-bangladesh-trade-relations-get- a-booster/
50. Bangladesh Embassy, Thimphu, n.29.

51. Ministry of Foreign Affairs, Kingdom of Thailand, *Bhutan-Thailand Friendship Park*. Available at: http://www.mfa.go.th/web/2651.php?id=23580
52. Tourism between Bhutan and Thailand, November 19, 2009. Available at: http://www.bhutantour.bt/bhutan-news/tourism-between-thailand-and-bhutan.html
53. Bisht, Medha (2010) Bhutan 2010: Foreign Policy Developments, Institute for Defence Studies and Analysis, December 30, 2010. Available at: http://www.idsa.in/idsacomments/Bhutan2010ForeignPolicyDevelopments_mbisht_301210
54. Bisht, Medha (2013). n.12
55. Bhutan Research, Bhutan – China Relations, Sino-Bhutan Rapprochement? Available at: http://www.bhutan-research.org/special-bhutan-china-relations
56. Savada, Andrea Matles (ed) (1991) *Bhutan: A Country Study*, GPO for the Library of Congress, Washington. Available at: http://countrystudies.us/bhutan/21.htm
57. Upreti, B.C. n.5.

CHAPTER 5

The Future Challenges Ahead of Bhutan

The administrative system in any transitional society which strictly follows its traditional, religious and cultural aspects for centuries is likely to face new challenges when adopting new and different socio-political aspects. Though Bhutan began to change its basic socio-political structure from 1950s onwards and became a parliamentary democratic country in 2008, the nation and people still undergo the traditional cultural and religious values in their daily life. Such a nation will encounter number of challenges and constraints in its structural and organizational sphere in its developmental and Modernisation process. Any democracy in the world requires a transparent administrative system, a vigilant parliament with full participation of the masses, an independent judiciary for promoting the idea of equality of law and a free press to criticize and collect input for the governing system. But while giving all such powers to the institutions, the possibility of being corrupted or having a biased view of such institutions is no less thus giving challenges to the administrative system in the country.

In the past four decades, Bhutan witnessed a number of changes and developments in economic, political, socio-cultural, technological and legal spheres in the country. The nation went through many stages of political and economic developments from the establishment of a unified nation under Shabdrung Ngwang Namgyal till the establishment of a democratic parliamentary government in 2008. The nation adopted and institutionalized a new system which was totally new and unknown to the people of Bhutan. In order to maintain the traditional and religious values of the country, the rulers tried to keep its cultural ethos alive when establishing the new administrative system and developments in Bhutan. Under the reign of Shabdrungs, the political system was controlled both by the temporal and religious heads. But after the establishment of the hereditary monarchical system, the power of religious heads began to shrink and later the spiritual aspect was left with no such powers they need to enjoy in the past. The Tshogdu under the Third King Jigme Dorji Wangchuk in 1953 was merely a consultative body and was more like a static political institution. Until the fourth king's Modernisation process, the national Assembly has not emerged as a modern political system that represents the people's will. In the modern world, this new democracy will be facing a number of challenges and problems related to its socio-cultural, political and economic aspects. Being a nascent democracy, Bhutan is struggling to find a place in the new world order. After the general election in 2008, the nation made a transition to a parliamentary democratic government that is supplanted with the concept of constitutional monarchy.

With the second general election at hand, some of the issues at present could prove to be the litmus test for the new democratic system and the political parties such as a balanced socio-economic development, youth employment, political rights for minorities and balanced foreign policy with its immediate neighbours like India and China. For the next government, socio-economic development will be the primary challenge.

Problems in Administration

Though the nation adopted a new administrative system in the year 2008 to lead the nation towards Modernisation and development while keeping alive its culture and tradition, the country still has a number of challenges before it. Bhutan stands on the threshold of new administrative constraints and challenges such as maintaining and protecting its unique identity, sovereignty and security as a viable nation-state in the South Asian region and in the world community of nations. Being the only surviving Mahayana Buddhism-inspired polity, the administrative system in Bhutan is the custodian of the unique social and cultural system that once extended beyond the Eastern Himalayas to a large part of Eastern and Southern Asia. Contrary to most of the developing and developed nations where colonialism and its legacy created an alien administrative structure, Bhutan has a new pattern of change in which they reformed its own institutions.[1]

1. Problems of Decentralisation in Bhutan

The decentralisation process is a part of gradually evolving initiatives for empowering people to participate in the decision making process of government. The government of Bhutan has successfully introduced this system in the nation and has been running it for the last one decade. But still the nation faces some challenges in its implementation such as division of power between the central and local government, the lack of accessibility of people in getting the services and the local elitism that prevail in the nation. As Bhutan experiments modern democracy, the successful functioning of the Department of Local Government (DLG) and its contribution to Good Governance of the nation are coupled with critical challenges to the present administrative system. The 10th five year plan of Bhutan examines critically the decentralisation process and its operation. The major challenges that will affect the pace and quality of decentralisation will be the weak institutional and human capacity at local levels. The government is facing the problems of inadequate resource base of local economies and institutions and the issues of the bureaucratic administrative systems and procedures that hamper the efficiency and effectiveness of local administration in Bhutan.[2] Another major challenge for the administrative system in Bhutan is the likelihood of a confrontation to happen in the local level other than the session of the National Assembly or the meetings of the Local Committee. Though the purpose of a decentralised political system is to analyse the value pluralism that permits diversity, it is not easy for the new born democracy to analyse comfortably within continuum of centralization and decentralisation of authority.[3]

2. *Corruption in the Administrative System*

The new government in power must take in to account the future challenges of political corruption in Bhutan, as the issue of corruption has been a major problem in all developing countries. With the introduction of a new political system the chances of corruption is more visible and more crucial as the political leaders in central or district level might use the legislative or executive powers for illegitimate private gain. The changed democratic government in Bhutan has to face challenges and problems like bribery, nepotism, patronage, etc. The delegation of power to the lower levels and local administrators must be clearly defined by the central authority to prevent the possibility of misuse of political power. As William Pitt, the Elder says, "Unlimited power is apt to corrupt the minds of those who possess it."[4] The nation was ranked 36th out of 178 countries according to the Transparency International Corruption Perception Index (CPI) in 2010.[5]

3. Centralisation and Authoritarian Nature of Administration

The central administrative system in Bhutan displays an increasing number of trained manpower and human resource management than at the local level. In the year 2003, over 50 percent of the total civil servants and bureaucrats were posted in the central sector and in addition the centre had most of the field posts with respect to the transfers and promotion of the staff. One can notice that the traditional Bhutanese polity was highly centralized by placing the royal households in to a hierarchy of service performers for the maintenance of foreign policy and defence of the country. Though the principle of decentralisation of administrative and financial powers has been established in Bhutan, the central government holds most of the key strategic and policy formulation authorities in the present era. This in future may result in centre-state conflicts and disturbance in the smooth functioning of government as defence and national security matters depend on decentralised coordination. Furthermore, it is clear from the history of Bhutan that various struggles and conflicts for power like the incarnations of Shabdrung have led to political crisis between penlops and monastic body for assertion of absolute power.[6] These historical facts and issues may haunt back if the existing government does not give much importance to such issues in the future.

4. *Role of Political Parties in Bhutan*

Being a new factor and alien to the Bhutanese politics, the role of political parties will be crucial in the coming years as it can cause a number of challenges to the political system of the country. The rulers of Bhutan were very cautious to avoid major risks of communal interference in the democratic process. This is the reason why the Fourth King has been very much conscious about restricting the role and forces of division of Bhutanese culture which have been fatal to the culture of consensus in the nation. Realizing the future challenges of party politics and its consequences, the constitution of Bhutan provides that party membership or establishment of a new party cannot be based on religion, sex, language, region or social origin. But still the establishments of a political party on this basis will be a challenge for the new government and administrative system in the future. Though the existence of progressives and conservatives has not generated political tensions, it is a matter of tension in the near future to the nation's political culture. The new government that came in to power in 2008 where the Druk Phensum Tshogpa (Party of Blissful Harmony, DPT) won forty-five seats out of forty-seven giving no place for a strong opposition in the National Assembly is a matter of concern. The absence of a real opposition will be a challenge for the present government. Some of the political observers feel that the introduction of democracy may create conflicts and divisions in the society where consensus played an important role in the past. As seen in other democracies, the chances of developing another political party in the state are an important challenge for Bhutan in the coming years.[7] As stated by Leo Rose:

> *"Part of the Tshogdu's weakness as a political institution, however, is the amorphous character of existing factional alignments. Here also the nonexistence of viable and enduring political association*

discourages the emergence of long-term programs and policies with a stable support base within the assembly. Moreover, under the Tshogdu's haphazard electoral system, there is limited continuity of membership, and only a small proportion of the people's representation in the Assembly at any one point in time would have had a lengthy experience in government."[8]

5. Problems of Elitism in Administration.

Bhutanese political system should provide a system in which the representatives of the people have to prove their ability to challenge the bureaucracy's elite position, so that the National Assembly can enjoy full authority in decision making. Furthermore the government also has to involve the local communities in the policymaking process for reducing the gap between rural and urban population and the authoritarian character of the central government. The history of elite domination in administration and bureaucracy should be wiped out by the new government by giving chances to young and new faces to the political sphere. As in any democratic nation, Bhutan has to be concerned about the challenges of elite domination in the governing body. The factors such as domination of royal family members in administrative and bureaucratic system and the representatives of the people being elected on the basis of rich family background will be a major challenge for the Bhutanese administrative system.

6. Problems of Dual Character of Sovereignty

Although the Fourth King gave up all his executive and administrative powers to the Royal Government of Bhutan, the Bhutanese people still consider him as the ruler and the monarch continues to keep a crucial role in the day-to-day administration in the nation. Under the new constitution of Bhutan, the Monarch is vested with significant power under the constitution and will remain as the last resort in any crisis. As the system of democracy was introduced in the nation not by a popular revolution but from the throne itself, the power and position of monarch in Bhutan is unchallengeable and the new government has to find a new balance towards a dual sovereignty. The responsibilities should be increasingly shared with the parliament and local committees and the powers of the executives in the nation would have to increase so as to successfully operate this matter.[9]

Future Socio-Cultural Problems in Bhutan

The traditional society in Bhutan has been defined as both patriarchal and matriarchal, but described as feudalistic and characterized by the absence of strong social stratification. The modern society changed in to nuclear family units from joint family units in a short period of time. Social status of a family is based on a family's economic status. The caste system prevails only among the Hindu Nepalese in the Southern Bhutan.[10] The challenges of Bhutanese society being divided on the basis of region or language are a major concern of the new government. The nation has to look forward to counter the challenges that are discussed below:

1. Use of Tobacco and Alcoholism Among the Youths

The Royal Government of Bhutan's laws for the prevention of drug trafficking and use of alcohol among youths in the country are concerned inadequate. Issues of increased cases of alcoholism in the capital worry the existing government. The negative effect of westernization of the people's lifestyle is considered as the major cause behind such incidents. The government should educate the people about the negative effects of the use of drugs and alcohol among the youth especially for those under the age of eighteen. The administrative system must try to reduce the use of alcohol inorder to reduce its adverse effects resulting in unemployment, poverty, relationship problems, divorce and parental separation, neglect and abuse of children, drunken brawls and domestic violence, crime, accidents and deaths. An alcohol-permissive society such as Bhutan's, may bring out an even bigger challenges than tobacco control in the nation under the new democratic government.[11]

2. *Poverty Eradication Programs and its Challenges*

Although Bhutan achieved successful progress to reduce poverty and alleviate the income and human dimensions of poverty, the government still has to look in to number of key challenges to the nation. The foremost challenge in front of the government lies in reducing the significant spatial disparities related to income and food levels, basic living conditions, income and food poverty variations between rural and urban areas, disparities in economic and employment opportunities, infrastructure and social services and ensuring equitable and balanced development to prevent inequalities in growth. All these factors cause enormous challenges for the country, a task made more difficult by the nature of scattered and highly dispersed population settlement in a harsh terrain for the government to fulfil. The democratic government should work for the subsistence nature of farming, increasing the levels of agricultural productivity and providing adequate rural infrastructure for the development. Full and strict commitment to the environmental sustainability could be an emerging challenge for the state with the increased pace of Modernisation and industrialisation in the country and for maintaining a careful balance with environment conservation and poverty eradication.[12]

3. The Issues of Unemployment

In any developing nation, there is a close linkage between poverty, employment and underemployment. The rapidly rising rates of educated youths who face unemployment and underemployment are a major challenge for the existing government in Bhutan. This may end up in high rate of crimes such as robbery, theft, drug abuse and prostitution in the country if not handled properly. The issue of unemployment is a major and recent phenomenon in Bhutan after the introduction of Modernisation and industrialisation, which the government has to take seriously to orient its youth for a better future. The trend of more youths migrating to the urban centres or job will result in worsening the present urban youth unemployment and result in high rate of crime in the state along with reducing the agricultural production in the state. The good governance framework under Gross National Happiness must provide for a qualified manpower to reduce the crime rate and juvenile delinquency in order to provide for the country's well-being and security in future.[13]

4. Development of Education in Bhutan

The reason behind unemployment is not lack of education but the quality of education in the country. Hence, the new democratic government should focus its governance in providing quality education to the people for a better future. Another stupendous challenge before the government is to enhance accessibility to primary education to the furthest reaches and remote areas of the country in the coming years. The government faces challenges of providing qualitative education to the people in a condition where dire shortage of good teachers, lack of basic infrastructure and the paucity of learning resources and facilities in the country prevail. Another immediate challenge that the government facing is the retention of children in the school as the incidental cost of sending children to school in both urban and rural communities appeared high. While addressing all these challenges in the education sector, the Royal Government of Bhutan should take an immediate and appropriate step towards improving the levels of enrolment, quality of education and the retention of children the school can be maintained by introducing more sustained inputs and committed resources. The Bhutan's Millennium Development Goals Needs Assessment and Costing Report 2007 estimated that education interventions would require the largest share (24.4%) of the total MDG resources needed. Between 1996 and 2015, the total education interventions are expected to cost about US $ 610 million in 2005 prices.[14]

5. Health Issues and HIV/AIDS

Despite providing improved amenities to the common people through different governmental programs, the nation still faces some basic health related issues. Difficulty in reaching out to the healthcare centre and providing adequate number of hospitals to the villages has become a serious issue in Bhutan. One of the primary concerns is that the nation needs to look for solution for expanding access to and improving maternal, neonatal, child health services and support programmes for remote rural communities. The government must address issues especially with regard to child health issues such as malnutrition and poor hygiene for rural mothers and children and improve the level of awareness and knowledge about it. Another key challenge for the government is the timely mobilization of adequate financial and technical support to implement new preventive measures in the nation. Bhutan has to address the challenges of enhancing institutional delivery and promoting access and utilization of infrastructure and medicinal care to the rural people.

The nation faces several issues and challenges with regard to the control of HIV/AIDS, its prevention, rehabilitation and care. The government should take steps towards promoting awareness among the public related to the issues and causes of this disease. The rising levels of HIV and TB co-infection should be dealt with a high priority in the health care. With regard to the latter, HIV/AIDS interventions are estimated to cost US$ 32.3 million between 2006 and 2015 or 5.9% of the total Health MDG intervention costs.[15]

6. Issues of Internet and Free Media

Today, one of the major issues that Bhutan faces is the problems of media and internet usage among youngsters and providing Information and Communication Technologies (ICT) throughout the nation. For all of these to happen, a lot of resources, political will and commitment and support from all agencies are required. In particular, financing ICT development in the country with sufficient restrictions is a challenge for the existing government.[16] Today the nation has access to many of the major global networks in the world through media and internet. Table 5.1 given below provides a clear picture of an increased number of internet users in the country from 2000 to 2010. This statistical description gives the government to take immediate necessary actions regarding the usage and control of internet usage in Bhutan for protecting its unique culture and tradition among the youth.

Table 5.1
Internet Usage and Population Statistics

YEAR	*Users*	*Population*	*% Pen.*
2000	500	8,12,184	0.0 %
2007	30,000	8,12,184	3.7 %
2009	45,000	6,91,141	6.5 %
2010	50,000	6,99,841	7.1 %
2011	1,48,770	7,08,429	21%

Source: http://www.internetworldstats.com/asia/bt.htm

Original source: International Monetary Fund.

The increasing rate of internet and visual media usage in the country may negatively affect the people, particularly children, and influencing them to act in destructive ways and that worries the government in Bhutan. Due to the fact that media is funded by the government, there is a concern, both among media professionals and citizens, that it could appear to be controlled and influenced by the state. Therefore, media professionals must do their best to report stories objectively and maintain credibility. The fact that the media industry is very young and the lack of trained and experienced media professionals will be a major challenge for the state. Today, mass media are attempting to reach a broad audience that is geographically spread out and isolated. It takes two weeks for newspapers to reach some areas. Real-time television broadcasts only reach some places in the Western region. Other areas receive delayed broadcasts. Due to these factors, rumours develop and are spread before people receive messages from the media. So, the government should take initiatives to provide access to the media both print and visual, throughout the nation effectively.[17]

The Future Economic Problems

The nation has so far successfully managed to ensure a harmonious balance between the modern economic forces and the traditional values along with the natural environment in Bhutan. As the country enters to a new phase of development and economic system, the challenges before the government and the people also got a global character as in any developing nation in the entire world community. Till the end of the monarchical system and beginning of the democratic parliamentary government, the development efforts and challenges was to a large extent, limited to basic tasks like building infrastructure, constructing roads and opening health care centres and schools. Today, under the new government in Bhutan, the focus has to be terminating the new challenges of ensuring the provision of equitable and efficient good quality social services. Under the new government the public outlay on health, education, water supply and sanitation accounts for more than 20% of the Government's expenditure. But as the population increases, and more and more people expect to have improved access to these basic social services, the burden on the exchequer can only increase. Due to the impact of modernisation, large scale migrations from rural to urban areas are expanding at an extraordinary pace. The nation should equip to deal with the issues such as influx of migrants, housing constrains, water and sanitation in the cities alone with a systematic urban planning. Realizing the adverse effects of the migration, the Royal Government of Bhutan should take initiatives to step up measures to meet the challenges deftly.[18]

1. The Challenges of Globalisation

The process of globalisation today has become an

inevitable and irreversible force in any developing nation in the world. Bhutan too confronts the relentless challenges of globalisation as with any other developing nations. The nation is facing a critical challenge to the core of its development philosophy, the Gross National Happiness, a formidable challenge for the great idea of wisdom and political acumen in the new era of Modernisation. Being exposed to the outside world for the first time in a much expanded way as never before, Bhutanese culture and tradition are confronted with crucial challenges under the process of globalisation. The government should give much importance to the people's reactions and must handle it sensitively in order to translate the fruits of globalisation to meet the needs of the people. The government should also generate mass consciousness of the values of Bhutanese culture and tradition among the youngsters to protect the society from the evils of globalisation. The challenge today before the administrative system in Bhutan is to devise mechanisms whereby the minimum standards are constantly evaluated and strictly enforced through various policy instruments throughout the nation.[19]

2. Problems of Streamlining Human Resource Management in the Country

The future success of any organizations relies on the ability to manage the human resources in the country in order to bring forward innovative ideas, perspectives, views and talent to the organization. Capitalizing on the diverse talents through proper human resource management in an organization will help face the challenges and problems by any nation. The government should analyse human resource management policies in different perspectives so as to prevent the challenges in job analysis, recruitment, types of interviews, career planning and development and methods to be adopted for the management of resources in the country. The administrative system should conduct macro and micro human resource planning to assess skilled human resource needs of the organizations within a specified time frame in order to formulate appropriate programs and policies in Bhutan. The nation must set goals based on analysis of manpower supply and demand to alleviate the problem and provide benchmark for determining the relative success or provide specific operation plan to achieve the results in the human resource management programs.

In Bhutan, the human resource development plans should function in order to achieve certain objectives and goals in the nation which is future oriented such as promotion of national self-reliance, preservation of national identity, emphasis on developing human resources in the private and public sectors and enhancement of the role of women in the development processes. The government should work for an integrated and intersectoral approach in planning the human resource development in the country for a better development. The new democratic government must strengthen and improve the infrastructures such as education and training in the country for a better future in the human resources management.[20]

3. Issues of Urbanisation and Industrialisation in Bhutan.

Bhutan is listed as the least urbanized countries in the world and thus the destabilizing effects of the urbanization frequently beset the nation's development processes. The urbanization in Bhutan leads to major problems like unemployment, mismatch of skills of the people, land degradation and air pollutions. Population pressure in urban areas increases inadequate infrastructure and aggravating tensions among the people and government in the country. The main challenging factor of urbanization before the existing government in the country is the physical environment constraints related to topography, climate and land use. The urban centres are under serious challenges due to migration of people from different parts of the country for employment and higher lifestyle that results pressure on government in expanding existing roads, telecommunication facilities, water supply and drainage, solid waste management, etc. for the increased population. According to CIA World Fact Book, about 35% of total population lives in urban areas of Bhutan in 2008 with 4.9% annual growth rate change for the period 2005-2010.[21] If these trends continue, it is estimated that the country's urban population will grow four-fold over the next 20-25 years totally challenging the existing cultural and social sustainability of the nation.[22]

The land degradation in Bhutan is man-made as well as a case of natural phenomenon as the nation progresses in its developmental curve. Land degradation in the country is mostly due to the displacement of soil material through water erosion and internal biophysical and chemical deterioration which results in visible negative effect of industrialisation. Loss of natural vegetation due to deforestation, shifting cultivation, encroachment into forest land, forest fire, etc. are some of the important factors that the democratic government should look into for sustainable development of the nation. Air pollution is another challenge before the government while adopting an industrialised based development policy. With the introduction of a number of industries in the nation, most of the forests have been cleared and the amount of carbon dioxide and other dangerous chemicals have mixed with the air and water in the last few years.

4. Developmental Issues

Political and economic changes with a rapid technological advancement in any country have ushered in new challenges and opportunities and have compelled the nation to re-examine its development policies. The population expansion, environmental issues, geographical factors, cultural history, refugee problems, disturbance from the insurgent group, growing poverty and economic disparities and protecting the unique national identity pose formidable challenges to Bhutan's sustainable development. In the era of growing interdependence with the onset of globalisation, the nation's development aspects are assuming a transnational nature. As a small landlocked country, Bhutan lacks economic and military resources. The external challenges that Bhutan faces are indeed daunting and in some cases threaten its developmental processes. The intrusion of militants group such as United Liberation Front for Assam (ULFA) and National Democratic Front of Bodoland (NDFB) who take advantage of the porous border forest lands of the South-Eastern Bhutan and of camp in eastern Nepal are some of the constraints to the country's development process as well as threat to peace, security and the territorial integrity of the nation. The issue of large-scale illegal migration through its porous borders is another serious challenge to the development process which the democratic government should look into as these problems cause disturbance in the country in the form of terrorist activities and violent demonstrations.[23]

Environmental Challenges Before the Democratic Government

Like any of the developing nations in the world, the issue of environmental sustainability in Bhutan faces a challenging future after the introduction of industrialisation and development. The environment in rural and urban settlements has deteriorated over the past two decades due to contamination of air, water and soil. These problems are compounded by a high rate of population growth in most urban areas and rapid industrialisation in the country resulting in the destruction of the forest area. Substantial inefficiencies in industrial and legal arrangements, strategic planning, insufficient resources and lack of civic responsibilities among the Bhutanese are some of the important issues that the government should take immediate step in protecting its natural environment.

For a country that is thinly populated, ecologically fragile, with limited resources and in the first stage of industrialisation, the problems of a sustainable environment are a major threat to the nation in the coming years. In Bhutan, the two urban centres such as Thimphu, Paro and Phuntsholing exhibit a complexity of environmental and social issues. Inadequate management of solid waste and wastewater are some the conspicuous environmental issues that the government should make appropriate legislation in the present atmosphere. The local and central administrative system should try to improve the existing insufficient infrastructure planning and services in the nation. The environmental sustainability in the urban areas further compounded with the population growth rate mostly due to rural-urban migration for better livelihood. Due to the fast growing urbanization process it is envisaged that by 2020 the issue of solid waste management and associated environmental problems will increase challenges to the government in Bhutan. The effect of rapid urbanization on the environment of Bhutan is well recognized by the Royal Government and it is trying to make a reputation as a clean and green country in the coming future.[24]

Though Bhutan relatively isolated and not too vulnerable to population pressure, the environmental and biodiversity aspects are not free from problems and challenges. The problem of deforestation is increasing as the people clear forest in several parts of the country trying to make room for agriculture, and that makes the tropical and sub-tropical zones of the south and the temperate zones of the interior under serious risk. In several parts of the country, livestock quantities exceed the natural carrying capacity of the land. The nation should encourage the people for sustainable agricultural activities that keep the ecology and bio-diversity unthreatened. In the wake of these deforestation activities, the wildlife is forced to survive within fragmented spaces that in the future can lead to loss of biodiversity and degradation of ecological issues. The government should introduce a new strategy for keeping the wildlife alive especially of the rare species in the Himalayan forests.

The Gross National Happiness Issues in Bhutan

Under the new pattern of development and urbanization in Bhutan, the implementation of Gross National Happiness (GNH) is challenged and is under serious threat. With the introduction of a globalised economical structure the contradictions between market economy and GNH is visible in the modern Bhutan. The increasing economic liberalization and social Modernisation have brought an influx of different cultures to Bhutan which causes some new conflicts of interests in the Bhutanese society that the government should be aware of addressing before the situation increases in severity. It is possible many of the conventional economic programs for a developed nation hold very little intrinsic interest and significance to the unique idea of Gross National Happiness.

The problems in the use of television and internet is another challenge for the GNH concept as the amount of time being consumed on television and internet has increased tremendously which results in the breakdown in the verbal interaction between family members causing a weak relationship even within the family. This is been illustrated succinctly by A.S. Evans, who wrote:

> *There is a Bhutanese folktale that poignantly, yet delightfully, portrays that happiness and prosperity are not necessarily one and the same. The story titled "Meme Haylay Haylay and His Turquoise" is about an old man who begins the day finding a priceless turquoise and exchanges the jewel with a horse, the horse for an ox, and the ox for a sheep, the sheep for goat, the goat for a rooster, and in the end the rooster for a song. The words of Buddhist master Shantideva summarize this story well: "The goal of every act is happiness itself, though, even with great wealth, it's rarely found".*[25]

The Western cultural norms such as materialism and individualism pose a direct threat to the original base of Gross National Happiness in Bhutan with the introduction of Modernisation. It was originally based on economic development while making conscious effect to preserve the traditional Bhutanese culture and prevent the society from the evil influence of a consumerist ideology and from any subsequent social and economic fragmentation. The government has to take necessary steps for protecting the unique culture and tradition of Bhutan so as not to endanger its development policies based on GNH and towards Modernisation of its economy. Such emphasis should be initiated for preserving and promoting the traditional aspects of Bhutanese culture so that the people can grow economically as well as spiritually by giving importance to happiness rather than Gross National Product.[26]

Conclusion

Threat to natural resources in Bhutan have increased

in the 21st century with the increase of economic growth, demographic changes and increased population growth. To face all these challenges, strong institutional, legal and policy framework, capacity building and awareness and innovative funding mechanisms should be developed by the government in the country. For Bhutan, the possibility of challenges to arise from different sources should be dealt with proper understanding of the situation in which the nation moves towards development. The government must keep its eyes wide open when it functionalizes the ideas of globalisation, industrialisation, Modernisation and urbanization in Bhutan. Coming out of the traditional character of isolation and Buddhist spiritual ideologies, Modernisation has been a credible alternative to revolution in Bhutan. The political visions and the leadership characters of the previous kings will remain an inspiration for the present democratic government in protecting the future challenges. The nation's state of development at the edge of modernity with a new democratic government at the centre and drafting a new written constitution will create an opportunity to monitor transition to a developed nation by tackling all the challenges in an orderly way.

NOTES

1. Mathou, Thierry (2008), *How to Reform a Traditional Buddhist Monarchy- The Political Achievements of His Majesty Jigme Singye Wangchuck, the Fourth King of Bhutan (1972-2006)*, Centre for Bhutan Studies, Bhutan.
2. The Royal Government of Bhutan , (2006), *10th Five year Plan*, Planning Commission, Bhutan.
3. Ura, Karma (2004) *Peasantry and Bureaucracy in Decentralization in Bhutan*, Institute of Developing Economies, Discussion Paper No.17, December 2004. p.1. Availabel at: http://

www.ide.go.jp/English/Publish/Download/Dp/pdf/017.pdf

4. Safire, William (2008) *Safire's political dictionary*, Oxford University Press, US, p. 566
5. Transparency International, 2010, *Corruption Perspective Index 2010 Results*. Available at: http://www.transparency.org/policy_research/surveys_indices/cpi/2010/results
6. Ura, Karma (2004), n.3, p.4.
7. Mathou, Thierry (2008), n. 1.
8. Rose, Leo E. (1977), *The Politics of Bhutan*, Cornell University Press, New York. p.165.
9. Mathou, Thierry (2008), n.1.
10. Mongabay, *Bhutan- Social System*, September 1991. Available at: http://www.mongabay.com/history/bhutan/bhutan-social_system.html
11. Dorji, Chencho (2005) *The Myth Behind Alcohol Happiness*, paper Presented at the Second Conference on Gross National Happiness, St. Francis Xavier University, Antigonish, Nova Scotia, Canada on June 20 to June 24, 2005. Available at: http://www.gpiatlantic.org/conference/papers/dorji.pdf
12. Royal Government of Bhutan, *Bhutan's Progress: Midway to the Millennium Development Goals*, Bhutan, November, 2008. Available at: http://www.undp.org.bt/assets/files/publication/MDG_Midway.pdf
13. Sebastian, Sarish (2011) *"Good Governance and Bhutan's political Structure: Problems and Prospects"* in Sigamani P. and N.U. Khan, (eds.), Reinventing Public Management and Development in Emerging Economies, Macmillan Publishers, New Delhi, India. P. 863-864
14. Royal Government of Bhutan, (2008), n.12.
15. Ibid.
16. International Development Research Centre, Canada. Available at: http://www.idrc.ca/its/ev-140931-201-1-DOTOPIC.html
17. Dorji, Kinley and Siok Sian Pek, (2005), THE MEDIA IN BHUTAN : In the service of the public, Paper Presented at the Second Conference on Gross National Happiness, St. Francis Xavier University, Antigonish, Nova Scotia, Canada on June 20 to June 24, 2005. Available at: http://www.gpiatlantic.org/conference/papers/pek-dorji.pdf
18. Bhutan National Human Development Report 2000, *Gross*

National Happiness and Human Development – Searching for Common Ground, The Planning Commission Secretariat Royal Government of Bhutan, Thimphu. p.30-32.

19. Wangchuk, Norbu, *Globalisation: A Challenge to Gross National Happiness*, Royal Institute of Management, Thimphu, Bhutan. Available at: http://www.rim.edu.bt/Publication/Archive/rigphel/rigphel1/globalisation.htm
20. United Nations, Human Resources Development, *Twelfth Meeting of Experts on the United Nations Programme in Public Administration and Finance*, New York, 31 July-11 August 1995. Available at: http://unpan1.un.org/intradoc/groups/public/documents/un/unpan000780.pdf
21. The Odora.com, *Bhutan People 2011*, January 13, 2011. Available at: http://www.theodora.com/wfbcurrent/bhutan/bhutan_people.html
22. South Asia Co-operative Environment Program. Available at: http://www.sacep.org/html/mem_bhutan.htm
23. The Royal Government of Bhutan, *9th Five Year Plan*, Planning Commission, Thimphu, Bhutan. P.50-51.
24. Clean Bhutan-RSPN, *Clean Bhutan Project*, 2007. Available at: http://cleanbhutan.rspnbhutan.org/?page_id=7
25. Evans, A. S. (2006) *Promoting "Gross National Happiness" in Bhutan Through Her Rich Oral Traditions. Journal of Bhutan Studies.* Vol. 15 (Winter 2006): p. 137.
26. Chua, Melissa (2008), *The Pursuit of Happiness: Issues Facing Bhutanese Youths and the Challenges Posed to Gross National Happiness*, Institute of South Asian Studies Internship Program, University of Singapore. Available at: http://www.isas.nus.edu.sg/Attachments/Research Attachment/Report%20-%20Melissa%20%2813%20Aug%2008%29.pdf

Chapter 6

Conclusion

"Whosoever desires constant success must change his conduct with the times." — **Niccolo Machiavelli**

In the modern world, no nation can afford to think or act separately without the cooperation of the other nation, as countries are coming closer with the new concept of globalisation and economic development through people's welfare. Under these circumstances, the tiny Kingdom of Bhutan is reconstructing its political and economic programmes since 1960s to develop a modern socio-economic and political structure protecting its unique tradition and culture. Being a land-locked nation, sandwiched between two Asian giants, Bhutan successfully adopted and changed to a modern nation without losing its tradition and culture. Though Bhutan is faced with many challenges on the process of modernisation, the rulers of the nation successfully managed those challenges with the unique principle of Gross National Happiness (GNH).

With the establishment of a Hereditary Monarchical

system in the country, Bhutan entered in to the world of change and development. Though the first two Kings followed the policy of isolation from outer world, they began to transform the inner political structure of Bhutan during their period. The Third King was the driving force behind the modernisation of the country by bringing Bhutan in to the outside world and started to go beyond the boundaries of the nation. He began to modernise the political system from monarchy to democracy. He introduced many institutions and delegated his power to those institutions and initiated the procedure to include the common men in decision-making process. During the reign of the Fourth King, the nation witnessed a number of democratic changes in the country and he provided a unique philosophy of Gross National Happiness (GNH) to the nation that would guide the nation and rulers in fulfilling the needs of time. He further stressed on enhanced foreign relations with other nations especially in the West and East to facilitate the process of modernisation and development. During his period, he delegated most of his powers to the parliament which was elected on the basis of adult suffrage.

The process of modernisation has totally changed the face of Bhutan in a short period of time surprising its neighbours and the entire world. The nation showed to the world that modernisation does not mean to abandon one's tradition and culture, but in developing one's own socio-political and cultural factors on the basis of set traditions and culture and keeping alive the spirit of unity and happiness. From the periods of Shabdrung to the present parliamentary government, one can easily find out that the nation has changed a lot in its social, political and economic fields without much change or transformation of its century old traditions and culture.

Bhutanese people share a common thread of simple

social, communal and spiritual values that makes the preservation and promotion of the nation's unique culture and tradition as the centrepiece for laying the foundation of the identity of the people as well as the kingdom. The nation gives high priority for the preservation and promotion of culture along with economic self-reliance, environmental preservation and good governance. Bhutan, though a small kingdom, provides for a unique paradigm with the main motivation force behind human effort as not only economic growth but also the cultivation of a humane society, the ultimate goal of the happiness of all people.[1]

Developmental activities are inevitable and important for any country in this globalisation era, but the governments of every country should manage to provide for a balance between the overall goals of sustainable development and environmental conservation and cultural preservation. Bhutan has been successful in managing its development and modernisation in its socio-political structure and in improving the living standards of the people by ensuring a harmonious balance between the natural environments and protecting its cultural heritage since 1961. In a short span of five decades, Bhutan witnessed numerous institutional changes in the political structure. This facilitated the enhancement of security, stability and advancement of the country from an isolated undeveloped nation in 20th century to a sovereign developing nation in the 21st century.

The process of modernisation undoubtedly depicts the planning and effect of institutional changes by the government which is consistent with the needs of time and aspirations of people. This thus provided for a capacity development, institutional development and empowerment of the political system of Bhutan. These developmental processes helped the nation to avoid any from of abuse of power and institutions in the country. The drafting of a new constitution for the Kingdom of Bhutan appears to be a golden step towards the modernisation of the political system of the country in the 21st century. Though the nation moved towards a democratic parliamentary system of government, the King has kept some defree of influence on the political sphere and in the nation's destiny. He still influences the lawmaking processes, the selection for the candidate of constitutional offices and him being the Supreme Commander of the armed forces. Hopefully, the peaceful experiences of the Bhutanese people with the new constitution and a stable democratic government will grant them a position in the international politics.[2]

The thinking of the people is gradually changing towards a modern socio-political life style as the country enters into the mainstream of development along with other nations. The use of internet and television is seeping in to the country and having a strong impact in the life of the Bhutanese people. In order to manage this inevitable development, the Royal Government of Bhutan has laid a higher priority on the preservation and promotion of culture and tradition. The foreign policy of the nation helped the nation to grow in a balanced development by choosing only limited nations for its relations who does not have any particular interest in the economy and politics of the nation. The nation has defined its developmental goals guided by the principles of GNH to maximise the happiness of the people and providing a better life style and good governance to them.[3] The modern democratic system of good governance placed the legislature as an important and prestigious organ of the government in the law making procedure. The parliament has tried to promote the welfare of the people through legislation and discussion regarding the development of all the sectors as well as organs of the government. Strengthening the principles of good governance, the democratic parliament through its organs reaching even to the grass root level understood the needs of the people. The beginning of participatory governance provided the Bhutanese citizens a sense of responsibility and belongingness in the decision making process.[4]

The modernisation process of the economy of the nation is necessary for the attainment of the goals of GNH. The social and political development in the recent past helped the nation to provide good governance than the neighbouring countries. Since 1960s, the nation showed an increasing momentum in the economic development as it opened its borders to the outside world. The globalisation effect made the economy of the nation to develop in to much more than the rulers expected. The following tables give information about the economic growth of the country from 1980 to 2012. In the near future, the concept of GNH will achieve a great place along with GDP, GNP and GNI. The example of Bhutan will be a guiding factor for the international community in developing its socio- economic and political sphere for the happiness of the people rather looking for temporal developments.

Table 6.1
Structure and Growth of Bhutanese Economy: 1980-2010

Year	*Contribution to Economy*				*Growth of Economy*
	Primary	*Secondary*	*Tertiary*	*Finance*	*Growth Rate in %*
1980-1985	43.73	17.07	39.22	2.25	8.05
1986-1990	38.66	21.80	39.56	3.00	10.14
19991-1995	35.08	26.24	38.66	2.54	4.70
1996-2000	31.56	30.68	37.76	3.38	6.34
2001-2005	26.52	34.88	38.62	3.92	7.64

2006-2010	21.01	39.47	36.37	5.74	9.32

Source: National Statistical Bureau of Bhutan 2010

Table 6.2
GDP Per Capita of Bhutan: 2005 to 2010

Year	*2005*	*2006*	*2007*	*2008*	*2009*	*2010*	*2011*
Per-capita GDP (USD)	1267.62	1350.15	1812.50	1854.52	1868.35	2186.89	

Source: National Statistical Bureau of Bhutan 2010

Table 6.3
Gross domestic product per capita at current prices

Year	*2009*	*2010*	*2011*	*2012*
Per-capita GDP (USD)	1921.78	2009.21	2121.17	2284.88

International Monetary Fund

Table 6.4
GDP by major Sectors in Current Prices, 2008-2011

Sector	*2008*	*2009*	*2010*	*2011*
Primary	11330.20	12550.70	13794.72	15401.10
Secondary	22365.30	24303.30	29396.61	32873.00
Tertiary	21017.40	24369.50	29286.28	37306.50
GDP	54713.00	61223.50	72477.61	85580.60

Source: National Accounts Division, NSB.

Table 6.5
Share of the GDP by major sectors in current process, 2008-2011

Sector	*2008*	*2009*	*2010*	*2011*
Primary	20.71	20.50	19.03	18.08
Secondary	40.88	39.70	40.56	38.41
Tertiary	38.41	39.80	40.41	43.59
Total GDP	100.00	100.00	100.00	100.00

Source: National Accounts Division, NSB.

Table 6.6
GDP growth rates by sectors, 2008-2011

Sector	*2008*	*2009*	*2010*	*2011*
Primary	2.53	1.60	1.13	4.00
Secondary	5.48	4.10	12.73	3.23
Tertiary	4.82	12.19	15.45	15.67
Total GDP	4.67	6.73	11.77	8.51

Source: National Accounts Division, NSB.

The modernisation is a recent phenomenon that needs to attain a smooth functioning and adaptation by the Bhutanese people. The process of urbanisation is moving fast in the country since sixties and seventies giving rise to all sorts of co-existence between tradition and modernity. The government and people in Bhutan look for a negotiated development between modernisation and tradition in order to preserve the identity and culture of the nation. The modernisation process should alleviate the problems of poverty as about 30 percent of the people live below poverty line according to the Census of 2005.[5] The government must take in to account the emerging issues of alcoholism among the youngsters due to the influence of west.

Bhutan stands on the threshold of many challenges in the modernisation process, as the concept is new to the people as well as the government. In the race towards development and modernisation, maintaining its identity, sovereignty and security as a nation state should remain as the primary concern for Bhutan. The nation under the parliamentary democratic setup has to share its powers between the central and local committees and political parties to find out a balance in the country. One of the major challenges faced by the government will be the wide gap between the rich and poor, educated and uneducated and rural and urban population. The political system of the country should try to involve all sets of people in its decision making process. As a major factor in the political development, the political parties will have to play a crucial role in the future in stabilizing the balance and strengthening the parliamentary system. The First General Elections in 2008 witnessed a new era in the political behaviour of Bhutanese politics as the Election Commission of Bhutan introduced a fractional debate rather duelling allegations of vote buying the elections. The Fourth King has showed an example to the entire world that reforming a traditional society does not necessarily mean the destruction of its culture or tradition, but a planned policy implementation and governance is needed.[6] In order to achieve smooth progress in the development process, Bhutan should be ready to face and adopt proactive measures against the challenges of inevitable forces of changes such as urbanisation, unemployment and pollution.

In the effort to make a modern state with the western principles, Bhutan has been doing almost unbelievably well in the past few decades. The nation holds a unique character of a nation that was never ruled by any colonial masters, but adopted the foreign ideologies and made a rapid and successful effort to build a modern state. The nation in the 21st century resembles a nation state where the politicians and the political institutions are severely restricted in their powers under the constitution giving shape to a perfect administrative unit. Leo E. Rose has analysed that the Bhutanese political system is unique because it cannot be compared with the other nation's political system. He argues that;

> *"Political reform, Bhutanese style, is a specially demanding challenge because there is no system to emulate, no similar situation to draw*

> *from. Bhutan is creating its won unique system of governance, an initiative which is as bold as it is risky. Political analysts would be hard pushed to identify another similar experiment of this daring and magnitude"*[7]

The Kingdom of Bhutan has adopted a multi-dimensional approach to modernisation and development by balancing the spiritual and material factors together. The unique principle of GNH, which guided the nation throughout its modernisation process, will help the nation to grow further and develop all section of the community. Modernisation is a difficult term to adopt and accept by a traditional society like Bhutan as every approach towards it challenges the basic culture and tradition of the nation. But, in a globalised world a nation cannot stand alone avoiding the factors of change and development. So the nation always endeavours to select the most beneficial aspects of the change in order to increase human happiness and providing the Bhutanese people the best life style.[8] The new democratic government of Bhutan in the last three years has chose diverse policies for development to steer the country towards modernisation, promotion of culture and preservation of environment. I would like to conclude my thesis pointing out that there is something more important than a society ruled by consumer or material values and principles. That is what the Kingdom of Bhutan shows to other nations in the international level that the promotion of happiness, identity, culture and tradition which are also as important as the material goals of globalisation and modernisation. The process of change in Bhutan will continue to gain momentum in the future and become a unique nation to preserve its century old tradition alive while modernising its socio-cultural and economic-political sphere guided by the principles of Gross National Happiness rather Gross National Product.

NOTES

1. Wangchuk, Dorji (2008) *Country Report: Bhutan*, Asia/Pacific Cultural Centre for UNESCO (ACCU). Available at: http://www.accu.or.jp/ich/en/training/country_report_pdf/08_09/country_report_bhutan_03.pdf
2. Hofmann, Klaus *Democratisation From Above: The Case of Bhutan*. Available at: http://www.democracy-international.org/fileadmin/di/pdf/papers/di-bhutan.pdf
3. Upreti, B.C. (2005), *Gross National Happyness and Foreign Policy of Bhutan :Interlinkages and Imperatives*, Paper Presented at the The Second International Conference on Gross National Happiness, St. Francis Xavier University, Antigonish, Nova Scotia, Canada on June 20 to June 24, 2005. Available at: http://www.gpiatlantic.org/conference/papers/upreti.pdf.
4. Sebastian, Sarish, (2011), "*Good Governance and Bhutan's political Structure:Problems and Prospects*" in Sigamani P. and N.U. Khan, (eds.), Reinventing Public Management and Development in Emerging Economies, Macmillan Publishers, New Delhi, India. P. 863-864.
5. Balasubramanian, N. and Jigme Nidup , (2007) *Role of Media in the Changing Socio-Political Situation in Bhutan*. Available at: http://www.bhutanstudies.org.bt/pubFiles/M-17.pdf
6. Mathou, Thierry (2008), *How to Reform a Traditional Buddhist Monarchy- The Political Achievements of His Majesty Jigme Singye Wangchuck, the Fourth King of Bhutan (1972-2006)*, Centre for Bhutan Studies, Bhutan.
7. Rose, Leo E. (1977), *The Politics of Bhutan*, Cornell University Press, New York, p. 188.
8. Thinley, Jigmi Y. *Values and Development: "Gross National Happiness"*, Text of the Keynote Speech Delivered at the Millennium Meeting for Asia and the Pacific, 30 October - 1 November 1998 Seoul, Republic of Korea

Bibliography

Books:

1. Acharya, Sanjay (1999) *Bhutan: Kingdom in the Himalaya*, Roli Books Publisher, India.
2. Alahari, S. Prasad (1997) *Modernism, Alienation and Media Behaviour*, T.R. Publications, Chennai.
3. Ardussi, John and Françoise Pommaret (ed) (2007) *Bhutan: Traditions and Changes*, BRILL, the Netherlands.
4. Aris, Michael (1994b) "*Conflict and Conciliation in Traditional Bhutan*" in: Michael Hutt (ed.) Bhutan: Perspectives on Conflict and Dissent, Kiscadale Publications (Kiscadale Asia Research Series No. 4), Gartmore.
5. Aris, Michael (1994a) The *Raven Crown: The Origins of Buddhist Monarchy in Bhutan*, Serindia Publications, London.
6. Aris, Micheal, (1980) *Bhutan: The Early History of Himalayan Kingdom*, Vikas Publications, New Delhi.
7. Belcher, B. M. (1998) *A production-to-consumption Systems Approach: Lessons from the Bamboo and Rattan Sectors in Asia*, in Wollenberg, E. and Ingles A. (ed) Incomes from the Forest: Methods for the Development and Conservation of Forest Products for Local Communities, CIFOR, Bogor, Indonesia.
8. Bernal, Martin (1987) *Black Athena: The Afro-Asiatic Roots of Classical Civilisation*, Rutgers University Press, USA.
9. Berthold, John (2005) *Bhutan: Land of the Thunder Dragon*,

Wisdom Publications, Somerville.

10. Bhardway, Vinod Kumar (1996) *Geography as a Factor in Bhutan's Development*, in Ramakant and R.C. Misra, (ed.), Bhutan – Society and Polity, Indus Publishing, New Delhi.
11. Bhattacharya, S. S. (1996) *Bhutan Towards Moderni-sation*, in Ramakant and R.C. Misra (ed.) Bhutan – Society and Polity, Indus Publishing, New Delhi.
12. Bhola, P.L. (1996) *Bhutan-Pakistan Relations*, in and R.C. Misra (ed.) Bhutan – Society and Polity, Indus Publishing, New Delhi.
13. Bhradwaj, Vinod Kumar (1996) *Geography as a Factor in Bhutan's Development*, in Ramakant and R.C.Mishra, Bhutan: Society and Polity, Indus Publishing, New Delhi.
14. Bisht, Medha (2010) Sino-Bhutan Boundary Negotia-tions: Complexities of the 'Package Deal', Institute for Defence Studies and Analysis, January 19, 2010. Available at: http://www.idsa.in/idsacomments/Sino-BhutanBoundary Negotiations_mbisht_190110
15. Bloom, William (1990) *Personal Identity, National Identity and International Relations*, Cambridge University Press, Cambridge.
16. Brown, Lindsay, Bradley Mayhew, Stan Armington, and Richard W Whitecross, *Bhutan: Lonely Planet Bhutan*, Lonely Planet Publisher, Great Britain.
17. C. Khanna, Vinod (1996) *Indo-Bhutan Relations in the Changing South Asian Context*, in Ramakant and R.C. Misra (ed.) Bhutan – Society and Polity, Indus Publishing, New Delhi.
18. C., Mathew Joseph (1996) *Political Economy of Ethnic Conflict in Bhutan*, in: Ramakant and R.C. Misra (ed) Bhutan – Society and Polity, Indus Publishing, New Delhi.
19. C., Mathew Joseph (1999) *Ethnic Conflict in Bhutan*, Nirala Publications, New Delhi.
20. Chakravarty, S.R. (1996) *Language and Literature in Bhutan*, in Ramakant and R.C. Misra (ed.) Bhutan – Society and Polity, Indus Publishing, New Delhi.
21. Choden, Tashi, (2004), Indo-Bhutan Relations Recent Trends, Journal of Bhutan Studies, Volume 11.
22. Choden, Tashi & Dorji Penjore (2004). *Economic and Political Relation Between Bhutan and Neighbouring Countries*, The Centre for Bhutan Studies, Thimphu.
23. Choudhury, Tapash and K. Roy, (1993) *State Building in Modern Bhutan (1616-1990): A Structural Functional Analysis*, in Manis

Kumar Raha and Iar Ali Khan (ed) Polity, Political Process and Social Control in South Asia: The Tribal and Rural Perspectives, Gyan Books, New Delhi.

24. Christine, Blanche, (1979) *Ancient Bhutan: A Study on Early Buddhism in the Himalayas*, Olschak Publisher, Swiss Foundation for Alpine Research.
25. Collister, Peter, (1987) *Bhutan and the British*, Serindia Publications with Belitha Press, London.
26. Crossette, Barbara (1995) *So Close to Heaven, The Vanishing Buddhist Kingdoms of the Himalayas*, Vintage Books, USA.
27. Das, B.S. (1995) *Mission to Bhutan: A Nation in Transition*, Vikas Publishing House, New Delhi.
28. Das, Nirmala, (1974) *The Dragon Country: The General History of Bhutan*, Orient Longman Publisher, India.
29. Deepa Mathur (1996), Socio-Economic Transformation in Bhutan: Prospects and Constraints, in Ramakant and R.C. Misra (ed) Bhutan – Society and Polity, Indus Publishing, New Delhi.
30. Dhakal, D.N.S. and Christopher Strawn (1994) *Bhutan: A Movement in Exile*, Nirala Publications, Jaipur.
31. Dixit, Kanak Mani (1994) *"Looking for Greater Nepal"* in Michael Hutt (ed.) Bhutan: Perspectives on Conflict and Dissent, Kiscadale Publications (Kiscadale Asia Research Series No. 1), Gartmore.
32. Dorji, Dasho Rinzin, (1989) A Brief religious, Cultural and Secular History of Bhutan, New York: The Asia Society Galleries.
33. Dua, M.R. and V.S. Gupta (ed.) (1994) *Media and Development:Themes in Communication and Extension*, Har-Anand Publications, New Delhi.
34. Dubey, Swaroop Rani (1996): *Buddhism in Bhutan and Sri Lanka: A Comparative Study*, in Ramakant and R.C. Misra, (ed.), Bhutan – Society and Polity, Indus Publishing, New Delhi.
35. Foote, Daisy (2007) *Bhutan*, Dramatists Play Service Publisher, India
36. Gillespie, Michael Allen (2008) *The Theological Origins of Modernity*, University of Chicago Press, USA.
37. Gupta, Bhabani Sen (1999) *Bhutan: Towards a Grass-root Participatory Polity*, Konark Publishers, New Delhi.
38. Gupta, S.S. (1996) *Indo-Bhutan Relations*, in Ramakant and R.C.

Misra (ed.) Bhutan – Society and Polity, Indus Publishing, New Delhi.

39. Gupta, Shantiswarup, (1974) *British Relations with Bhutan*, Panchsheel Prakashan Publishers, India.
40. Hutt, Michael (2003) *Unbecoming Citizens: Culture, Nationhood, and the Flight of Refugees from Bhutan*. Oxford University Press, New Delhi.
41. Jayapalan, N. (2000) *India and Her Neighbours*, Atlantic Publishers and Distributors, New Delhi.
42. Jigmi Thinley (1996): Current Situation in Bhutan, in Ramakant and R.C. Misra (ed), Bhutan – Society and Polity, Indus Publishing, New Delhi.
43. John W. Garver (2001) *Protracted Contest: Sino-Indian Rivalry in the Twentieth Century*, University of Washington Press, Seattle.
44. Joseph, Mathew C. (1999) *Ethnic Conflict in Bhutan*, Nirala Publications, New Delhi 1999.
45. Keane, John (2009) *The Life and Death of Democracy*, Simon and Schuster, London.
46. Kennedy, Timothy (2009) *Where the Rivers Meet the Sky: A Collaborative Approach to Participatory Development*, University of Alaska Press, Alaska.
47. Kharat, Rajesh (2005) Foreign policy of Bhutan, Manak Publications, New Delhi.
48. Kharat, Rajesh (2009) *Indo-Bhutan Relations: Strategic Perspective*, in K. Warikoo (ed), Himalayan Frontiers of India: Historical, Geo-Political and Strategic Perspectives, Taylor & Francis, New York,
49. Kohli, Manorama (1982) *India and Bhutan: a Study in Interrelations, 1772-1910*, Munshiram Manoharlal Publisher, India.
50. Kohli, Manorama (1993) *From Dependency to Interdependence: A Study of Indo-Bhutan Relations*, Vikas Publishing House, India.
51. Kristof, Nicholas D. And Sheryl WuDunn (2001) *Thunder From the East – Portrait of a Rising Asia*, Vintage Books, New York.
52. Kymlicka, Will (1995) *Multicultural Citizenship: A Liberal Theory of Minority Rights*, Clarendon Press, Oxford.
53. Labh, Kapileshwar (1974) *India and Bhutan*, Volume 1 of Studies in Asian History and Politics, Sindhu Publications, India.
54. Labh, Kapileshwar (1996) *Political Development of Bhutan: Emerging Trends*, in Ramkant and R.C. Mishra (ed) Bhutan;

Society and Polity, Indus Publishers, New Delhi.

55. Lijphart; Arend (1977) *Democracy in Plural Societies: A Comparative Exploration.* Yale University Press, New Haven and London.
56. M.D. Dharamdhasani (1996) *Economic Development and Modernisation in Bhutan,* in Ramakant and R.C. Misra (ed) Bhutan – Society and Polity, Indus Publishing, New Delhi.
57. Mahendra P. Lama (1996) *Bhutan: A changing Development Paradigm,* in Ramakant and R.C. Misra (ed) Bhutan – Society and Polity, Indus Publishing, New Delhi.
58. Manorama Kohli (1996) *Ethnic Crisis in Bhutan: Implications,* in Ramakant and R.C. Misra (ed) Bhutan – Society and Polity, Indus Publishing, New Delhi.
59. Marshall Cavendish Corporation, (2007) *World and its People: Eastern and Southern Asia,* Marshall Cavendish, India.
60. Mathou, Thierry (1994) *"The Growth of Diplomacy in Bhutan 1961-1991: Opportunities and Challenges"* in Michael Aris and Michael Hutt (eds) Bhutan: Aspects of Culture and Development, Kiscadale (Kiscadale Asia Research Series No. 5), Gartmore.
61. Meenakshi Misra & R.C. Misra (1996) *Bhutan's Foreign Policy in the New Context,* in Ramakant and R.C. Misra (ed.) Bhutan – Society and Polity, Indua Publishing, New Delhi.
62. Mehra, G. N. (1974) *Bhutan: Land of the Peaceful Dragon,* Vikas Publishing House, India.
63. Parmanand (1992) *The Politics of Bhutan: Retrospect And Prospect,* Pragati Publications, New Delhi.
64. Parmanand (1996) *Bhutan's Problem of Ethnicity: Causes, Consequences and Prospects,* in Ramakant and R.C. Misra (ed.) Bhutan – Society and Polity, Indus Publishing, New Delhi.
65. Rabgye, Sonam T. (1996) *Indo-Bhutan Relations,* in Ramakant and R.C. Misra (ed.) Bhutan – Society and Polity, Indus Publishing, New Delhi.
66. Rahul, Ram, (1971) Modern Bhutan, Vikas Publications, India.
67. Rahul, Ram, (1997) *Royal Bhutan: A Political History,* Vikas Publishing House, India.
68. Ramphel, Norbu (2000) *Bhutan: The Emergence of a Nation-State,* Anmol Publications, New Delhi.
69. Ramakant and Ramesh Chandra Misra (ed) (1996) *Bhutan: Society and Polity* Indus Publishing House, New Delhi.

70. Rennie, Frank and Robin Mason (ed) (2008) Bhutan: Ways of Knowing, IAP, USA
71. Rizal, Dhurba P. (2001) *Bhutan: Decentralisation and Good Governance*, Adroit Publishers, New Delhi.
72. Rizal, Dhurba P. (2002) *Administrative System in Bhutan: Retrospect and Prospect*, Adroit Publishers, New Delhi.
73. Robert, Geoffrey K. (1971) *A Dictionary of Political Analysis*, Longman, London.
74. Rose, Leo E. (1977) The Politics of Bhutan, Cornell University Press, New York.
75. Rustomji, Nari (1978) *Bhutan: The Dragon Kingdom in Crisis*, Oxford University Press, London.
76. Schicklgruber, Christian and Françoise Pommaret-Imaeda (ed) (2000) *Bhutan: Mountain Fortress of the Gods*, Serindia Publisher, London.
77. Sebastian, Sarish, (2011) *"Good Governance and Bhutan's Political Structure: Problems and Prospects"* in Sigamani P. and N.U. Khan, (eds.) Reinventing Public Manage-ment and Development in Emerging Economies, Macmillan Publishers, New Delhi.
78. Shakya, Tshering (1999) *The Dragon in the Land of Snows – A History of Modern Tibet since 1947*, Pimlico, London.
79. Sharma, Jai Prakash, 1996, The Nature and Direction of Political Change in Bhutan, in Ramkant and R.C. Mishra (ed), Bhutan; Society and Polity, Indus Publishers, New Delhi.
80. Singh, Nagendra, (1972) *Bhutan: A Kingdom in the Himalayas; A Study of the Land, Its People, and Their Government*, Thomson Press Publication Division, India.
81. Sinha, A.C. (1991) Bhutan – Ethnic Identity and National Dilemma, Reliance Publishing House, New Delhi.
82. Sinha, A. C. (2001) *Himalayan Kingdom Bhutan: Traditions, Transition and Transformation*, Indus Publishing Company, New Delhi, 2001.
83. Sinha, A. C. (1994) *Bhutan in 1993: Continuing Ethnic Stalemate.* Asian Survey 34(2), University of California Press, USA.
84. Tatsuo, Inoue (1999) *"Liberal Democracy and Asian Orientalism"*, in Joanne Bauer and Daniel Bell (eds) The East Asian Challenge for Human Rights, Cambridge University Press, Cambridge.
85. Thinley, Jigmi Y. (1994) *"Bhutan: A Kingdom Besieged"* in Michael Hutt (ed.) Bhutan: Perspectives on Conflict and Dissent, Kiscadale Publications (Kiscadale Asia Research

Series No. 4), Gartmore.

86. Thurman, Robert A. F. (1996) *"Human Rights and Human Responsibilities: Buddhist Views on Individualism and Altruism"* in Irene Bloom et al. (eds.) Religious Diversity and Human Rights, Columbia University Press, New York and Chichester.
87. Upadhyay, Shashi (1996) *Bhutan and SAARC*, in Ramakant and R.C. Mishra (ed), Bhutan; Society and Polity, Indus Publishers, New Delhi.
88. Upreti, B.C. (1996) *The Nepali Immigrants in Bhutan: Growing Conflict Between National and Ethnic Identitities*, in Ramakant and R.C. Mishra (ed), Bhutan; Society and Polity, Indus Publishers, New Delhi.
89. Upreti, Sonia, (1996) *Status of Women in Bhutan*, in Ramakant and R.C.Mishra (ed) Bhutan: Society and Polity, Indus Publishing, New Delhi.
90. Ura, Karma (2002) *"Perception of Security,"* in Dipankar Banerjee (eds.) South Asian Security, Future: a Dialogue of Directors Regional Strategic Studies Institutes, Regional Centre for Strategic Studies, Colombo.
91. Ura, Karma (2004) *Deities, Archers and Planners*. Centre for Bhutan Studies, Thimphu.
92. Ura, Karma and Ajia Keizai Kenky?jo (2005) *Peasantry and Bureaucracy in Decentralisation in Bhutan*, Institute of Developing Economies and Japan External Trade Organization, Thimphu.
93. Verma, Ravi, (1988) *India's Role in the Emergence of Contemporary Bhutan*, Capital Publishing House, New Delhi.
94. Yeshey Zimba (1996) *Three Decades of Planned Development*, in Ramakant and R.C.Mishra (ed) Bhutan: Society and Polity, Indus Publishing, New Delhi

Documents

1. Bhutan National Human Development Report (2000) *Gross National Happiness and Human Development – Searching for Common Ground*, The Planning Commission Secretariat, Royal Government of Bhutan, Thimphu.
2. *Civil Society Organizations Act of Bhutan* (2007). Available at: http://www.judiciary.gov.bt/html/act/Civil%20Society%20Org%20Act.pdf
3. Clean Bhutan-RSPN, *Clean Bhutan Project, 2007*. Available at:

http://cleanbhutan.rspnbhutan.org/?page_id=7

4. Constitution Drafting Committee of Bhutan. Available at: http://www.constitution.bt/html/members/members.htm
5. Country Reports on Human Rights Practices 2003. Available at: http://www.state.gov/g/drl/rls/hrrpt/2003/27945pf.htm (26.02.2004).
6. Decentralisation Outcome Evaluation Report. Available at: http://www.undp.org.bt/assets/files/publication/dec_OER.pdf
7. Dorji, Tenzin (1995) *Assessment of non-timber forest resource utilisation in Eastern Bhutan*. Field Document. No.UTF/BHU/008/BHU/Third Forestry Develop-ment Project, Forest Services Division, Thimphu, Bhutan.
8. Linder, Wolf and Anne-Claude Cavin (2003) *Decentralisation and Local Governance in Bhutan*, Report on a fact finding mission for the Swiss Agency for Development Cooperation, March 2003, Thimphu.
9. Ministry of External Affairs, India, *Annual Report 2010-2011*. Available at: http://meaindia.nic.in/mystart.php?id=500417371
10. Ministry of Planning, Royal Government of Bhutan (1996) *Eighth Five-Year Plan 1997-2002*. Royal Government of Bhutan, Thimphu.
11. Norbu, N. 2000. Sustainability of Chir pine Forests under Resin Tapping and its Socio-economic Impacts in Bhutan. FRDD, DoFS, MoA, Thimphu, Bhutan.
12. Planning Commission, Royal Government of Bhutan (1987) *Seventh Five-Year Plan 1987-1992*. Royal Government of Bhutan, Thimphu.
13. Planning Commission, Royal Government of Bhutan (1999a) *"Bhutan 2020: A Vision for Peace, Prosperity and Happiness (Part I)"*. Available at: http://www.undp.org.bt/Vision2020.pdf.
14. Planning Commission, Royal Government of Bhutan (1999b) *"Bhutan 2020: A Vision for Peace, Prosperity and Happiness (Part II)"*. Available at: http://www.undp.org.bt/Vision2020_part2.pdf
15. Planning Commission, Royal Government of Bhutan (2002) *Ninth Five-Year Plan 2002-2007*. Royal Government of Bhutan, Thimphu.
16. Royal Government of Bhutan, *Bhutan's Progress: Midway to the*

Millennium Development Goals, November, 2008, Bhutan. Available at: http://www.undp.org.bt/assets/files/publication/MDG_Midway.pdf

17. Royal Government of Bhutan (1999) *Enhancing Good Governance: Promoting Efficiency, Transparency and Accountability for Gross National Happiness*, Thimphu 1999.
18. Royal Government of Bhutan, *Local Government Act of 2009*. Available at: http://www.nab.gov.bt/downloadsact/Dzo74.pdf
19. Royal Government of Bhutan, *10th Five Year Plan 2008-2013*. Available at: http://www.educationfasttrack.org/media/library/Country_Documents/Bhutan/Bhutan_10th_Five-Year_Plan_2008-2013.pdf
20. Royal Government of Bhutan, *Election Act of Bhutan 2008*. Available at: http://oag.gov.bt/wp-content/uploads/2010/05/Election-Act-of-Bhutan-2008both-Dzongkha-English.pdf
21. Royal Danish Ministry of Foreign Affairs, *Strategy for Danish Development Co-operation with Bhutan 2003-2007*. Available at: http://www.um.dk/NR/rdonlyres/71E4DE11-7CA4-48F9-8B99-8A6DAAD3E3B5/0/BhutanDenmark_partnership.pdf
22. Strengthened Institutional Capacity of the Election Commission of Bhutan. Available at: http://www.undp.org.bt/Strengthened-Institutional-Capacity-of-the-Election-Commission-of-Bhutan.htm
23. Thai Bhutan Friendship, April 29, 2009. Available at: http://www.bhutantour.bt/bhutan-news/thai-bhutan-friendship.html
24. The Constitution of the Kingdom of Bhutan. Available at: http://www.constitution.bt/
25. The Druk National Congress, *Draft Constitution of Bhutan: Suggestions for Better Future*. Available at: http://www.bhutandnc.com/constitution1.pdf
26. The Permanent Mission of Bhutan to the United Nations in New York. Available art: http://www.un.int/wcm/content/site/bhutan/cache/offonce/pid/4154
27. Transparency International (2010) *Corruption Perspective Index 2010 Results*. Available at: http://www.transparency.org/policy_research/

surveys_indices/cpi/2010/results

28. UNDP (2003) "*Human Development Index*" at: http://www.undp.org/hdr2003/pdf/hdr03_HDI.pdf.
29. United Nations, Human Resources Development, *Twelfth Meeting of Experts on the United Nations Programme in Public Administration and Finance*, New York, 31 July-11 August 1995. Available at: http://unpan1.un.org/intradoc/groups/public/documents/un/unpan000780.pdf
30. World Bank, *Bhutan Economic Update 2010*, April 2010. Available at: http://siteresources.worldbank.org/BHUTANEXTN/Resources/Bhutan_Brief_April_2010.pdf
31. 76th Session of National Assembly, Proceedings and Resolutions, 29th June to 30th July 1998. Available at: http://www.gnhc.gov.bt/

Articles:

1. Acocella, Joan, "*Little People*". The New Yorker, August 18 & 25, 2003.
2. Archibugi, Daniele (2009) "*Democracy for Export: Principles, Practices, Lessons*", 5 March, *Open Democracy net*.
3. Andrea Matles Savada, (ed) (1991) *Bhutan: A Country Study*, GPO for the Library of Congress, Washington. Available at: http://countrystudies.us/bhutan/42.html
4. Bloom, Alexis (2001) *Television Comes to Bhutan*, The New York Times, on 3.05.2001.
5. Bray, John (1993) *Bhutan: The Dilemmas of a Small State*. The World Today 49(11).
6. Chakravarti, Balaram, (1980) *A Cultural History of Bhutan: From Padmasambhava to the Present Times, Volume 2 of A Cultural History of Bhutan*, Hilltop Publisher, Chakravarti.
7. Chhetri, Pushkar, *Bhutan-Bangladesh Trade Relations Get a Booster*, Bhutan Observer, 18 January, 2011. Available at: http://www.bhutanobserver.bt/bhutan-bangladesh-trade-relations-get-a-booster/
8. Chua, Melissa (2008) *The Pursuit of Happiness: Issues Facing Bhutanese Youths and the Challenges Posed to Gross National Happiness*, Institute of South Asian Studies Internship Program, University of Singapore. Available at: http://www.isas.nus.

edu.sg/Attachments/ResearchAttachment/Report%20-%20Melissa%20%2813%20Aug%2008% 29.pdfD:\thesis\final thesis\thesis final in one file\full and final\Chapter 7.doc

9. Dorji, Chencho (2005) *The Myth Behind Alcohol Happiness*, Paper Presented at the Second Conference on Gross National Happiness, April, 2005. Available at: http://www.gpiatlantic.org/conference/papers/dorji.pdf
10. Dorji, Kinley and Siok Sian Pek (2005) *The Media in Bhutan: In the Service of the Public*, Paper Presented at the Second Conference on Gross National Happiness, April, 2005. Available at: http://www.gpiatlantic.org/conference/papers/pek-dorji.pdf
11. Dorji, Tshering, *Gross National Happiness in Bhutan*. Available at: http://ezinearticles.com/?Gross-National-Happiness-in-Bhutan&id=5198079
12. Evans, A. S. (2006) *Promoting "Gross National Happiness" in Bhutan Through Her Rich Oral Traditions*, Journal of Bhutan Studies. Vol. 15 (Winter 2006)
13. Hasrat, Bikrama Jit, (1980) *History of Bhutan: Land of the Peaceful Dragon*, Education Department, Bhutan,
14. Hutt, Michael (1996a) *Bhutan in 1995: Weathering the Storm*. Asian Survey 36(2).
15. Hutt, Michael (1996b) *Ethnic Nationalism: Refugees and Bhutan*, Journal of Refugee Studies 9(4).
16. Hutt, Michael (1997) *Bhutan in 1996: Continuing Stress*. Asian Survey 37(2).
17. Karma Galay (2001) *Bhutanese Context of Civil Society*, in Journal of Bhutan Studies, Summer 2001, Vol.3, No.1.
18. Karma Ura (2004) *The Bhutanese Development Story*, *Kuensel*, 23 January 2004.
19. Kaul, Nitasha (2008a) *"Monarchies in Transition in Asia"*, paper presented at Centre on Democracy, Development, and Rule of Law (CDDRL), Stanford University, 5-6 June.
20. Kaul, Nitasha (2008b) *"Power to the People"*, *The CSD Bulletin*, 15 (2), Summer Issue.
21. Kaul, Nitasha (2008c) *"Bhutan is Neither Authoritarian Nor Stuck in a Time Warp"*, *Guardian*, 27 March.
22. Kaul, Nitasha (2008d) *"Democracy is all you need?"*, *The Edinburgh Journal*, 24 April.
23. Kuenga Tshering, *Gross National Happiness: Its Assumptions And*

Applications in Bhutan, Bhutan. Available at: http://www.friendsofhumanity.ch/uploads/pdf/article_gnhinbuhtan_feb09.pdf

24. Mathou,Thierry (1999) *Bhutan: The Political Reform in a Buddhist Monarchy*, Journal of Bhutan Studies ,Volume 1, Number 1, Autumn 1999, Thimphu.
25. Mathou, Thierry (2000) *The Politics of Bhutan: Change in Continuity*, Journal of Bhutan Studies, Vol.2, Nr.2, Thimphu.
26. Mathou, Thierry, (2008) *How to Reform a Traditional Buddhist Monarchy- The Political Achievements of His Majesty Jigme Singye Wangchuck, the Fourth King of Bhutan (1972-2006)*, Centre for Bhutan Studies, Bhutan.
27. Mathou, Thierry (2004) *"Bhutan-China Relations: Towards a New Step in Himalayan Politics"*, in The Spider and The Piglet: Proceedings of the First International Seminar on Bhutanese Studies, The Centre for Bhutan Studies, 2004, Thimphu.
28. McDonald, R. (2005) *"Towards a New Conceptualisation of GNH and its Foundtations"*, *Journal of Bhutan Studies*, Vol. 13, Thimphu.
29. Pain, Adam and Deki Pema (2000) *"Continuing Customs of Negotiation and Contestation in Bhutan"*. Available at: http://www.bhutanstudies.org.bt/journal/vol2no2/v2n2customs.pdf
30. Parmanand (2002) *Bhutan's Neighbours – Cooperation with India, Boundary Dispute With China*, The Statesman, 24.08.2002.
31. Petech, Luciano, *"The Rulers of Bhutan c. 1650–1750"*. Oriens Extremus. Zeitschrift für Sprache, Kunst und Kultur der Länder des Fernen Ostens, vol. 19, Hamburg, 1972.
32. Pelvar, Sonam, *One up for e-governance* in Bhutan Times. Available at: http://www.bhutantimes.bt/index.php?option=com_content&task=view&id=1415&Itemid=94
33. Rinzin, Chhewang, Walter J. V. Vermeulen and Pieter Glasbergen (2006) *Public Perceptions of Bhutan's Approach to Sustainable Development in Practice*. Available at: http://www.geography.ryerson.ca/jmaurer/108BhutanGNH1.pdf
34. Savada, Andrea Matles (ed) (1991) *Bhutan - A Country Study*, Federal Research Division, Library of Congress, Section 1. Available at: http://lcweb2.loc.gov/cgi-bin/query/r?frd/cstdy:@field(DOCID+bt0020)
35. Schell, Orville (2002) *Gross National Happiness*, in Red Herring, 15.01.2002; reprinted in Frontline World http://www.pbs.org/

frontlineworld/stories/bhutan/gnh.html

36. Stehlik, Vladimir (2000) *Bhutan and the Impeding Gush of Ego*, in Himal South Asia, August 2000. Available at: http://www.himalmag.com/aug-2000/
37. Windrel, Thomas *Bhutan the Making of a Modern state*. Available at: http://www.winderl.net/countries/bhutan/Bhutan%20-%20Towards%20a%20Modern%20State.pdf.
38. Thinley, Lyonpo Jigmi Y. (1998) *Values and Development: Gross National Happiness. Gross National Happiness*, The Centre for Bhutan Studies, Thimphu.
39. Tshering, Namgay, *DDC Plans Electronic English-Dzongkha Dictionary* in Bhutan Observer, March 18, 2011. Available at: http://www.bhutanobserver.bt/ddc-plans-electronic-english-dzongkha-dictionary/
40. Upreti, B.C., *Gross National Happyness and Foreign Policy of Bhutan :Interlinkages and Imperatives*. Available at: http://www.gpiatlantic.org/conference/papers/upreti.pdf
41. Ura, Karma (2001) *"Perceptions of Security"* at: http://www.bhutanstudies.org.bt/journal/vol5/v5-9.pdf (13.01.2004), pp. 113-
42. United Nations, *Kingdom of Bhutan: Public Administration Profile*, February 2005. Available at: http://unpan1.un.org/intradoc/groups/public/documents/un/unpan023230.pdf
43. Wangchuk, Kinley (2010) *"Why Bhutanese Trade with Thais"*. Bhutan Observer, 10-05-2010. Available at: http://www.bhutanobserver.bt/2010/readers-voices/05/why-bhutanese-trade-with-thais.html.
44. Wangchuk, Norbu, *Globalisation: A Challenge to Gross National Happiness*, Royal Institute of Management, July 2002, Vol. I. Thimphu, Bhutan. Available at: http://www.rim.edu.bt/Publication/Archive/rigphel/rigphel1/globalisation.htm
45. Wangyel, Tashi *"Rhetoric and Reality: An Assessment of the Impact of WTO on Bhutan"* in The Spider and The Piglet: Proceedings of the First International Seminar on Bhutanese Studies, The Centre for Bhutan Studies, 2004, Thimphu.

Websites Refered

1. Bangladesh Embassy, Thimphu: http://www.bangladesh embassy.bt/index.php?option=com_ content&view=

article&id=14&Itemid=14
2. Bhutan Broadcasting Service: http://www.bbs.com.bt/bbs/?p=4104
3. Bhutan Observer: http://www.bhutanobserver.bt/246-candidates-register-for-functional-test/
4. Civil Society organizations Authority of Bhutan: http://www.csoa.org.bt
5. Department of Information Technology & Telecom, Bhutan: http://www.dit.gov.bt
6. Druk Phuensum Tshogpa (DPT): http://www.dpt.bt
7. Embassy of India, Thimphu: http://www.indianembassythimphu.bt/mega.html
8. Embassy of Japan, India: http://www.in.emb-japan.go.jp/Japan-Bhutan-Relations/silver_jubilee_celebrations_2011.html
9. Encyclopedia of Nations: http://www.nationsencyclopedia.com/World-Leaders-2003/Bhutan-FOREIGN-POLICY.html
10. Federal department of Foreign Affairs, Switzerland: http://www.eda.admin.ch/eda/en/home/reps/asia/vbtn/bilbhu.html
11. Government of Canada: http://www.canadainternational.gc.ca/india-inde/bilateral_relations_bilaterales/canada_bhutan-bhoutan.aspx?lang=eng
12. Index Mundi: http://www.indexmundi.com/bhutan/executive_branch.html
13. India-Bhutan Relations: http://meaindia.nic.in/meaxpsite/foreignrelation/bhutan.pdf
14. International Finance Corporation: http://www.ifc.org/ifcext/southasia.nsf/Content/Bhutan
15. Ministry of Foreign Affairs, Royal Government of Bhutan: http://www.mfa.gov.bt/
16. Ministry of Foreign Affairs of Japan: http://www.mofa.go.jp/region/asia-paci/bhutan/index.html
17. Ministry of Foreign Affairs, Kingdom of Thailand: http://www.mfa.go.th/web/2651.php?id=23580
18. Mongabay, Bhutan- Social System, September 1991. Available at: http://www.mongabay.com/history/bhutan/bhutan-social_system.html
19. People's Democratic Party of Bhutan: http://www.pdp.bt

20. Royal Civil Service Commission of Bhutan: http://www.rcsc.gov.bt/VisionMission.asp
21. Royal Court of Justice, Judiciary of Bhutan: www.judiciary.gov.bt
22. South Asia Co-operative Environment Program. Available at: http://www.sacep.org/html/mem_bhutan.htm
23. The Constitution of the Kingdom of Bhutan: http://www.constitution.bt/
24. The Odora.com, Bhutan People 2011, January 13, 2011. Available at: http://www.theodora.com/wfbcurrent/bhutan/bhutan_people.html
25. http://www.himalaya2000.com/bhutan/history/early-history.html
26. http://www.keystobhutan.com/bhutan/bhutan_history_pre.php
27. http://www.keystobhutan.com/bhutan/bhutan_history_buddhism.php
28. http://bhutansiam.com/history.html
29. http://www.bhutanmajestictravel.com/bhutan-100-years-of-monarchy
30. http://advbhutan.com/about-bhutan.htm
31. http://www.bhutan2008.bt/en/node/276
32. http://countrystudies.us/bhutan/21.htm
33. http://countrystudies.us/bhutan/19.htm
34. http://countrystudies.us/bhutan/22.htm
35. http://countrystudies.us/bhutan/39.htm
36. http://countrystudies.us/bhutan/42.htm
37. http://www.britannica.com/EBchecked/topic/64215/Bhutan/25023/Agriculture-and-forestry
38. http://www.nationsencyclopedia.com/Asia-and-Oceania/Bhutan-INDUSTRY.html
39. http://www.economywatch.com/world_economy/bhutan/export-import.html

Index